Warrior
Origins

The author training in the morning snow on London's Primrose Hill, overlooking the city.

Cover Illustrations:
Early nineteenth-century Japanese *tsubas* (sword hand guard), made of iron and decorated in high relief in silver, gold, *shakudo* (a gold/copper alloy also known as hakudo), copper and *shibuichi* (an alloy of three parts copper to one part silver). One piece (on the front and back) is credited to Egawa Toshimasa and depicts Sojobo, the King of the Tengu (a mythical semi-divine mountain spirit) clad in a mountain priest costume accompanied by one of his Tengu whilst teaching martial secrets using scrolls to the young warrior Minamoto no Yoshitsune – the legendary founder of Yoshitsune Ryu Ninjutsu. On the book spine is the Japanese Thunder God Raijin, or Raiden, with his *tomoe* (Japanese swirl) patterned drums, shooting down thunder and lightning. (This piece is decorated with patinated copper alloy, gold and copper inlay, credited to Kingyokudo Myochin Hirosada, 1857.) This character has inspired popular modern 'thunder god' personalities in contemporary martial arts computer games and gameplay media including 'Lord Raiden' in the *Mortal Kombat* series. Photos © Victoria and Albert Museum, London.

Warrior Origins

The Historical and Legendary
Links between Bodhidharma's
Shaolin Kung-Fu, Karate
and Ninjutsu

Dr Hutan Ashrafian

No matter how you may excel in the art of te ['*art of the fist*' or
Karate],
And in your scholastic endeavours,
Nothing is more important than your behaviour
And your humanity as observed in daily life.

Nago Ueekata Chobun名護 親方 寵文(1663–1734), also known
as Tei Junsoku程順則. Okinawan scholar and government official.

First published 2014

The History Press
The Mill, Brimscombe Port
Stroud, Gloucestershire, GL5 2QG
www.thehistorypress.co.uk

British Library Cataloguing in Publication Data.
A catalogue record for this book is available from the British Library.

ISBN 978 0 7509 5618 5
Typesetting and origination by The History Press
Printed in Great Britain

Contents

About the Author

Hutan Ashrafian is a doctor, martial artist and historian. He has three decades of experience in Karate and has practised a wide range of traditional martial arts and sport combat systems. He has a particular interest in the evolution of Karate, Kung-Fu, Zurkhane and Ninjutsu. He has studied Chinese-Okinawan martial cross-fertilisation and practises several founding styles of Karate. He

holds a 5th Dan Black Belt in the Okinawan Karate style of Goju-Ryu, Dan grades and instructorships in several other systems including Shito-Ryu, Seiki-kai and Shotokan. He has the *Soke* title ('official inheritor') in the Okinawan style of Gusuku-Ryu ('Way of the Fortress'). He has successfully competed in both Karate and Judo, winning an array of gold, silver and bronze medals at World Junior, University, European and World Masters levels, and currently trains with

The author, Hutan Ashrafian.

the Jindokai International Martial Arts Association at the London School of Oriental and African Studies (SOAS) Dojo. Following qualification from medical school he was elected Fellow and council member of the Royal Asiatic Society and awarded membership of the Royal College of Surgeons of England. He completed a PhD in surgery and metabolic physiology and is currently a practising surgeon and clinical lecturer at Imperial College London.

Acknowledgements

I dedicate this book with my deepest affection to my parents Jamshid and Susan and to my older brother Houman, with whom I began my journey in the martial arts, and also to our incredible first instructor Yoshihiro Itoshima, to whom we are eternally grateful for building the foundations of our Karate knowledge and practice.

Particular gratitude goes to Professor Stephen Chan OBE, 9th Dan Chief Instructor and President of the Jindokai International Martial Arts Association and a close friend, who has been guiding my martial journey from Westminster School and the international competition circuit through to the present day and onward. His exceptional abilities in the martial arts, world expertise on international relations, humanities and academia are a constant source of inspiration to me and countless others.

My yearning to understand the martial arts that I see and practise has been fed by training with dedicated, enthusiastic, like-minded individuals. As a result, I would like to express my deepest gratitude to the multitude of fellow martial artists (of all styles) I have had the pleasure of training alongside over the years; you have all been a massive inspiration.

The final stages of this book have coincided with my training at the Jindokai International Martial Arts Association at the London

School of Oriental and African Studies (SOAS) Karate and Kobudo Dojo (located in the university 'Dungeon'). I would therefore like to express deep appreciation to my Dojo mates: Dr Ranka Primorac, Peter Ayres, Katy Crofton, Dr Matthew O'Donnell and, of course, Dr Steve Taplin.

Special thanks to Gavin J. Poffley, my fellow Karate-ka and friend with whom I relish sparring competitively on the mats and discussing esoteric aspects of martial arts; I thank him for his expertise in Japanese, his ability to translate the most complex of texts and his help in proofreading this manuscript. I am also thankful to the wonderful Dr Leanne Harling for her translation of my vision of the cover, whilst also contributing to the proofreading.

I very much appreciate the recent international martial conferences conducted under the auspices of Col (Ret.) Roy Jerry Hobbs, 10th Dan Hanshi and Chief Instructor of the Dentokan Sekai Bugei Renmei, Inc., whose enormously broad martial expertise remains every motivating; the enlightening Brian Rogers and the inimitable Stuart Lawrence, who stayed open-minded to my crazy 'fortress' style of Karate whilst delighting in a heady mix of Okinawan, Chinese, Japanese and North American Goju styles! Thanks also go to Richard Thomas and Dr Alistair MacPherson from my time at Westminster School and Wayne Otto, the world Karate champion of champions and former England Karate coach for the magnificent competition sessions in London's Crouch Hill, who have all been exposed to my hybridisation of history and martial arts and have contributed to my Dan grades and medals. I thank Sylvain Guintard (Revd Kuban Jakkôin), 8th Dan in 'Ninpo' Budo-Taijutsu, yambushi priest of Shomudo hermitage, for our discussions on the *Yamabushi* and all things Ninja.

I am indebted to Professor Richard N. Frye, with whom I have studied the ancient world from east to west for many years. His encyclopaedic knowledge of all things Persian and his effortless familiarity with the world of the orient have proved massively valuable.

My inquisitiveness about the martial arts has in part been derived from my career in medicine and science and thanks goes to my surgical colleagues and mentors, Professor Thanos Athanasiou and Professor Lord Ara Darzi.

This project would not have been possible without the significant knowledge freely shared by the multitude of martial artists with whom I have trained, and their open, welcoming culture that nourished fruitful discussion and was an inspiration to write this book.

Hutan Ashrafian
London

Preface

The martial arts are as old as as man. From the dawn of civilisation, we were able to advance ourselves beyond a condition of savage hand-to-hand aggression to a state of intelligent conflict resolution. Contests evolved from a haphazard demonstration of brute force to satisfy primal urges towards the higher goals of stability, protection and law enforcement. That is not to say that atrocities did not occur as they do today, but rather there was an increased appreciation of using force for good. A well-known example is that of Cyrus the Great of Persia, who invaded Babylon in 539 BCE in part to free all slaves, permit religious tolerance and to encourage international dialogue. Such a show of martial strength was based on the premise of what has been called the first ever bill of human rights, the Cyrus Cylinder c.539–530 BCE (a copy of which currently resides in the United Nations), and resulted in worldwide acknowledgement of the invader's humanity at that time, which endures to the present day.

This show of martial strength was based on centuries of knowledge, even in Cyrus' era, and in addition to the prerequisite strength of arms it was also based on strategy, skill and teamwork. These latter aspects of martial arts are now considered as accepted universal fundamentals, and they have been repeatedly refined into a multitude of schools, styles and systems.

Of the unarmed martial arts, there are currently four main systems or disciplines that fulfil the three criteria of (i) being practised by a large number of international students, (ii) having a traceable ancient history and (iii) having a worldwide impact. The so-called 'foundation schools' are Kung-Fu, Karate, Taekwondo and Ninjutsu. Kung-Fu is also known as Shaolin or Wushu Kung-Fu/Gung-Fu (or Gongfu, a Cantonese word meaning 'effort' or 'perseverance' that only took on the meaning of 'Chinese unarmed martial arts' quite recently; another common term is 'Chuan Fa'). These schools of course overlap and vary tremendously, such that Kung-Fu represents an umbrella term to cover myriad Chinese schools representing the huge Chinese populace, whereas Ninjutsu is not practised by large populations, but nevertheless has penetrated modern culture and society to an extraordinary degree. Dedicated training in any of these arts leads to an age-old set of questions: how did each particular school commence? Where and when did it occur and why? The goal of this book is to investigate and clarify the legendary and historical origins of these martial arts, paying particular attention to occasions when their records coincide and agree.

Certain concepts regarding the history and development of the martial arts are increasingly becoming accepted and each style's origin is being scrutinised much more closely than before. Simply reading books such as Sun Tzu's *Art of War* or the *Hagakure* is no longer enough; now there is a desire to know why these books were written, in what context, and by whom. This book is not intended to be a reference work describing every legend and record of each martial arts style and substyle, but has been written to equip the reader with facts and concepts that can be applied over a wide field; and if a practitioner, to the interpretation of his or her own art, whatever that may be. It contains a number of key descriptions of pertinent schools, techniques and individuals intended to communicate to the reader relatively complex temporal associations in martial arts evolution. I have kept these as accurate as possible, but have purposefully aimed to keep my descriptions succinct so as to not to render them overly intricate.

This book is not intended as a practical manual of fighting arts; such 'training manuals' already exist in large numbers (and will necessarily differ greatly in training techniques, as this text will hopefully clarify).

The aim is to elucidate and integrate knowledge regarding the mainstream martial arts and consider possible connections and common origins, a subject discussed in nearly every martial arts club or dojo, but one that always seems to need deeper understanding. At a practical level, the comprehension of many of the advanced forms in Karate, Ninjutsu and Kung-Fu would be incomplete without knowing their original interpretation. At an epistemological level therefore, we need to comprehend the origins of our martial knowledge and skills. The book aims to equip the reader with the knowledge of how each particular school commenced, when, and why.

In the vast majority of cases, the historical record of these arts is incomplete, particularly the farther we go back in time. As a result, many martial artists have to view their historical provenance through the intermingling of some history with a wider influx of legends. The use of these legends of course lends itself to almost effortless dissemination in dojos and training halls, as they follow a straightforward oral tradition. Consequently, much of our comprehension of the development of martial arts is based on conjecture. I have written this book to offer the reader a framework within which to consider the development of modern martial arts, and am aware that there will always be new facts (and even more legends) to replace or add to the current record. I also make use of several biological analogies that convey concepts of martial art evolution. I have made comparisons using Darwinian and neo-Darwinian concepts to portray ideas and thoughts. To this end, I have reflected the application of evolutionary biology in the title of this book as a respectful tribute to Charles Darwin's seminal treatise *On the Origin of Species*. I have aimed to bring new insight into the evolution of martial arts using existing legends and history through the creation of martial arts evolutionary trees.

Transliteration:

The transliteration within this book has been a particularly interesting consideration. Sources include Middle Persian, Farsi, Sanskrit, Japanese, Korean and both Cantonese and Mandarin. I have attempted to keep to accepted philological standards where possible, but have on occasion deviated to the popular interpretation of terms where appropriate. Any inconsistencies herein are in all cases my fault rather than errors by those who advised me on the manuscript.

1

Enter the Dharma

The enigmatic origins of the martial arts are a preoccupation of martial artists worldwide. Attending the training halls of the most prominent and popular styles from around the globe including Kung-Fu, Tai Chi, Karate and Taekwondo, you will hear an almost universal claim that these schools have a lineage that can be traced back to a monk known best in the English-speaking world by his Indian name: Bodhidharma (Damo in Chinese, Daruma Taishi in Japanese). The fact that this monk is also considered to be the father, or first patriarch, of Zen (Chan) Buddhism adds to these origins stories a feeling of legitimacy; and also assumes for the fighting arts a spirituality, in the association with Zen philosophy and ascetic practices.

Instructors of all levels and grades proudly list their personal lineage of training, reverentially putting pictures of their particular style's forefathers on the wall and almost always acknowledging that Bodhidharma was the first of all. The monk is also depicted proudly alongside the more recent forefathers, with a short explanation that he had 'created' the first martial art of Shaolin Kung-Fu, which eventually evolved into many different schools and other martial arts, such as Karate. Many Japanese dojos to this day are inaugurated by the painting of eyes on Bodhidharma dolls, whose subsequent auspicious open-eyed presence will favour the martial enlightenment of their students. (In Japan this is actually a widespread practice outside of the martial arts too, especially for shop openings and during election campaigns.)

The 'creation story' of the martial arts in many clubs is typically recounted thus. Bodhidharma was travelling from India to China, when he encountered a group of weakened and sickly monks at the Shaolin Ssu (Young Forest Temple), the site where the practices known as Shaolin Boxing, Wushu or Kung-Fu would later originate. As a result, he designed and instigated a series of health-giving exercises in the monks' daily routines (some based on the movements of animals). The monks then flourished physically, and continually practised these exercises, which eventually became known as Kung-Fu. As most of the Asian martial arts claim descent from this style of fighting, Bodhidharma is largely credited as 'the father of all martial arts'. Zen Buddhist schools often use the same story but usually ask the first Zen question, why did Bodhidharma travel to the East?

In view of the current popularity of martial arts, it is no overstatement to say that billions of people worldwide readily consider Bodhidharma as the originator of their martial art, sport, or even Buddhist religion. However, the direct evidence to support these claims is not clear. There are of course a wide variety of legends ascribed to Bodhidharma, no doubt having been told, retold and modified for hundreds, if not thousands of years. Travelling to various clubs around the world, both in the East and West, provides the practitioner with interesting insights about the evolution of these legends, as they form a patchwork of narratives regarding this monk's life. There is currently a significant lack of firm historical details regarding Bodhidharma, and any true morsels of evidence are overwhelmed by the surfeit of legendary stories to such an extent that discriminating between history and legend is like untying the Gordian knot. Is it possible to dissect out the real history from the fiction? Unsurprisingly, varying groups of martial artists and historians are polarised regarding Bodhidharma; some unquestioningly pronounce their faith in the truth of his legendary exploits whilst others question whether he even existed. Is there any tangible evidence of his existence, or his origins and his deeds? What was his contribution to the founding, establishment and development of the martial arts and what has his impact been to this day?

By the fifth century CE of the Julian calendar, the world as we know it was beginning to take shape, with the foundations of institutions, philosophies and cultures that we would readily recognise today. In Western Europe, the Roman Empire was gradually declining and the Anglo-Saxons were settling in Britain. Technological and social sophistication and refinement were international phenomena that were being constantly and independently reinvented, so that in the Americas, for example, the Maya were building massive stone temples comparable to those of the ancient Egyptians, although with completely different technology.

The East was no different and China had its Southern and Northern dynasties, whilst in Persia the empire of the Sassanids was comfortably established. The famed Silk Road between them that allowed the mutually beneficial transmission of goods and culture had already been in existence for many centuries and with the political and military strength of these territories, communication and exchange was flourishing. In India, a 'golden age' was taking place, and both religion and science were thriving (the concept of the number zero having been invented during this time).

In these times of cultural development and transmission of ideas, religion was taking a prominent role. The Persians were adhering to their ancient religion of Zoroastrianism, considered by many as the world's oldest monotheistic belief system, whilst St Augustine of Hippo, who had himself studied Zoroastrianism and its Gnostic-type offshoot of Manichaeism, had written the important Christian work: *The City of God* (De Civitate Dei). Hinduism, which had existed for several millennia, was constantly expanding, and the newer religion of Buddhism had commenced a late but continual expansion, particularly through its Mahayana school.

It is through Mahayana Buddhism that we first come across the name of Bodhidharma. Although historically this religious sage is understood to have studied the Mahayana way, he is largely famed for and credited with founding the Zen (Chinese: Chan) strand of Buddhism, and instigating the exercises and forms that he subsequently taught to monks at Shaolin.

Opinions are split as to the importance of these proto-martial exercises as although the legends of Bodhidharma allude to the fact that he introduced and created the basic forms of the martial arts, he is also reputed to have achieved his spiritual self-enlightenment not through their practice but through contemplation and meditating for years on end. This gives credence to those Zen Buddhists who believe in a more formal and conservative practice of meditation without the incorporation of martial arts or strenuous exercise. Furthermore, the Zen (Chan) Buddhism of the famed Shaolin monks is more akin to some sects of Buddhism in Tibet, Korea and the smaller schools of Japan than it is to Chinese and mainstream Japanese schools of martial arts and Buddhism. The Shaolin School can be seen to have Taoist influences, and uses a large amount of martial practice to augment and accompany meditation. The martial arts are used to strengthen the body, allowing deep meditation to occur. Other schools of Zen believe in more of a deep and continued static meditation, allowing the mind to empty.

The fact that both martial artists and Zen Buddhists independently claim their philosophy as coming from the same Bodhidharma lends some credence at least to the idea that one or a group of monks started their school at approximately the same time and place in northern China. Indeed, with the many years of rewriting history, and political propaganda, one could easily imagine that martial artists and Zen Buddhists could have come up with different and independent originators of their disciplines, which later became confused and unified into the same individual. But the fact that both strongly adhere to the one unified Bodhidharma theory reinforces the implication that it was indeed one of the same group of monks, bearing the name Bodhidharma, who founded both disciplines.

Variations of the name Bodhidharma are listed in various Asian languages as:

Sanskrit:	Bodhidharma or Bodhi Dharma
Chinese – Cantonese:	Pou Dai Daat Mor or Daat Mor
Chinese – Mandarin (Pinyin):	Pu Ti Da Mo or Da Mo
Japanese:	Daruma or Daruma Taishi
Vietnamese:	Bo de dat ma
Korean:	Dalma or Boridalma

This name is accepted by many as not being his birth name but an adopted name when he entered the Buddhist order, probably given to him by his master or seniors, as in Sanskrit it means 'he who has reached enlightenment'.

As mentioned previously, there is no lack of conflict regarding the authenticity of the legends of Bodhidharma, a not uncommon finding when dealing with the posthumous chronicles of influential figures. However, it is important to note that there is an almost complete unity in the belief of the single figure of Bodhidharma as the first forefather, even though the context can be subject to speculation. The fact that he started what we know today as the Asian martial arts and first passed it on to the Shaolin monks is generally accepted in folklore. However, some claim that although he was the first Patriarch of Zen Buddhism in China, he was not the first patriarch or originator of this strand of Buddhism in India, and indeed posit that he learned and adopted Zen as a disciple from one of the Indian patriarchs before taking it to China. Others say that Zen existed in China before Bodhidharma and that he came later, and was simply effective at promoting, teaching and disseminating this new form of spirituality. The orthodox view, however, is clear: Bodhidharma was the originator of Zen Buddhism and the first Zen Buddhist patriarch in the world.

2

Shaolin and Kung-Fu

As it is practically impossible to date the origins of the various legends attributed to Bodhidharma himself, they are reported here in a loose chronological order of the monk's life. Actual historical evidence is scrutinised in Chapter 3.

We are told virtually nothing about Bodhidharma's childhood and he is generally described as appearing on the stage of history as a middle-aged or even as an elderly man (**Figure 1**). He is reputed to have had piercing blue eyes and very dark black hair. His hair was copious, especially on his chest, seen coming out of his monk's robes, which made him notable in China as the presence of such hair made him stand out when compared to the comparatively bare-chested Chinese men.

He is shown sometimes wearing an earring and is portrayed as having a very prominent nose, which together with his blue eyes added to his reputation as an outsider or alien. Blue eyes are another rare trait in the ethnic Chinese (and also in the indigenous peoples of neighbouring India and Persia) and his eyes became an important subsequent characterising feature in artistic representations, where they are usually illustrated as bulging out. This effect adds to the aura he is attributed with in the chronicles, as having the almost superhuman ability to attain a profound meditative state with a steely and unremitting stare.

Most legends state that Bodhidharma came from south-east India and was born *c.*440–470 CE on 5 October (Chinese lunar calendar). Another date given is 482 CE. He is described as the third son of a 'great king'. More specifically, this is thought to be King Sugandha from a dynasty known as the 'Sardilli', or, according to the theory favoured by most narratives and South Indologists, the Pallava King Simhavarman (ruling between 436–460 CE) who was based in the region of Tamil Nadu in the ancient city of Kanchi or Kanjeevaram (today's Kanchipuram). This is significant, as at one point in history Kanjeevaram was a Buddhist kingdom. Some legends give Bodhidharma's birth name as 'Bodhitara' or 'Bodhipatra'.

Some claim that he was born into the priestly caste (Brahmanas), whilst others describe him as originating in the warrior caste (Kashatriyas). The stories that adopt the latter go on to state that he learned armed and unarmed combat such as Kalarippayattu, Vajra Mushti, Kuttu Varisai or any of the indigenous martial arts

likely to have come from what were then known as the Dravidian combat schools.

Those who believe in his Brahminic origins say that he trained in various schools of Yoga (Devanagari), specifically the four branches of yoga explained in the Sanskrit text *Bhagavad Gita* (Song of the Lord, *c.*400–100 BCE). These are *Karma yoga* (action and exercise),

Figure 1: Image of Bodhidharma in the cave.

Jnana yoga (knowledge), *Bhakti yoga* (religious devotion) and *Raja yoga* (meditation).

As he was the third son, this allowed him the freedom to adopt a religious life, as the first royal son typically would be responsible for the family lands and inheritance of leadership, whilst the second would be expected to devote himself to the military and matters of national defence. Although this is a tenable theory, such a practice was never strictly adhered to and would be highly variable. A good example would be the case of Siddhartha Gautama, the founding Buddha, who was the first son of a king but adopted the religious life, leading to his founding of Buddhism. Furthermore, there would have been no onus on a young Bodhidharma to specifically adopt Buddhism, with Hinduism or one of ancient India's many other religions being a more likely choice. Whatever his status at birth or origins, Bodhidharma somehow experienced and later converted to Buddhism, allegedly after his father's death, giving up worldly belongings in favour of a more simple monastic life.

His master, the sage Prajnatara (also known as Prajnadhara or Panyata) was the twenty-seventh patriarch of Indian Buddhism, apparently in a direct line of descent from the Buddha himself. A Mahayanist, he is reputed to have come from Magadha in the ancient Indo-Aryan kingdom of Mahajanapadas, one of the four main kingdoms of ancient India. Siddhartha Gautama himself travelled southward to Magadha during his journeys before becoming the Buddha, and in 326 BC Alexander the Great's army reputedly mutinied at the thought of fighting at Magadha, therefore forcing Alexander to turn south and ultimately return homeward via Persia.

Bodhidharma, being an astute and gifted student, rapidly progressed in his Buddhist schooling and in time was acknowledged as an 'enlightened master', becoming the twenty-eighth Patriarch of Indian Buddhism. Some Zen legends differ, stating that at the flower sermon on Vulture Peak the Buddha did not speak and just silently held up a flower. He saw that only an individual disciple, a monk named Kasyapa, was smiling and that it was he alone who had understood the teaching that day. This event is accepted as the first 'transmission of the lamp', a direct communication of mind without words, with Kasyapa receiving the Dharma directly at that time and the Buddha renaming him Mahakashyapa to commemorate it. According to some Zen schools, this therefore makes Mahakashyapa the first Zen patriarch, and Bodhidharma the twenty-eighth.

Prajnatara asked Bodhidharma to travel to China, as he believed Buddhism had begun to perish there, and he wanted Bodhidharma to further develop Mahayana there, maybe establish Sarvastivada teachings or even introduce Zen to that continent. Alternatively, others say that Buddhism was declining in India and that Prajnatara asked Bodhidharma to transmit Buddhism to China to ensure the continuation of their school of Buddhism. His journey was difficult, the elements were harsh and he endured various difficulties with thieves and robbers. Some Chinese legends inform us that he commenced his journey in 470 CE aged 117 years, bringing with him books on martial arts.

There are a variety of routes suggested for the journey. Most legends allude to Bodhidharma walking via the Silk Route or, alternatively, through Tibet and the Himalayas. Other legends have a sea route, via the Bay of Bengal, sailing to Guangzhou (Canton), and from there to the capital, Jiankang (an ancient name for Nanjing). He was said to be 120 years old at that time, the journey having taken approximately three years, with an estimated date of arrival of 473–527 CE, most accounts alluding to 520 CE.

Once in China, Bodhidharma meets a local military administrator named Shang Yao (or Shao Yang), who informs the ruling monarch of the time of his presence. This was Emperor Wu of Liang (also known as Liang Wudi, 464–549) of the South dynasty, who subsequently asked Bodhidharma for a royal audience (he reigned 502–549). The emperor was well read and a devout Buddhist, and was keen to meet distinguished foreign Buddhist monks in order to discuss religion and to display his charitable contribution to many Buddhist works, monks and temples. He had commissioned the translation of many sutras from Sanskrit to Chinese, all in reverence of the Buddha. He would have been keen to learn new Buddhist concepts and reinforce his beliefs, maybe even getting the monk to strengthen his Buddhist and royal authority, or help him set up more monasteries and temples.

The emperor, believing in karma (good begets good and bad begets bad), is famed for having asked the monk what merit he had earned for erecting numerous Buddhist temples and completing various charitable deeds in the name of the Buddha. Bodhidharma replied that he had earned nothing at all, going on to explain that superficial and worldly deeds are not the path to enlightenment, and implying that the emperor's deeds had not been altruistic but rather self-adulating, negating any karmic benefits.

A second question was posed: what is the fundamental concept of Buddhism? To which Bodhidharma famously replied, 'vast emptiness'. A final question was posed: who did the monk think he was? This insinuated that he had not realised the high social standing and authority of his host. The final answer by the monk continued in its simplicity: he had no idea of who he was.

The two characters parted company in a civilised but frosty fashion, although some do say that the emperor actually had Bodhidharma banished from his kingdom. There is, however, no story of any compulsion or violence being used.

After leaving the palace and city of Nanjing, Bodhidharma headed north, some say with the aim of visiting Lo-yang, a capital of ancient North China. In doing so, he had to cross the mighty Yangtze River. The local community did not want the monk to leave them or to cross the river, so they set all their boats adrift to prevent his passage. He famously overcame this impasse by using a single reed, throwing it on the water, then stepping onto it whilst in a state of meditation. By doing so, he himself acted as a sailboat, and let the river breeze transfer him across to the other side.

Once in the north of China, he eventually came to Henan province, and whilst there, he passed through Dengfeng, entering the 20-square-mile Song mountain range of thirty-six peaks, where he climbed either Bear's Ear Mountain (Xiong Er Shan), Mount Xiaoshishan (Mount Songshan) or another of the peaks. The range and the peaks are today actually known as one entity, Lofty Mountain (Song Shan), being one of the Taoist Five Great Mountains. On this mount was the site of the ancient Shaolin Temple (Xiaolin-si or Shaolin Ssu – Young Forest Temple), built during the reign of Emperor Xiao Wen Di of the Northern Wei dynasty (386–534 CE) by imperial decree (495 CE). Bodhidharma came across this monastery, which had been in existence for approximately forty years when he arrived, and sought admission, but was duly refused by the monks in the temple and by the abbot (some call him Fang Chang or 'Head Monk') for unstated reasons. We are simply told that many people applied for entry, so admission was complicated and difficult. The legends are very unclear, usually specifying a date of 526 or 527 for arrival at the Shaolin Temple, although some say that the date 526 or 527 came after a period of nine years of meditation, after which Bodhidharma finally entered the monastery on that date (see p. 26).

Bodhidharma, being an enlightened master of Buddhism, was not troubled by this exclusion from the temple, and he would regularly return in the evenings to discuss Buddhist concepts with the monks. Nonetheless, the monks continually refused him admission. Impervious to this denial, he is then said to have found an undisturbed small cave, one or two miles from the site of the temple, some say the Five Breasts Peak, where he sat cross-legged inside in silent Zen meditation, facing its rock wall continuously for nine years. His meditative state was augmented by keeping his eyes wide open in a permanent stare. Nine is an auspicious number, representing enlightenment, longevity and lucidity.

The intensity of his gaze over the nine years is purported to have burnt holes into the cave wall, with his sitting body also forming a corresponding shadow in the rock face. These were supposedly still in existence years after Bodhidharma's death, and were even shown to travelling scholars and monks, such as Du Mu (1459–1525), who purportedly saw them in the winter of 1513.[1] The monks who noticed this elevated level of spirituality and strength understood this to be a superhuman Buddhist feat, and finally not only permitted him entry to their temple, but rather beseeched him to join them. Variations on this meditation story exist, such as those that report Bodhidharma's limbs withered away from lack of use and nutrition, but he stayed very much alive. Others say he did not actually meditate for nine years against a wall, but that he meant that his mediation style would be 'wall perceiving', or fixed as a rock.

Others narrate that he was called the 'wall gazing Brahman', and used to meditate inside the cave near Shaolin for two to four hours on a mat of leaves at dusk and dawn, exercising, living and contemplating at times in between. Some claim his meditation was actually inside the Shaolin Temple itself, in one of its rooms or halls.

Alternatively, after seven years, he fell asleep during his uninterrupted meditation, and when he woke up, so as to never interrupt his mediation again, he cut off or ripped off his own eyelids, hence his depiction in later years as having 'bulging eyes'. Some versions of this story have it that the cut-off eyelids were thrown onto the ground and from them sprouted China's first green tea plants. Some explain this through the idea that tea was introduced during the Tang dynasty and was used by Buddhist monks to stay awake during long hours of meditation, so the legend linked the tea with their spiritual master Bodhidharma.

During his time of meditation, he was exposed to the elements, harsh winters and winds. Many wild and dangerous animals would come his way, but he would remain motionless, deep in meditation, and ultimately he came to no harm.

On entering the Shaolin Monastery, with most Shaolin masters quoting a date of arrival of 526, Bodhidharma was reputed to be 66 years old. The monks had continued with their Buddhist teachings and ideals with dedication, having also adopted some of Bodhidharma's intensive meditation style. However, as worthy as this seemed, he observed that the monks were unable to follow the rigorous meditative practices that he had developed and endured. For one, they would be seen to fall asleep sometimes out of sheer physical exhaustion during meditation, or else their physical weaknesses would not allow their minds to attain an adequate meditative state.

Furthermore, their overall appearance was not of healthy individuals on the path to spiritual enlightenment, but rather of weak and feeble bodies, with wearied faces, constantly drowsy after periods of concentration and generally fatigued by their daily routine, rendering them unable to continue in their daily copying and translating of scrolls, let alone attaining the highest state of enlightenment or 'nirvana'.

As a result, he decided to teach them the basic forms and modes of exercise that he had devised and developed during his breaks from heavy meditation in the period of the nine years. These form the basis of today's Shaolin 'Heart-Mind-Fist', and may have been inspired by some of the animal movements that Bodhidharma observed during his meditative years, or possibly a modification of his exercise, yogic and martial arts teachings from India.

These include:

The Change of the Tendons or The Change of the Sinews, or The Muscle Change Classic.
The Marrow Washing.
The Eighteen Hand Movements, or 18 Lo-Han Hands (十八羅漢手) or Eighteen Hands of Buddha (*shihpa lohan shou* – enlightened hand exercises, performed by using the technique of 'dynamic tension').
The 'Sanchin' kata – 'Three Conflicts', 'Three Battles' or 'Three Gods' (although the latter is erroneous, mistaking the 戦 chin character for 神 *shin/kami*: 'divine'. This is a form of Okinawan Karate, which is performed by using the technique of 'dynamic tension'. 三戦 Sanchin is an Okinawan dialect word with origins in China, and the sixth-century Chinese would almost certainly not have called it that. However, this skill is probably the forerunner of the modern practice that came to be known in Karate circles as 'Sanchin'.

The first two were later recorded as the *Yi Gin Ching* or *I Chin Ching* (Book of Changing Muscle/Tendon), and the *Xi Shui Jing* or *Hsi Sui*

Chin (Book of Washing Marrow). These have been ascribed directly to Bodhidharma, though no proof of this exists.

All three exercises are practised to this day, and are considered the founding elements of two arts, the 'external' Shaolin Boxing, Shaolin Fist Law (or Shaolin Ch'uan Fa in Mandarin) and the Wudang 'internal' Chi Gung. It is said that Bodhidharma taught these as strength-giving exercises, and he maintained a policy of no violence, according to Buddhist teachings. These exercises were to be practised every day in order to enhance the circulation and physical fitness and vitality. Some of the exercises were more suited to pairs or groups of monks, and quickly adopted the name of Temple Boxing, today called Chinese Temple Boxing.

Around 900 CE, a nobleman and Shaolin graduate by the name of Chueh Yuan (or Chueh Yan Shang-jen), further developed the Bodhidharma's original 18 Lo-Han Hands into seventy-two movements, and later expanded them with the Shensi province Shaolin master Li-Shao to make 170 strokes, named after various animals, well-known today as crane, dragon, leopard, snake and tiger. He later combined them with the *Chi Na* (joint locks, grapples and pressure-point system) of the Shaolin master Pai Yu-Feng to form a series of 173 hand and foot movements that we know today as Shaolin Gung-Fu, which later became known in the West as Kung-Fu.

In the thirteenth century a Taoist monk by the name of Chang Sang Feng, who was probably exposed to Shaolin teaching, advanced the internal aspects of his teaching to become the forefather and champion of what we call Tai Chi Chuan. It is interesting to note that, like Bodhidharma approximately 700 years before him, Chang Sang Feng is first mentioned only in religious texts,[2] later credited with the creation of the martial arts. In fact, his legends first came to prominence during the Ming dynasty (1368–1644), because of a close association between the ruling monarchs and court with Taoism. The first literary association of him with Kung-Fu or Chinese Boxing is Huang Zongxi's (1610–1695) *Epitaph for Wang Zhengnan* (1669), which is important in the history of the martial arts, as it is the first to give us the delineation of Chinese Temple Boxing[2, 3] as hard or 'external', such as Shaolin Kung-Fu, or soft, 'internal', such as Tai Chi Chuan.

Following Bodhidharma's time with the Shaolin monks, for an undisclosed period, he is said to have left the Shaolin Monastery and visited other temples and locations in China. He is reputed to have travelled as far as Okinawa, Japan and even Korea, to bring them Zen. It seems unlikely that he actually went to Japan and certainly not Okinawa, considering its relatively small size and that Okinawa remains relatively uninfluenced by Buddhism to this day. Indeed, both in China and Japan, there are Bodhidharma dolls, or Daruma (the Japanese name) good-luck dolls, painted with the characteristic dark hairy features (chest and body) to denote his Indian or 'Western' appearance. The classic Daruma doll in Japan is rotund and, pretty much, just a stylised head, with heavy eyebrows and whiskers. His eyes are coloured later, for example painting one pupil at the beginning of a year or at the making of a wish, and the other when the wish has come true. In art, his eyes are typically depicted as blue and bulging. As mentioned earlier, his nose is big and his body is very hairy, with thick black hair, particularly prominent on his chest. Again, this depicts his Western or Indian origins.

It was during his period of nine years of deep meditation that Bodhidharma was approached by many monks asking to be his disciple. Bodhidharma was dismissive of all of these individuals until one of them, known as Huike or (Shenguang Huike), persisted with his requests and questions regarding Buddhism. Bodhidharma typically would not answer, remaining in complete silence.

Huike, in order to prove his dedication and commitment to Bodhidharma as a sage, then stands in snow in the middle of the night in front of the Shaolin Monastery, undergoing extreme mountainside hardship in order to prove himself. Bodhidharma still denies him discipleship. Then, in the act of a complete devotee, Huike cuts off his left arm and prepares to cut off the other, at which point Bodhidharma accepts him as a follower, informing his new pupil that his determination to get training and enlightenment was as strong as his own.

It is in remembrance of Huike that Zen Buddhists perform the gassho (a Japanese term literally meaning 'aligning of palms') greeting with one hand. Huike goes on to become the twenty-ninth Patriarch of Buddhism, after Bodhidharma, and as a result the second Zen patriarch in China.

The legends that describe Bodhidharma finishing at the Shaolin Monastery and departing, relate that before he had identified his first disciple he had attained masterful enlightenment, thus allowing him to become the twenty-eighth patriarch. Two main narratives exist: one is that of the Four Students. During his time in China, he had only a few disciples, many say only four or five, and the first account gives us the names of four students, three monks and one nun.

This is the *koan* exercise performed by Zen Buddhists to help convey their understanding of Buddhism to their students, and was actually chronicled during the Song dynasty in the *Ching-te Ch'uan Teng-lu*, the most prominent of the 'Transmission of the Lamp' *Teng-lu* texts, compiled by Tao-Yuan, presented to Emperor Zhenzong in 1004 and subsequently published by imperial decree in 1011.

In this account, after a long period in China, stated to be as wildly different as four and sixty years, but usually as nine, Bodhidharma tells four of his top students that the time has come for him to ask if they can convey their comprehension or understanding. One of them, Daofu, says that they should neither be affixed nor separated from letters, thus allowing the Way to function with freedom. At this Bodhidharma explains that he had attained his skin. Next, the nun Zongchi explains that her comprehension is akin to the delight of seeing Akshobhya Buddha land just once and not again. To this Bodhidharma explains that she has attained his flesh. Following the nun, the next disciple, Daoyu, states that the four Great Elements are originally empty and the five Skandhas do not exist, thus he did not see anything to be attained. The master comments that Daoyu has attained his bones.

Finally, when it was Huike's turn, he simply got up, came forward, made one (or three) full bows, stood up and returned to where he was, to which Bodhidharma exclaimed that Huike had attained his marrow. With this, Bodhidharma confirmed Huike as the second Patriarch of Zen in China, transmitting the Dharma at that time and giving him the robe.

An alternative story explains that Bodhidharma reproached Huike as he had continually persisted in asking so many questions, explaining that true enlightenment does not come from the teachings of another individual but from within. Huike appeals to his master, saying that his soul is not yet pacified, at which time Bodhidharma requests that his disciple bring forth his soul so that he might pacify it. Huike responds that he cannot carry out the request as he knows not where his soul is, as he has attempted to find it over many years unsuccessfully.

At this the master replies that by definition his soul is and would be pacified forever as a result. Up to this point, the story can be found in the 'Four Practices' section of *The Two Entrances and Four Practices* text (see p.43). Immediately following this occurrence, it is narrated that Bodhidharma transmitted the Dharma to his disciple, entitling him the twenty-ninth Patriarch of Zen and the second Patriarch of Zen in China, giving him the begging bowl and the robe. With this, Bodhidharma left the Shaolin Temple.

As with what is known of Bodhidharma's birth and life, the details of his death – the time, location and his age – are varied and unsure. He may have travelled extensively, and even returned to India and passed away there. Some explain that he passed away in his fifties whilst others insist that he was over 150 years old. The cause of his death is similarly unknown; theories have been proposed of a natural death or poisoning by jealous monks. Others claim that Bodhidharma went to Japan, teaching for a further 200 years before dying aged over 250.

There are stories of him having gone to Chen Sung (One Thousand Saints) Temple to propagate the Dharma, passing into Nirvana in 528–539, and his subsequent burial on the Song mountain range; a number claim interment at a site on Bear's Ear Mountain (Xiong Er Shan). Nearby, a stupa was built for him in the Pao Lin Temple. Many years later, Emperor Dai Dzong (reigned 762–779) of the

Tang dynasty posthumously titled Bodhidharma 'Yuen Che Perfectly Enlightened Great Master', also renaming the stupa as 'Kong Kwan Contemplator of Emptiness'.

Supposedly three years after Bodhidharma's death, a Chinese emissary (whom some call Song-yun – an envoy of one of the later Wei dynasties) travelling in the Central Asian mountains (the Pamirs) saw Bodhidharma travelling west, carrying a staff from which hung a single sandal. Conversing with the great sage, the emissary was told by the man he believed to be Bodhidharma that he was returning to India. He also informed the emissary that his monarch would soon die. On returning to China, the prediction became true, and subsequently the news of this story travelled far. Monks at the Song mountain range who had buried Bodhidharma opened his tomb to examine the deceased monk's remains in order to refute the fable. On opening the tomb, they noticed that there were no remains whatsoever, other than a single sandal.

Of note, a small number of legends subscribe to the fact that he was of Persian or Iranian stock, explaining that this was the reason for his Aryan looks (blue eyes, characteristic nose etc.), the name Iran being an equivalent of Aryan and literally meaning 'land of the Aryans'. These legends are complicated as they claim that Bodhidharma became the first Patriarch of Zen by combining Mahayana Buddhism with Sufism to create Zen Buddhism. Although the Sufic teachings according to some religious scholars have some superficial similarities to Zen, they do not fundamentally correlate. The Sufic influence on the origins of Zen can also be historically discounted as Sufism was not practised until at least the lifetime of the Prophet Muhammad (570–632), with Sufism as we know it not occurring until much later, particularly with reference to its spread to China. The legend that Bodhidharma was of Persian origin is, however, a convincing one, and will be discussed in Chapter 3.

The historical record

The written history of Shaolin Kung-Fu through the interpretation of the original Chinese evidence has been well addressed by other scholars[4] and is beyond the scope of this text. As stated earlier, the *Yi Gin Ching* is not considered authentic and the Shaolin Stele from 1517 is attributed not to Bodhidharma but rather the Bodhisattva Vajrapani's Kimnara King. Some authors claim that martial arts and martial artists came to the Shaolin Monastery and it was they who developed Shaolin. It is also claimed that some of the martial-artist monks were practising their techniques before Bodhidharma arrived, although the evidence for these findings is lacking. Although the bibliographies in the *Book of the Han Dynasty*, the *Records of the Grand Historian* and the *Spring and Autumn Annals of Wu and Yue* all record martial arts in existence in China before Bodhidharma's arrival, none of these allude to the concept of a recognised Shaolin Kung-Fu. Furthermore, although subsequent accounts of Shaolin monks do exist, it is not until the mid- to late-sixteenth century that we have formal accounts of Shaolin martial techniques and training, and it is possible that some of the earliest Shaolin victories may have been ascribed to militarily experienced individuals working on behalf of the monks in warfare.

During the Tang dynasty (618–907 BCE) evidence from a stone stele reveals that in 610 and 621 the monks were able to defend their monastery from outlaws and supported the subsequent Emperor Taizong of Tang (the second Tang emperor) to victory in the Battle of Hulao.

In the following three periods, very little is reported on Shaolin:

907–960 the Five Dynasties and Ten Kingdoms era;
960–1234 Song, Liao, Jin and Western Xia dynasties;
1271–1368 Yuan dynasty.

In the subsequent Ming dynasty (1368–1644), the lacuna in Shaolin descriptions is filled by an exponential rise in reports of fighting Shaolin monks. For the first time, the monks are reported as being experts in hand-to-hand combat, spear and staff weaponry. Cheng Zongyou's *Exposition of the Original Shaolin Staff Method* is dated to approximately 1610 and published in 1621.[4]

During the mid-1500s, Shaolin monks were enlisted to defend the Chinese mainland against Japanese Wokou (possibly a mistaken transliteration of the Japanese word wakou/wako), pirates.[5] Zheng Ruoceng lists at least four battles where the monks were involved:

1. Gulf of Hangzhou (1553);
2. Wengjiagang on the Huangpu River delta (1553);
3. Majiabang (1554);
4. Taozhai (1555).

The monks won a massive victory at Wengjiagang, suffering only four casualties compared to 100 for the pirates. Conversely, the largest defeat was at Taozhai, with four monks dying and subsequently being commemorated by a statute near Shanghai (Mount She).

Figure 2: Shaolin monks outside the original Shaolin Temple.

We have very little evidence as to the time and form of dissemination of these Shaolin Kung-Fu arts and their likely derivatives into the hard and soft styles. The monastery (**Figure 2**) was visited by authors such as Yu Dayou in approximately 1560 and we know that he, for example, returned home with two monks who then disseminated their arts to fellow monks in Yu Dayou's monastery.

The development of styles

The subsequent development of each style takes a unique path, each with a host of unique legends. In summary, these are depicted in **Figure 3 (overleaf)**. Whether through Bodhidharma or via indigenous Chinese martial skills, Shaolin is traditionally divided into five substyles:

1. Crane
2. Dragon
3. Leopard
4. Tiger
5. Snake

The combination of these represents the original Shaolin style. This is then divided into the soft internal Kung-Fu (Wudang) that eventually develops into Tai Chi (although controversially there is a school of thought proposing that Tai Chi Chuan developed independently of Shaolin) whilst the harder style of Kung-Fu becomes northern Shaolin Monastery Kung-Fu. This northern Shaolin style later evolves into the southern styles, but the northern styles are also divided into a number of seven foundation sects to become all the common hard Kung-Fu styles of today, including White Crane, Praying Mantis and Wing Chun.

Still further legends of the development of Shaolin exist,[6] whereby Bodhidharma dies in approximately 534 CE and the Shaolin Monastery falls into disarray. However, the third abbot then rein-

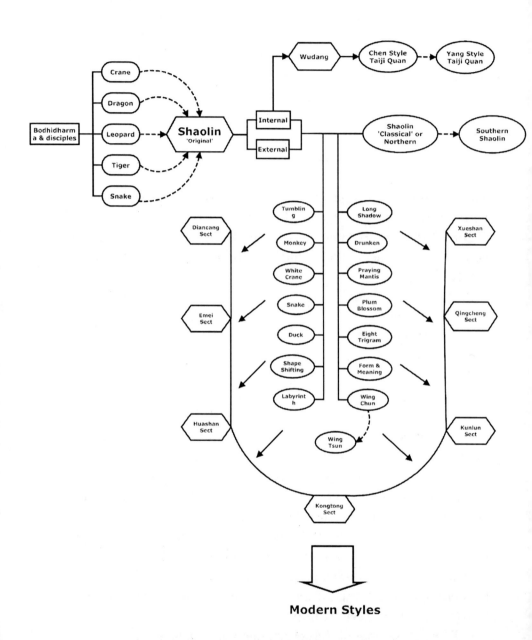

Figure 3: The development of Kung-Fu styles.

troduces martial arts and meditation, where the monks base their skills on the movements of animals such as snake attacks, tiger-claw strikes, ape fighting snakes and crane striking frogs. As the concept of Zen Buddhism spreads, a second southern Shaolin Monastery is founded in Fukien, which subsequently becomes more influenced by Taoism. Cultural links would be established with Tibetan monks and some would create formal styles such as the Crane of the monk Ordator.

Monks from the northern and southern Shaolin would then go on to the Five-Formed Fists and the Essence of Five Fists (五形拳 alternative translations of the same term). Finally, due to a conflict of political interest, a senior monk, Pak Mei (white eyebrows), betrays his fellow monks and the northern temple is burned. Later, however, Pak Mei and his disciples revive the temple and they continue to train under his leadership. The several surviving monks (or guardians) go on as five elders (one of whom was Pak Mei) to develop the myriad Kung-Fu styles including Hung Gar, Praying Mantis, Dragon and Wing Chun. The southern stylists were responsible for the addition of Taoism into the compendium of arts such that they would develop arts such as Tai Chi, Hsing I and Bagua Zhang (the trinity of internal arts, the *neija chuan*).

Legendary techniques of the Shaolin

The Shaolin monks have been reported to demonstrate superhuman abilities and skills. Many of these legendary skills of the Shaolin warriors are ascribed to the continuous development of internal energy, or *Chi*. These can be used to develop seventy-two identifiable skills (**Figure 4**).

Today the Shaolin Monastery continues to exist, although now there are numerous competing Shaolin schools claiming so-called authenticity. The modern Shaolin Temple is now widely regarded as a government-funded tourist attraction with only a marginal relevance to the original practices. Some historians see it as merely a

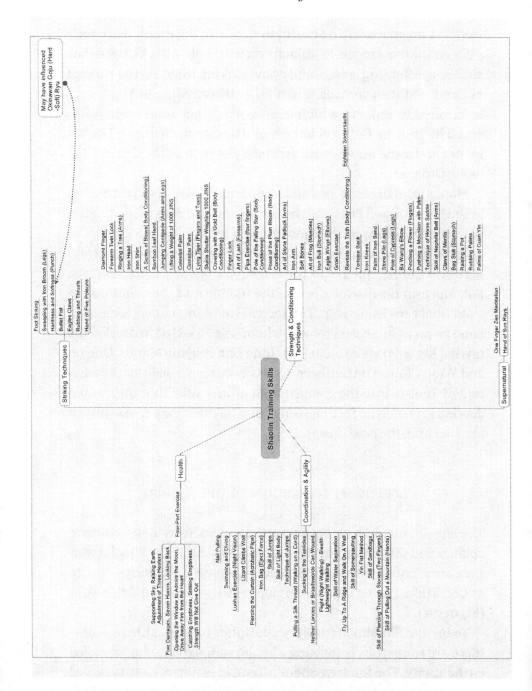

Figure 4: Shaolin Training Skills (derived from the *Training Methods of 72 Arts of Shaolin* written by Jin Jing Zhong from 1934 and the *Treasured Secret Book* by monk scribe Wu Toy San Ling Kung), (Quoted from Chow & Spangler, *Kung Fu: History, Philosophy and Technique*, 1982)

manufactured history for recreation and pleasure, for the benefits of tourism and a cultural novelty. The recent visit to the temple by foreign dignitaries and presidents is an example of such a use.[7] There are political activists such as the controversial New Zealander and pro-Chinese campaigner Rewi Alley who see the modern Shaolin Monastery as useful for educational and political aims in China and the West.[222] It is claimed that his 'rediscovery' of the Shaolin monastery led to the re-invention of modern Shaolin to accommodate a national and touristic craving for Eastern martial arts.

The spread of Kung-Fu to the West through television series such as *Kung Fu* starring David Carradine in the 1970s and the first English text on Shaolin (Robert W. Smith's book *Secrets of Shaolin Temple Boxing*,[9] based on the *Shaolin Nei-Kung Mi-Chueh* 'Secrets of Shaolin Internal Work'), also contributed to a kind of self-fulfilling prophecy as the idea of Shaolin was embellished for popular entertainment. The modern Chinese Wushu that the Shaolin monk display teams show is very different to what went on before the Cultural Revolution and most likely represents a Wushu gymnastic/acrobatic hybrid (likely based on Chinese Opera). Nevertheless, the monks are now world-renowned and demonstrate their skill around the world. Current skills typically demonstrated to tourists and in public demonstrations include *Di-Tan Quan* (ground fighting skills), tiger form and drunken monkey techniques. The skills demonstrated include the rolling fist and dropping, single-finger press-ups, head tumbling, back dropping and leopard fist. As a result of the worldwide popularity of the martial arts of prominent Kung-Fu celebrities such as Jackie Chan, Jet Li, Stephen Chow and, of course, the colossal Bruce Lee (whose mysterious death is described in Appendix 1 of this book), Shaolin and other Kung-Fu styles are practised and venerated worldwide.

3

Unravelling the Silk Road

There are no authenticated writings by Bodhidharma himself and what is known about him is largely limited to several Chinese manuscripts from a variety of sources over a period of 500 years.[10] As with the analysis of any historical texts, one is always wary of the evolution of factual history into pseudo-history and legends. One is increasingly apprehensive of the accuracy of later texts, particularly as they are written against the background of polarised sociopolitical Chinese Chan Buddhism at the turn of the first millennium.

We first come across his name in a Chinese text entitled *A Record of the Buddhist Monasteries of Lo-yang*, written by Yang Hsüan-chih (Yang Xuanzhi), a writer and translator of Mahayana Buddhist manuscripts in the sixth century. He is generally accepted to have lived from 493 to 534 and probably for some years after, whilst he compiled the book. Although seventh-century Chinese scholars considered him to express a strong anti-Buddhist sentiment, of this we cannot be sure, although what we do know is that at the time many manuscripts were being written with an indirect, or hidden, political message – in this case a criticism of 'the enemies of Wei legitimacy and the Han aristocracy in 549'.[11]

The author mentions Bodhidharma twice. First when he is describing the well-known Yung-ning Monastery, constructed by

Empress Dowager Ling of the Hu family in the first year of the His-p'ing period:

> At that time there was a monk of the Western Region named Bodhidharma, a Persian Central Asian. He travelled from the wild borderlands to China. Seeing the golden disks [on the pole on top of Yung-ning's stupa] reflecting in the sun, the rays of light illuminating the surface of the clouds, the jewel-bells on the stupa blowing in the wind, the echoes reverberating beyond the heavens, he sang its praises. He exclaimed: 'Truly this is the work of spirits.' He said: 'I am 150 years old, and I have passed through numerous countries. There is virtually no country I have not visited. But even in India there is nothing comparable to the pure beauty of this monastery. Not even in the distant Buddha's realms of ultimate things.' He chanted namah, or homage, and placed his palms together in salutation for days on end.[12, 13]

The second mention is when describing the Hsiu-fan Temple (Temple for the Cultivation of Goodness): he noted that there was 'a statue of Vajrapani (a fierce holder of the Thunderbolt Sceptre) guarding its gate. Pigeons and doves would neither fly through the gate nor roost upon it (or were not allowed to do so). Bodhidharma said that the statue catches the true character, or bore a striking resemblance to Vajrapani.'[12, 13]

The construction date of the Yung-ning Monastery has been put around 516 CE, though it is reputed to have had a short existence. Its pole with the golden disks, and eventually the whole monastery, were damaged by wind and then later by fire from a military encampment, said to have been there between the years 526–528 by various authors.[12, 14] This is our first and last true placing of this monk in time; he was likely to have been in Lo-yang some time between 516 and 528.

Yang Hsüan-chih's invaluable contemporaneous account of the monk gives us some clear information about Bodhidharma:

He was a Persian or Central Asian from the West.

He was of advanced age, and Yang Hsüan-chih documents that he claimed to be 150 years old, implying he was older than this when he died.

He was likely to have been in Lo-yang during the years 516–528.

He had travelled extensively in the ancient world, probably travelling via India.

He had adopted Buddhism (likely Mahayana), although the national religion of Persia at that time was Zoroastrianism.

Bodhidharma and Yang Hsüan-chih conversed and as the latter would probably only have spoken Chinese and some Indian dialects, this implies that Bodhidharma as a Persian spoke one of these two languages.

He chanted 'namah' – described by orientalists in this context as a Buddhist chant, though in the languages of Middle Persian or Pahlavi, the vernacular of the Persian Sassanid Empire (of the time), it was a well-known term for a book or letter (*Namag*)[15] from which prayers and chants were memorised, read and recited by the educated priest class. Examples include *Arda Wiraz Namag* (Iranian 'Divina Commedia') and the *Khwaday Namag* (Book of Kings). Indeed the word 'Namaz' used by Muslims across the world to mean 'prayer', does not originate from the Arabic (which uses the word 'Salat' for this meaning), but from the Middle Persian root 'Namag'. No corresponding connotation with comparative relevance exists in Sanskrit, whereby the term 'nama' usually means 'name',[16] sometimes 'holy name' but rarely if ever is it associated with the meaning of 'prayer'. Bodhidharma may have been vocalising in Persian or chanting Persian prayers.

As he is mentioned twice in the *Record of the Buddhist Monasteries of Lo-yang*, some scholars consider that there may have been two Bodhidharmas, although this seems unlikely.

Our next source for Bodhidharma is a Zen Buddhist follower, and therefore he would already harbour some degree of favourable bias in his writing about the monk. By the time he writes, the Chinese disciple T'an-lin identifies Bodhidharma as the first Patriarch of Zen Buddhism, and thus referred to him by his new title, that of the Dharma Master, or the Tripitaka Dharma Master Bodhidharma.

T'an-lin was a Sanskrit scholar, and although traditionally seen as one of Bodhidharma's direct disciples, he is now viewed as a second-generation disciple, being a follower of one of the two most widely accepted of Bodhidharma's direct disciples, probably the monk Hui-k'o (Huike).[12] He wrote a short biography of Bodhidharma, which acted as a preface to some of the core teachings of Zen Buddhism ascribed to Bodhidharma, namely the *Treatise on the Two Entrances and Four Practices*.

The *Treatise on the Two Entrances* is fundamentally important to the understanding of the evolution of Zen,[17] and was probably composed by a group of unknown eighth-century Zen Buddhists. The *Biography*, by T'an-lin, acted as a preamble, equivalent to contemporary 'About the Author' information. The *Biography* implicitly reinforces the association of the text with Bodhidharma, so as to assure readers that the source of the work was that of Zen's first patriarch, the Tripitaka Dharma Master Bodhidharma. The *Biography* in itself is quite clear:

The Dharma Master was a South Indian of the Western Region. He was the third son of a great Indian king. His divine insight was clear; whatever he heard, he understood. His ambition lay in the Mahayana path, and so he put aside his white layman's robe for the black robe of a monk. He merged with the sagely lineage and made it flourish. His dark mind was empty and quiescent. He comprehended the events of the world. He understood both Buddhist and non-Buddhist teachings. His virtue surpassed that of the leaders of the age.

Lamenting the decline of the true teaching in the outlands, he subsequently crossed distant mountains and seas, travelling about propagating the teachings in Han and Wei. Of scholars who had extinguished mind, there were none who did not come to have faith in him but those who clung to characteristics and preserved views to ridicule him.

At the time his only disciples were Tao-yü and Hui-k'o. These two monks, even though born later, showed a superior aspiration for the lofty and distant. Fortunately they met the Dharma Master and served him for several years. They reverently requested him to inform them; they readily perceived the master's intention. The Dharma Master was moved by their pure sincerity and instructed them in the true path: thus quieting mind; thus giving rise to practice; thus according with things; and thus [implementing provisional teaching] devices. This is the quieting of mind of the Mahayana Dharma. Make no mistake about it. Thus quieting mind is wall-examining. Thus giving rise to practice is the four practices. Thus according with things is protection against derision. Thus [implementing] devices is to implement devices without attachment. This brief preface draws upon the meaning in the following text. [*The Two Entrances and Four Practices* commences here].[12]

T'an-lin is generally accepted to have lived between 506 and 574 BCE.[10] From his *Biography* of Bodhidharma we can derive various insights about Zen Buddhism (unfortunately not within the remit of this book) and we can also extract and comment on the factual information given regarding the elusive monk:

T'an-lin's work contradicts Yang Hsüan-chih, as T'an-lin claims that Bodhidharma was a native of India, the country where the 'original' Buddha, the founding father Siddhartha Gautama, was born, without Persian heritage.

Bodhidharma was of royal pedigree, being the third son of a great king.

Some scholars suggest that by defining him as a royal from South India would imply that he was of the Indian Kshatriya warrior caste.[12]

He originated his Buddhist training in the Mahayana School.

He wore a dark robe.

To get to North China, he crossed distant mountains and seas.
He had two main disciples named Daoyu and Huike who studied
under him for several years.

The works by Yang Hsüan-chih and T'an-lin together form the
foundations for most of the subsequent Bodhidharma biographical
texts. Amongst these is the seventh-century, three-volume *Further
Biographies of Eminent Monks* by Dao Xuan (596–667), in which the
famous monk is again recorded as being of 'South Indian Brahman
stock' (Indian Priest class).[18]

Dao Xuan's work is an important literary source, his work
describes hundreds of prominent monks whose histories we can
cross-reference and analyse. The monks coming from various geog-
raphies and schools means that their lives by definition were quite
varied, and therefore their biographies give us a broad insight, if at
the expense of a little depth. The work was first completed in 645 CE,
but Dao Xuan continued to work on the manuscript until his death
in 667, adding in approximately 150 more biographies.[12] This is
highly beneficial, as once word was out that the book had been completed, other scholars could have contacted and met with Dao Xuan,
correcting any errors or omissions, and giving information for new
additions and entries.

Whilst compiling his work, it is clear that Dao Xuan combined
both the works of Yang Hsüan-chih and T'an-lin to derive his work
on Bodhidharma, reiterating Yang Hsüan-chih's documented age of
Bodhidharma as being over 150.

Dao Xuan also is more specific than either of the first two biographies with regard to Bodhidharma's route from East to West, writing that he 'first arrived at Nan-yueh during the Song period. From
there he turned north and came to the Kingdom of Wei'.[18] By doing
so, he strongly suggested that Bodhidharma went by boat to China.
Nan-yueh (also known as Nanyue or Nam Viet) was the name of
an ancient kingdom that covered a large area of southern China
(modern Guangdong, Guangxi and Yunnan) and North Vietnam. Its
capital was Panyu (Cantonese Poon Yu), on the site of, or very close to,

the location of modern Guangzhou (formerly Canton City). It was and still is an extremely significant port on the coast of southern China, and if Bodhidharma had travelled by land, Guangzhou could not be his first entry point into China. The fact that Guangzhou was the location of his first contact with China therefore indicates sea travel.

The chronicle next informs us that this all occurred during the Liu Song dynasty (420–479), the first of the four Southern Chinese dynasties. Bodhidharma next travels north towards the seat of the Northern Wei dynasty, also known as the Tuoba Wei or Yuan Wei (386–534). By doing so, he must have crossed the Yangtze River that divided China into North and South. As the reign of the Northern Wei dynasty started earlier than that of the Liu Song, and fell at a much later date, then mathematically one can pinpoint Bodhidharma's arrival into China as during the time when both dynasties coexisted. This would correspond to the lifetime of the Liu Song dynasty, somewhere between 420 and 479, if we accept Dao Xuan as an accurate source. The legends discuss his meeting with Emperor Wu of Liang (reigned 502–549), a not impossible time frame, but the monk would have been in China for at least twenty-three years before going to the emperor's court.

Dao Xuan tell us that 'he lived at no fixed abode' and 'spread/taught the word of Zen wherever he went'. He is further mentioned in the section on meditation, critiquing on his particular method of 'Mahayana wall-gazing',[10] and also later alluding to his existence in the biography of his disciple Huike (whom we encountered in the legends above). The segment on Huike that was written during the first composition of Dao Xuan's work includes a passage regarding Bodhidharma's death:

Sakya Seng-k'o, also known as Hui-k'o, family name Chi, was a man of Hu-lao [Honan]. In external learning he looked into the classics and histories; in Buddhist learning he penetrated the texts of the canon. In the end, thinking of the capital of the path, he silently scrutinized the fashions of the times. In solitude he accumulated great illumination, and his intellectual awakening far surpassed that of the crowd. Still, perfecting the path is not something done anew by each practitioner, and people valued having a transmission from a master. In unison the prestigious ones criticized him: 'his path is merely one of expedience and lacks a real strategy. He seems to possess understanding, but is not lofty. Who could possibly moor himself to the essence of his teaching?'

When he reached forty years of age, he encountered the Indian monk Bodhidharma, who was travelling about propagating the teaching in the area of Mount Sung and Lo-yang. Hui-k'o came to cherish him, realising that Bodhidharma embodied the path. In a single glance Bodhidharma was pleased with him, and he came to serve Bodhidharma as his master. To the end of the master's life he received the purport of the teachings. He trained for six years, making a subtle investigation of the one vehicle. Principle and phenomena fused; suffering and joy became unobstructed. His understanding was not of the provisional sort, for his wisdom emerged from a divine mind. Hui-k'o treated sensory objects in the manner of a potter, grinding up the duality of purity and defilement, shaping it as if were clay, and coming to a realisation. The resilient strength of his pottery was due to his power and dynamism, not to the qualities of the mound of clay.

Bodhidharma died at Lo River Beach. Hui-k'o concealed the body [or buried the body without the proper ceremonies] on a bank of the river, but Bodhidharma had enjoyed a fine reputation in the past, and so a proclamation was transmitted throughout the imperial domain. This brought monks and laypeople to come and politely ask if they could follow the master's model. Hui-k'o then unleashed his astounding discourse and presented his mind essence: 'Though you may be able to spread the verbal formulation of Bodhidharma's teaching throughout the world, the intention behind it will not be established. Abstruse books are but a look from afar. You have not even begun to experience it in your minds!'

Later, at the beginning of the T'ien-p'ing era [534–7], he went north to Yeh, the new capital of the Eastern Wei, and opened many secret parks.[12]

So Bodhidharma received a relatively unceremonious ending, particularly for a man of his exalted standing and divine spirituality, as such a high priest could expect to be afforded a lavish funeral with many well-wishers, onlookers and dignitaries present. A prominent funeral procession and an aptly tranquil and exalted site would have been the norm, not simply a cave by the riverbank, as Dao Xuan intimates. As this happened before Huike went north to the capital of the Eastern Wei dynasty (534–550) during the Tianping era (534–537), then the latest possible date of death is 537. However, this can be honed further, as according to some scholars,[19] the Japanese edition of the Chinese Buddhist Canon (*Tripitaka Koreana* or *Palman Daejanggyeong* in Korean), commonly known as the *Taisho Shinshu Daizokyo*, describes an incident relevant to the date of Bodhidharma's death. In 528, following a battle between rebel and loyalist forces, the victorious rebels sought to eliminate all those associated with one particular loyalist who had perished during the conflict. This loyalist had a nephew called Seng-fu who studied under a Dharma master, both of whom could have been characterised as 'associated' with the dead loyalist uncle. Although we do not know from the text who was rounded up, what it does say is that there was a 'political mass execution'. Importantly, this mass execution occurred at Ho-yin (also known as Lo-pin).

Lo-pin therefore could correspond to Dao Xuan's Lo riverbank, and it is not unreasonable to assume that a mass execution would occur at a riverbank for ease of body disposal, or a mass burial could occur at such a site after the executions. As the text mentions a certain Seng-fu and his Dharma master as being connected with the reviled individual, then we can assume these two individuals would at least be targets for execution, if not actually executed. The Dharma Master alluded to in the text may have been Bodhidharma, who died at Lo-pin, and due to the the mass burial received only a 'simple' burial in a cave from his devout disciple Huike. We shall never know for sure.

Lastly, Dao Xuan gives an almost satirical insight into Bodhidharma's disciple Huike, for he tells us that the well-known story of the disciple having cut off his arm to prove his devotion and the depth of his desire to study spiritual enlightenment under Bodhidharma may not be completely accurate. He relates that although the tale was used by many Buddhist masters in their *koan* teaching exercises to exemplify degrees of self-sacrifice and devotion,[20] more or less with glee he says this was a yarn, and that actually thieves had cut off his arm.

Dao Xuan's *Biographies* give us the following:

Bodhidharma came from the Indian Priest class.

Bodhidharma lived for over 150 years.

He travelled from West to East.

He first arrived in China at Nan-yueh during the Liu Song period, at a large port not bordering other countries, implying the route was by sea.

Bodhidharma travels north towards the Northern Wei dynasty and by doing so must have crossed the Yangtze River.

Bodhidharma received a relatively unceremonial burial.

By deduction, his arrival must fall during the years 420–479 (corresponding to the time of the Liu Song dynasty).

By deduction, the latest possible date of death is 537.

Correlating the monk story from the Chinese Buddhist Canon and Dao Xuan, the date of death may be 528.

After Dao Xuan, in the late seventh century a document entitled *The Epitaph of Faru (or Fa-ju)*, written for the Zen monk of that name (638–689), who was a prominent disciple of the fifth Zen patriarch, mentions Bodhidharma as the first Zen patriarch in a chronological lineage down to Hung-jen (Hong-ren), who is listed as the fifth Zen patriarch.[10] Unfortunately, we do not know the epitaph's author. This text is important, as it is the first that considers a chronological lineage, rather than simply mentioning Bodhidharma and his immediate disciples.

The *Song of Enlightenment*, a later ancient Buddhist text of the famed Buddhist master Yung-chia Hsuan-chueh (or Yongjia

Xuanjue, 665–713) mentions Bodhidharma. The authorship of the manuscript is usually attributed to this prominent disciple of the sixth Zen patriarch, Huineng (638–713),[21] and was probably written during the T'ang dynasty. It continues the concept of Zen patriarchal lineage, but this time starting with the Father Buddha (Sakyamuni Buddha or Gautama Buddha) as the original instigator of Zen, subsequently making Mahakasyapa the first Zen patriarch, leading to Bodhidharma as the twenty-eighth patriarch and so on:

> Mahakashyapa was the first, leading the line of transmission;
> Twenty-eight Fathers followed him in the West;
> The Lamp was then brought over the sea to this country;
> And Bodhidharma became the First Father here:
> His mantle, as we all know, passed over six Fathers,
> And by them many minds came to see the Light.[22]

So the text assures all Zen Buddhists that they follow a lineage directly from the father Buddha (even if other schools of Buddhism disagree) and to strengthen this argument, it 'demotes' Bodhidharma and denies his position as the father of Zen, and rather portrays him as the twenty-eighth patriarchal transmitter of it. The text implies that although he is great, Bodhidhama cannot be compared to the supremely enlightened Father Buddha, and Zen itself gains more acceptability. It encourages followers to deduce that the father of Zen Buddhism was the father of *all* Buddhism, Gautama Buddha. The text has cultural and political biases but we can draw two conclusions from it:

> Bodhidharma was from, or must have travelled from, India (the fact that he came from the same nation as the Father Buddha strengthened the public perception of his 'Zen' authority).
> He came to China by sea.

Near the Shaolin Temple itself there is a testimonial dating from 723 (under the Tang dynasty 618–907) known as the Song Mountain Shaolin Temple Stele (Shaolin si bei).[1, 23] Measuring 3.44m by

1.28m, this monumental stone structure of engraved inscriptions informs us about a number of local political and economic issues, and famously recounts that combative Shaolin monks assisted the then-future Emperor Li Shimin in his struggle against his adversary Wang Shichong. It briefly mentions the monk Bodhidharma and Huike, stating that they 'once lived on this mountain [Mount Song]'; although there is no explicit mention or association of them with the word 'Shaolin' or its temple, some might argue that this is implied.

Other Shaolin references during the Tang dynasty (618–907) fail to mention the great Buddhist monk. These texts include the King of Qin's *Proclamation to the Abbot of Shaolin Temple* (621), *Edict Granting Fields to the Shaolin Temple* (632) and *Record of Repairs Performed at the Shaolin Temple* (683). This absence has caused the many martial arts historians much angst over the centuries, although this author does not necessarily find it to be such an obstacle. Simply the fact that Bodhidharma went to the Shaolin Temple and taught the monks exercises that later became Kung-Fu does not necessarily mean that he should be mentioned in every text. Importantly, it is widely accepted that it was not he who got the temple constructed, but another Indian Buddhist monk named Batuo, of the school of Nikaya Buddhism. Batuo is never credited as having started Zen and only ever rarely as having started Shaolin Kung-Fu, but is credited only as the instigator of the temple itself. Even he is not mentioned in many of the above texts, so why would Bodhidharma be? Not every Vatican document mentions St Peter.

The most detailed Chinese biography of Bodhidharma is written in the tenth century. The *Anthology (or Collection) of the Patriarchal Hall* (Tsu-t'ang-chi or Zutangji, compiled in 952) uses information from previous authors, but also adds to them. A version is extant in Korea, in the format of a wood block from 1245.[24] The sources from which it draws are unknown, but are likely corrupted by passage of time and bias. The anthology is the one most responsible for the vast quantities of legends about the famous monk.

In this source, we come across the Indian name Prajnatara, identifying him as the twenty-seventh Patriarch of Zen and master in India, and thus recognising Bodhidharma as the twenty-eighth Patriarch of Zen and master in China. It states that Bodhidharma arrived on Chinese soil in 527 by sea from India, the journey taking three years, which means that his arrival did not occur during the Song period, but during the Liang dynasty.

He initially attended the Liang court (based at today's Nanjing), and an encounter with Emperor Wu of Liang was largely unproductive as he presented himself as obdurate in his interpretation of his school of Buddhism, somewhat offending his host and leading to a non-violent dismissal from court, either directly by the emperor, or self-imposed. He left Nanjing and eventually crossed the Yangtze River to reach the kingdom of the Northern Wei dynasty. This subnarrative can actually be found in an earlier appendix to a text recording the teachings of Shen-hui (684–758), a prominent disciple of Huineng (the sixth Zen patriarch).[25, 26]

The *Anthology of the Patriarchal Hall* then contradicts both Yang Hsüan-chih and Dao Xuan, stating that rather than being over 150 at death, he was actually exactly that age when he died. He was buried on Mount Xiong'er to the west of Luo-yang.

As described earlier, three years after this interment a Chinese official of one of the later Wei dynasties, named Songyun, was travelling through the Pamir mountain range when he encountered Bodhidharma. The monk was carrying a staff, from which hung a single sandal, and he claimed to be travelling to India. During the conversation he informed Songyun that his ruler would soon pass away. On Songyun's return to China, Bodhidharma's prediction became true. As a result his tomb was reopened, revealing the presence of only a single sandal but no bodily remains.

Until now, no mention of Bodhidharma had explicitly connected him to the Shaolin Temple, fighting monks, Kung-Fu or even the wall gazing. In 1004 an additional manuscript containing the 'Biography of Bodhidharma' was produced, entitled *Jingde Records of the Transmission of the Lamp (Jingde chuandeng lu)*. This work by Dao Yuan has an entry concerning Bodhidharma that is almost identical to that of the *Anthology of the Patriarchal Hall*, other than adding that his master (Prajnatara the twenty-seventh patriarch) renamed Bodhidharma, changing the monk's original name of 'Bodhitara' that he had before becoming a Buddhist disciple.

In the *Jingde Records of the Transmission of the Lamp* we first come across a mention of Bodhidharma and the Shaolin. It states that in year 10 of the Taihe period of Emperor Xiao Ming Di of the Northern Wei dynasty, he [Bodhidharma] dwelled at Lo-yang and later went to the Shaolin Temple, and there he positioned himself opposite a wall for nine years, without uttering a word during that whole period. It goes on to say that after the nine years, he died in his upright seated position. We have to question the text's accuracy as it seems to be historically self-contradicting. For example, the Taihe period (477–499) falls under Emperor Xiao Wen Di (471–499), and not under the reign of Emperor Xiao Ming Di (516–528). There is no mention of Shaolin fighting skills. According to the text, it was in year 10 of the Taihe period that Bodhidharma was at Lo-yang and then went to Shaolin. This means a date of 487, which conflicts with our historical knowledge that Shaolin was built in 495, implying that Bodhidharma went to Shaolin seven years before it was built.

This confusion, however, may be resolvable. First, the *Jingde* text tells us that Bodhidharma dwelt or lived in Lo-yang in year 10 of the Taihe period (487); it does not say how long he was there before he went to Shaolin. He may well have lived in and around Lo-yang for a few years before moving on. Remember that Yang Hsüan-chih saw him twice at Lo-yang, therefore Bodhidharma would not have been there for a short 'tourist visit', but probably for a substantial period. This would mean, then, that after a few years at Lo-yang, exceeding the 487 date and also passing 495, he could have gone to Shaolin.

Although we might discern some facts from the *Jingde* text, it is clearly not our best historical source for chronology, in view of its internal discrepancies. It was suggested earlier that the longer these texts are written after the life of Bodhidharma, the more inaccurate they become. We know that Bodhidharma is mentioned by Yang Hsüan-chih as a contemporary, and we can therefore date

Bodhidharma's time in Lo-yang from his account, falling some-where between 516 and 528.

At the beginning of the second millennium Zen was spreading internationally. The earlier biographies were being spread, repeated and reinforced so that, for example, by the thirteenth century, the Japanese Zen monk Keizan Jokin (1268–1325), the fourth-generation teacher of the monk Dogen's school of Soto Zen, inscribed a well-known legend in his *Denkoroku* or *Transmission of Light*.[27] In it, he includes fifty-three koans pertaining to the events occurring for the transmission of the Dharma amongst the fifty-three patriarchs of the Ts'ao-tung (Soto) line of Zen. Within this, he mentions Bodhidharma in koan 29, and says he was born as the third son of a South Indian Rajah of the warrior caste. Following his father's death, he approached Prajnatara, the twenty-seventh Indian Patriarch of Buddhism, in a line directly from the Buddha, and asked for holy induction to become a Buddhist monk and disciple. Following his subsequent spiritual enlightenment, his spiritual master Prajnatara put it to him that after his death Bodhidharma should travel to China to locate and develop (worthy) new followers.

Bodhidharma fulfilled his master's request, eventually traversing the Yangtze River into North China and reaching the Shaolin Monastery, where he educated the monks for nine years, whilst also guiding four main disciples. Of these, one became enlightened – and he was Huike.

As already pointed out, however, quite a lot of these texts have agendas that detract from their objectivity, as the authors desire to strengthen their arguments about why their school of Zen should be adhered to. The authors of the later stories would have obtained copies of the earlier biographers' works and amended their content to suit. This problem remains with us today.

From these later biographies we can discern the following:

Bodhidharma is the twenty-eighth Patriarch of Zen.
His master was called Prajnatara, who in turn was the twenty-seventh Patriarch of Zen.

Bodhidharma arrived in China by sea.

His journey was from India.

The journey took three years.

The date of arrival in China was 527.

He encountered Emperor Wu of Liang at Nanjing (464–549, reigned 502–549).

He crosses the Yangtze River to get to the Northern Wei dynasty (386–534).

He dies aged 150 years.

He is spotted three years after death and predicts the demise of one of the later Wei rulers.

He was born Bodhitara, and subsequently was named Bodhidharma by his master Prajnatara on becoming a Buddhist.

He dwelt at Lo-yang in year 10 of the Taihe period before going to Shaolin.

He spent nine years sitting upright meditating against a wall.

By deduction, if his entry into China was 527, and he spent nine years meditating against a wall, then he must have lived to at least 536.

According to some, if he encountered the official of the 'last' Wei dynasty three years after his death, and if the last Wei dynasty is recorded as ending in 554, then his date of death would be 551.

According to my interpretation, actually the last Wei dynasty ended in 534, though its emperor for whom Bodhidharma made the prediction died in 535, implying a date of death of 532.

Even this does not stand scrutiny, as these are for the last Wei emperor, and the later biographies only specify that Bodhidharma predicted the death of one of the 'later' Wei kings. This is difficult to pinpoint as in the last eighteen years of the dynasty (516–534) there were seven kings: Xiao Ming Di, Youzhu, Xiao Zhuang Di, Chang Guang Wang, Jie Min Di, An Ding Wang and Xiao Wu Di.

If we try to discern the information gathered from Bodhidharma himself, we need to consider the texts directly attributed to him, already mentioned briefly in the legends surrounding the monk. These are *Yi Gin Ching* or *I Chin Ching* (Book of Changing Muscle/Tendon), and *Xi Shui Jing* or *Hsi Sui Chin* (Book of Washing Marrow). We cannot reliably identify their original sources.

Over the centuries, it seems that these texts have 'always' been attributed to Bodhidharma, with each generation reinforcing this truth, or myth. An early twentieth-century popular novel is an example of this process, *The Travels of Lao Ts'an*, serialised between 1904 and 1907 in *Illustrated Fiction Magazine*.[3, 28] Following the popularity of this text, another appeared, which also claimed Bodhidharma as the father of Kung-Fu, written anonymously and entitled *Shaolin School Methods*, serialised in 1910 by a Shanghai newspaper.[29] This text, which expanded on Bodhidharma as the Father of Kung-Fu, also gained great popularity, not only because of its martial arts content, but also because of its political message, expressing a strongly anti-Manchu sentiment. As with many other successful books, the mixture of politics, history, legend and heroic action led to literary success, and primed the market for a very widespread book entitled *Secrets of Shaolin Boxing*, published in 1915.[3, 30] This text, written by a so-called 'Master of the Study of Self Respect' continued the by now successful tradition of anti-Manchu and anti-Imperial sentiment, clearly defining Bodhidharma as the instigator of the aforementioned exercises, informing us that all our martial arts are derived from these exercises via this sage.[31] This book influenced all subsequent texts and well-known histories of the martial arts,[3] such as the 1919 classic, Guo Shaoyu's *History of Chinese Physical Culture*.[32]

The anonymity of the text by definition undermines its credibility, particularly in view of the lack of sources, and authors from the East and West have been keen to question whether any information or teachings therein, or the texts it draws on, are from Bodhidharma, adopting the stance that they are spurious.[33–42]

Many current Shaolin masters claim that the texts actually originated in south-east China in Zhejiang province at Mount Tiantai, where the famous Sino-Japanese school of Mahayana Buddhism originated (Tendai Buddhism) and where supposedly the Daoist monk Zining wrote them around 1624 during the Ming dynasty. He has been accused by two military generals of falsifying forewords to the texts, the Tang's Li Jing and the Southern Song's Niu Hao, an unlikely co-authorship for the time.

The texts themselves have their own legend. After Bodhidharma left the Shaolin Monastery, he left an iron trunk there, which was subsequently opened by the monks. Inside they found two manuscripts, *Yi Gin Ching* and *Xi Shui Jing*. The former was taken by Bodhidharma's first disciple Huike, the latter was taken and studied by the monks, who practised its teachings assiduously and as a result improved their own health and developed their own skills, thus propagating the art of Shaolin Kung-Fu.

Clearly, it is impossible to say who wrote the texts, especially as we only first hear of them as late as the fifteenth century. It is quite possible that Bodhidharma did not write them; he is also said not to have written any for Zen Buddhism, which rather reinforces the idea. Others could have written them as a result of his direct teaching or, if not, the works could be the result of a few authors wishing finally to put to paper a long tradition of martial arts teaching that had previously only been taught by action, speech and demonstration. Either way, there is currently no way of knowing their origin, but it would be incorrect to say that the exercises definitely did *not* come from Bodhidharma.

We simply don't know.

Separating fact from fiction

Extracting viable truths regarding Bodhidharma is difficult. For example, if we look at Huike in the historical references, we find that he studied under Bodhidharma for several years (T'an-lin), or is it six years (Dao Xuan)? Or maybe four, or sixty years (various *Four Student* koan legends)?

If we are to ascertain any facts with even a modicum of accuracy, it makes sense to concentrate on the earliest historical texts. First, Hsüan-chih was a contemporary; second, the further we go forward in time, the more the legends are subsumed into the 'history'. Third, the mention of Bodhidharma later on, once he has amassed popularity, will perforce be biased: he will be commandeered to reinforce an argument of one nature or another. That he was the 'First Patriarch of Zen' or the 'Father of the Martial Arts', means that anyone wanting to make a statement about these two topics can add authority to anything they write by invoking the name Bodhidharma, or somehow associating the monk with themselves. This can be illustrated by the fact that so many temples have claimed to have been visited by the monk.

We need to think of the broader picture, for between the first 50–100 years of Bodhidharma's lifetime he is only and exclusively mentioned in Chinese texts. He cannot be found in any Indian, Japanese or Korean text, though he is later, with the spread of Buddhism. Although he was probably in India, or as the majority believe, he was actually an Indian, and he was the twenty-eighth Patriarch of Buddhism, he is not found in any first-millennium Sanskrit or Indian texts.

Searching through the three largest libraries in the world, namely the Library of Congress, the British Library and Bibliothèque Nationale de France, no such text can be found. This is a consistent finding, even for libraries with a strong geographical relevance for Bodhidharma, including the National Library of China, the National Library of India and the National Diet Library of Japan. Modern experts in Buddhism are confident[43] that Bodhidharma is not mentioned in any Sanskrit or any Indian text. The following question, therefore, cannot be avoided: if Bodhidharma existed, and he came from India, the son of a 'great king' no less, then why do the Indian texts fail to mention him?

We shall never know definitively that he existed. However, the fact that a number of bona fide historical sources describe him – *alongside* his numerous legends – leads us to believe that he was real.

The fact that no early non-Chinese sources mention him warrants further analysis. Thankfully, we do have evidence of other foreign monks in China at around the time of Bodhidharama,[20] a good and relevant example here would be the monk Batuo,[44] also noted to be of Indian origin and named Buddhabhadra. In the *Deng Feng County Recording* (Deng Feng Xian Zhi), there is an entry on him regarding his arrival in China from the West in 464 CE to preach Nikaya Buddhism. He is credited as instigator of the Shaolin Monastery, eventually built in 495 by royal decree of Emperor Xiaowen (467–499) of the Northern Wei dynasty. Although the monastery would have initially been designed as a temple and centre for the translation of Indian Buddhist texts into Chinese, some say that Batuo, on becoming founding abbot and patriarch, also set up a fighting and exercise system, eventually establishing the concept of elite fighting monks.

The fact that Batuo is considered as a possible candidate for 'Founding Father' of Shaolin is awkward, in that his role is viewed as significantly less important than that of Bodhidharma, even though he set up the monastery in the first place! In fact, it would have been easy to identify him as Shaolin Kung-Fu's great luminary without having to include Bodhidharma in *any* legend. Bodhidharma's prominence in Zen and Shaolin Kung-Fu lore does imply a significant contribution.

Like Bodhidharma (according to some sources), Batuo was originally a monk from India; however, we do not necessarily expect to find him in any Indian texts, as initially he is not described as being anything but a devout monk who travels to China to spread the word of his Buddhism. Bodhidharma, on the other hand, is given the significant spiritual title of twenty-eighth patriarch, in line to the Buddha himself, also coming from a royal background. If there would be anyone whom ancient Indian scholars would want to write about, it would be him. So why not? And why is he often termed 'Barbarian from the West', or depicted with a big nose, bulging, piercing blue eyes and white skin? These are not typical attributes of an Indian, and the Chinese authors and artists at the time would have been acutely aware of this: India bordered China and the two had an ancient and scholarly understanding of each other.[45]

Indeed, ever since T'an-lin's *Biography*, where Bodhidharma was pronounced an Indian, our suspicions should arise. T'an-lin and all Buddhist biographers after him had an overarching agenda – to prove Bodhidharma's lineage as Patriarch of Zen and direct transmitter of the lamp, in line from the Buddha himself: 'the Pope of Buddhism', if you will. Thus it made sense to make his country of origin the same as that of the Father Buddha. It made sense to call him princely and from the warrior caste (either as per the legends[12] or the later Japanese text of the *Denkoroku*) as, again, Gautama Buddha was one such. Alternatively, those who claimed his origins were from a priest caste would be seeking to ensure his spiritual heritage.

If, however, we return with an objective mind to the only contemporary account of Bodhidharma, that of Yang Hsüan-chih's *A Record of the Buddhist Monasteries of Lo-yang*, he is quite clear in his description: 'Bodhidharma, a Persian Central Asian'.

As Bodhidharma is not yet named a Patriarch of Zen or the founder of Shaolin Kung-Fu, Yang Hsüan-chih is probably our most unprejudiced and honest source. He is clear in his statement, and it would be arrogant of us to say that this author could not tell the difference between an Indian and a Persian. Both of these cultures traded and regularly exchanged goods and scholarship. There is good evidence of all three cultures knowing each other well from ancient times,[46] not least through the ancient Silk Road and by sea. There is no reason, therefore, for Yang Hsüan-chih to give disinformation, and even if he were, why would he pick Persia as the origin of the monk? The concept of a Buddhist monk coming from Persia in those times would be rare, and such a fabrication would have been so obvious that the work of Yang Hsüan-chih would have been quickly discredited, without us ever having heard about it in the modern era. Indeed, it would be most difficult for Yang Hsüan-chih to distort any information regarding Bodhidharma, as the two were contemporaries, and the readers of Yang Hsüan-chih's manuscript at the time could have verified for themselves Bodhidharma's Persian origins.

This contemporary nature of his description therefore precludes any dishonesty on the part of Yang Hsüan-chih.

What can be said is that so many authors take differing stances on Bodhidharma's original Indian caste that we can largely discount all of them. The fact that he was an Indian royal, being the third son of a great king, is a consistent story. It is also rather insightful, and may represent a shred of truth. For although some would claim that the princely nature is attempting to associate him with the princely history of the father Gautama Buddha, the chronicles differ in that Gautama Buddha was the first-born prince: why, then, would the biographers make Bodhidharma, the twenty-eighth patriarch, any less than the first-born? Why would he be the third son? Furthermore, although many fictions could be constructed for Bodhidharma, defining him as a prince even 200 or 300 years after his death would have been difficult, and indeed manuscripts and coins listing royalty did exist at his time.[47, 48] From time immemorial, royal lineage has been universally important across cultures. Guides or rules to succession are a foundation step to stability in any society and come to include the concept of divine birthright. Had Bodhidharma not been a prince, it would have been obvious for many years after his death. Whether from India or Persia, falsifying Bodhidharma as a prince would have been difficult, and again, an unusual thing to do – very few other priests are accorded the same royal background. This allows us to surmise, therefore, that Bodhidharma was likely a royal prince, and furthermore the third prince in a royal line.

4

Prince of Persia

Before undertaking to date Bodhidharma, one must exclude unrealistic longevity. Many of the biographers quote an age of 150 or older, which is impossible for the first millennium. Bodhidharma himself may have either knowingly or unknowingly communicated an incorrect age to his followers, let alone the various biographers wanting to add a superhuman quality to their Zen master. Once the numerical age of 150 was used, it became very difficult to 'shake off', and so subsequent authors could only confirm it, being unwilling to contradict the sensational claim. As we have so little accurate and comparable data regarding Bodhidharma's age, we shall not use this given figure but look at corroborative facts concerning the estimation of his lifetime.

For ease of calculation, the following postulations are also represented pictorially in **Figure 5** (see p. 65). To start with, if we look at the contemporary account of Yang Hsüan-chih, we know by deduction (explained above), that the monk must have been alive and in Lo-yang (China) between 516 and 528 **(Box a)**. This is our most accurate date, around which we must base everything else. Importantly, although the next biography we come across chronologically is written by an author who lived during the 516–528 period, namely T'an-lin's (506–574), he never documented any direct information about Bodhidharma, or ever alluded to having personally met him, taking his information from disciples who had encountered the sage. This makes T'an-lin a second-generation disciple. This implies, there-fore, that although Bodhidharma and T'an-lin lived in the same era, T'an-lin probably became a Zen Buddhist scholar after Bodhidharma had died or left, giving the latest date of death or disappearance of Bodhidharma as 574, that of T'an-lin's death. It is extremely likely, however, that Bodhidharma died or disappeared well before this, as it would be unlikely that T'an-lin would have become a Zen Buddhist and written his biography in his final years. So Bodhidharma would have died or disappeared some time before. We therefore use T'an-lin's last year as our very latest date of death for Bodhidharma, with the actual date of death likely occurring before T'an-lin's Zen Buddhist conversion, so many years before, but not of course before T'an-lin's birth in 506 **(Box b)**. To put T'an-lin's age of conversion to Buddhism into context, Dao Xuan tells us that Bodhidharma's first top disciple, Huike, met his master when aged 40.

Dao Xuan gives us more hard data and, as explained above, deduction reveals that Bodhidharma's arrival must fall during the years 420–479, corresponding to the time of the Liu Song dynasty **(Box c)**, and furthermore the latest possible date of death is 537, which on correlating the monk story from the Chinese Buddhist Canon and Dao Xuan, gives us a likely date of death of 528 **(Box d)**.

From the *Anthology of the Patriarchal Hall* and the *Jingde Records of the Transmission of the Lamp*, we get the date of arrival in China as 527, and as Bodhidharma encountered Emperor Wu of Liang at Nanjing during his reign of 502–549, he would have been in China at some point during this time **(Box e)**. Although the corrobora-tion of his 'sighting after death' legend is not germane to this arith-metical calculation, even the dates of the legend fall within the time period accorded to the meeting with the reign of Emperor Wu of Liang at Nanjing (502–549). Furthermore, the *Jingde* text, although alluded to already as inaccurate, does give us one date as year 10 of the Taihe period (487), when Bodhidharma was at Lo-yang before going to Shaolin; for completeness, this date has been included.

That said, it is clear that we get our most historically accurate range of time from arrival to death or disappearance as 420 to 537 **(Box f)**. This period of 134 years still seems unrealistically long. Huike left to go to the Eastern Wei dynasty during the Tianping era (534–537). The entry in the Chinese Buddhist Canon giving a date of mass execution and therefore Bodhidharma's death in 528 is reasonable. Scrutinising Bodhidharma's date of arrival in China is more interesting, however.

We have already concluded that following Dao Xuan, Bodhidharma arrives in China during the Liu Song dynasty (420–479), then visits the Northern Wei dynasty (386–534). As the Liu Song dynasty falls entirely within the Northern Wei dynasty, and as Bodhidharma is noted to have visited both, then by deduction, he must have arrived some time in the shorter of the two time spans, namely that of the Liu Song (420–479).

We can thus discern the time range of arrival and start to pare it down. Bodhidharma's travel to China and arrival during the Liu Song dynasty may not have been a coincidence. The earlier periods of this Southern dynasty had been famous in the ancient world for their contribution to the sciences (mathematics and astronomy) and the arts (poetry and painting), leading to the reign of Yuanjia (425–453) being termed one of the 'golden ages' of the Southern dynasties. During these times, there was also a period of great Buddhist expansion, scholarship and cultural enlightenment.[49] Indeed some prominent members of court such as the official Xie Lingyun were Buddhists themselves, and it may have been to this place, with such a reputation, that the Buddhist monk was headed.

The dynasty became politically unstable, with a number of political deaths and assassinations. Emperor Wen (reigned 424–453), Emperor Xiaowu (reigned 453–464) and Emperor Ming (465–472) ruled for twenty-nine, eleven and seven years respectively. Many of the emperors were tyrannical despots with an appetite for bloodshed and murder. Ming, who incidentally may be the inspiration for the Flash Gordon comic character of the same name (*Ming the Merciless*[50] and not the Chinese Empire of the same name 1368–

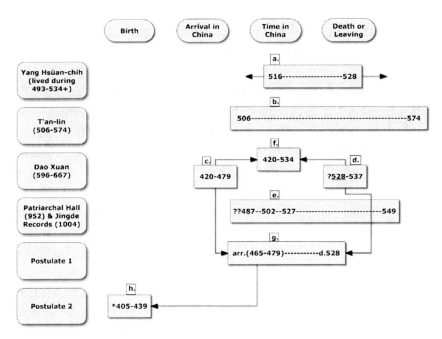

Figure 5: Pictorial representations of various calculated dates for Bodhidharma's birth, arrival in China, time in China and death or leaving China, corroborated from his ancient historical biographies.

1644) was particularly known to be cruel and savage. The last two emperors of the dynasty after him (Houfei and Shun) only ruled for two years each.

It could be that Bodhidharma initially travelled to the Liu Song dynasty in the belief that he could practise his Buddhism under an enlightened regime, but on arrival found it to be a politically unstable fire nest of danger and unpredictability. This may have forced him to leave the Liu Song in favour of a more stable political environment, namely the Northern Wei dynasty.

If we extend this postulation, he may have arrived in China during the reign of Ming or the later two Liu Song emperors, placing his arrival at the latter end of the dynasty of 465–479. This date means that Bodhidharma arrived in China beween 465 and 479 **(Box g)**. Finally, if we were to reasonably assume Bodhidharma arrived in China between the ages of 40 and 60, then using the 465–479 arrival date, his date of birth would be between 405 and 439 **(Box h)**.

A unique history of brotherhood – a possibility for the origins of Bodhidharma

The idea of a Persian noble travelling to China between the fifth and sixth centuries is reasonable. The Persian Empire at that time was under the rule of the Sassanid dynasty who ruled from 224 CE until the Muslim Arab Conquest in 651.[48, 51, 52] This empire is considered amongst the greatest of ancient Persia and is famed for its cultural achievements, its commitment to the Zoroastrian religion and its military might. It defeated the Roman Empire under Emperor Valerian in 260.

Communication between the Sassanid Empire and China was surprisingly well established and had even been in existence during the previous royal Persian dynasty of the Parthians (third-century BCE to third-century CE). Prior to this, there are examples of cultural links and linguistic interacton between these empires, such as the Old Persian word maguš and the Old Chinese word myag, meaning wizard, around the eighth century BCE.[53] The Sassanid and the Chinese would trade via the Silk Road and both empires would share artisans and musicians. Diplomatic ties were so close that when the Arabs invaded Persia, the Chinese gave protection and support to the last Persian emperor, Pirooz II and his son Narsieh. Although the emperor's bid to reinvade Persia was unsuccessful, the Chinese continued to offer support to the Persian royal house and Narsieh became a member of the Chinese Royal Guard, and his family and descendants were accorded royal status for many years.

Even before the time of the Sassanids, there is a Buddhist legend of an earlier Persian–Chinese connection, in which An Shih-kao (or An Shigao, *c.*168 CE) renounces his hereditary claim to the Persian royal throne to instead become a Buddhist missionary monk.[54] This story would fit perfectly with that of Bodhidharma – other than the time, which is about 400 years too early, dating to the Persian Parthian or Arsacid Empire. The legend of An Shih-kao has little corroborative Persian evidence, but the story of the so-called 'Parthian Marquis' may have subsequently been mixed with those of Bodhidharma, adding weight to the idea that Bodhidharma was Persian.

Further evidence of ancient Sino-Persian relations is the recent discovery of a Chinese version of the Cyrus Cylinder. The original cylinder written in Akkadian script is a foundation-deposit cylindrical tablet representing the Persian invasion of Babylon in 539 BCE by Cyrus the Great. Its text proclaims the importance of repatriating refugees and deportees, in addition to restoring religious buildings. According to the Torah and the Bible, Cyrus the Great is said to have assisted in the freeing of the Jews from captivity and their return to Judea and Israel, so that today he is considered as the only gentile to hold the title of 'Moshiach' (Messiah). Although the historical evidence for this is not fully established, the Cyrus Cylinder has been called 'the world's first charter of human rights'. Although the cylinder's role as such is controversial (it has similarities to the older Mesopotamian royal inscriptions of Marduk-apla-iddina II and Sargon II), its importance in the ancient world has been generally accepted.

The Chinese version[55] of the Cyrus Cylinder, written in cuneiform on fossilised horse bones, was first identified in 1928 and formally presented to Beijing's Palace Museum (of China's Forbidden City) in the 1980s. They were subsequently assessed by experts from the British Museum in 2010. Although their authenticity is still under scrutiny, early analysis reveals the bones to be authentic and likely to have been derived from a version of the cylinder in Persia, as opposed to Babylon. If these pieces are authentic, it reveals a deep relationship and familiarity between the Chinese Empire and the Persian Empire dating as far back as the sixth-century BCE.

The possibility of Bodhidharma's life starting at some point between 405 and 439 is interesting when considered against the backdrop of the Sassanid royal household (**Figure 6**). The empire was exposed to an influx of spiritual philosophy and concepts leading to religious turmoil. There was support for the religions of Zoroastrianism, Manichaeism and Christianity. There was also turbulence in the inheritance of kingship.

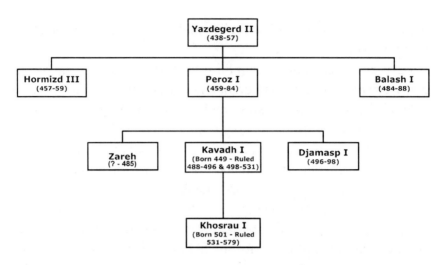

Figure 6: Chronology for the known kings and princes of the Sassanid Dynasty in the fifth and sixth centuries CE.

In two successive generations two sons from one king would both lay concurrent claims to the throne. These were Hormizd III and Peroz I and, subsequently, Kavadh I and Djamasp I. Both cases led to an internal struggle for the empire, and on both occasions the victorious brother would forgive his rival and continue to provide him with the privileges of royalty. This is uncommon in other royal dynasties of the ancient world, where competitors even within the same family would be executed or assassinated. Interestingly, Kavadh I initially loses the throne to his brother Djamasp I, but then subsequently regains it and continues to rule for another thirty years.

Although there is no direct mention of Prince Bodhidharma in the Sassanid dynasty or lesser vassal states, there is the possibility of the existence of an unnamed minor Persian prince who might have had some secondary claim to the throne, may have contributed on the wrong side of a royal contested battle for the Persian throne, may even have harboured unorthodox religious beliefs. Accordingly, he would have retained his freedom and title, but may have left the empire by volition or under some encouragement to explore and visit the neighbouring Indian and Chinese lands, to avoid any potential title claims. Once in China, the local scholars of the time such as Yang Hsüan-chih would have recognised this royal visitor as Persian, one who may have adopted Buddhism on his extended journey from Persia to India and on to China.

Subsequent authors may have become confused concerning the prince's travels via India and assumed this was the starting point of his journey, hence ascribing his origins to India. It would be a misinterpretation of fifth-century Chinese civilisation to suggest that Yang Hsüan-chih could not accurately differentiate between Southern Indians and Persians.[13] These cultures had been well-known to each other for centuries at the time of Bodhidharma, and Yang Hsüanchih's manuscript is not recognised as suffering from cultural or ethnic bias. In summary, Bodhidharma's description as a Persian in sixth-century China is likely to be based on a valid observation.

5

Zurkhane (House of Power) and Kalarippayattu

If Bodhidharma was a Persian prince who travelled from Persia to India then to China, then his derivation of Shaolin can have been taken from either his access to indigenous Persian martial arts or, alternatively, via exposure to Indian martial arts in his travels, or possibly from both.

Two prime candidates for these original martial arts can be considered to provide both the traditional exercise elements and as being in the correct locations and era. On the Persian side there is the ancient martial art of Zurkhane, and on the Indian side there is the martial of Kalarippayattu and its progenitor arts.

Zurkhane (House of Power) or Varzesh-e Pahlavani (Sport of the Heroes)

Ancient Persia and Iran has a long-standing tradition of the veneration of legendary heroes. These champions are best described in the *Shahname* (or 'Book of Kings') written by the Persian poet Ferdowsi around 1000 BCE, based on a much older Middle Persian text known as *Xwaday-namag*. His epic poem narrates the mythical and historical legends of the Persians from prehistory, through the Zoroastrian era until the Arab Muslim Conquest. Much of the story focuses on heroes with superhuman powers who compete in chivalrous combat, which can take place in battles but more importantly are in hand-to-hand combat and wrestling.

The greatest heroic warriors are given the title *pahlavan* – an ancient Persian word that can be derived from its Indo-European roots and that can also be found in ancient Sanskrit and Indian languages. The greatest pahlavan, according to the Persian epic, is Rostam – a local king of Sistan of the house of Nariman, seen to some extent as an Iranian Hercules. He was so massive at birth that his mother required a Caesarian section; and he was so powerful and massive that he needed divine intervention to ensure he would not make an imprint into the earth as he walked. Pahlavans such as Rostam fought according to an unwritten code of chivalry based on loyalty and honour.

In its current form, the martial art of Zurkhane is practised through the ancient tradition of the pahlavans and involves the veneration of the Imam Ali, according to more recent Shia Islam and also Sufi orders. The greatest Zurkhane sportsmen are given the title pahlavan and adhere to strict principles of purity in practice and mind.

Zurkhane, also known as Varzesh-e Pahlavani, gained widespread acclaim and became the national sport in Turkey (known as *Pehlivani*), and was widely practised in India (known as *Pehlwani*). This sport regained popularity in India under the Mughal Empire (1526 to the mid-nineteenth century) where the court was heavily influenced by Persian culture and art.

The sport itself is practised in a pit (approximately 4ft deep) known as the *gowd*.[56] Here the sportsmen train, led by an *ostad*, following the rhythm of the *morshed* (or traditionally a *zaerbgir*) whose song sets the rhythm, and the training is accompanied by his drumbeat (*zaerb-e-zurkhane*). Zurkhane (translated as 'house of power') is also the name for the building or house where training is done. The spiritual strength and dedication it calls for has parallels with the ancient Persian divine warrior sprit of Verethragna ('smiting of resistance') that continued as the hypostasis or 'giver of victory' in the Zoroastrian religion,[57] and has some influence of the Shahname and modern Zurkhane stylists.

The chivalrous code of Zurkhane is embodied in the concept of *jaevan-maerdi* or ('youthful manhood'). This represents the four characteristics of a true warrior:[56]

> *shojaa-at* – bravery;
> *hekmat* – wisdom;
> *edale-at* – justice;
> *efaet* – chastity.

These are achieved through:

> *vafa* – loyalty;
> *sadgh* – honesty;
> *aamin* – trustworthiness;
> *saekha* – generosity;
> *tavazo* – humility;
> *nashiyat* – advice;
> *hedayat* – guidance;
> *towbe* – penitence.

The ultimate goal is to become like one's hero pahlavans. Although the title of pahlavan was traditionally a military rank, it is used to venerate distinguished Zurkhane practitioners, according to open competition. The world champion is the *Jehan-Pahlavan*, and there is now an international federation running the sport.

Training in the sport consists of basic cardiovascular drills of running, stretching, body strengthening exercises and wrestling/grappling (**Figure 7**). Push-ups are performed on a wooden block known as the *takhteh-ye-shena* (swimming board). Each flexion-extension movement can be straight, as in the traditional manner, or rotating (known as *pichidan*).

Ancient training weapons include:[56]

The *mil*, a wooden equivalent to the ancient *gorz* (Iranian club),
   which is also seen in ancient India.
The *kaebade*, or iron bow, used for strengthening.
The *sang*, which translates as 'stone' and is in fact a wooden
   shield wielded to improve strength and accuracy.

Much of the training in Zurkhane is in its powerful, dynamic and
intricate wrestling techniques. Wrestling, known as *koshti*, is performed according to either international or local rules (*Koshti-Kaj*).

Interestingly, the place where the training takes place, the zurkhane, is not too dissimilar from a warrior monastery; men enter
the zurkhane to advance their physical capabilities whilst adhering
to their spiritual and religious beliefs. Attendance at training is led
by rank and with respect to age. The lowest rank is the *nowcheh*, fol-

Figure 7: Zurkhane; unarmed grappling and wrestling in Persia during the Qajar era
in the nineteenth century. (Photograph taken by Antoin Sevruguin)

lowed by the *nowkhasteh*, and then the *pahlavan*. A leading champion is entitled *pahlavan-e-pahlavanan* (hero of heroes). Uniforms consist of decorated loincloths or sturdy training shorts (on occasion made of leather).

If Bodhidharma did have an acquaintance with Zurkhane, it would have been a much older version than is currently practised. Nevertheless, there are distinct areas of overlap between exercises performed in the gowd and those of the Eighteen Hand Movements, or 18 Lo-Han Hands of the Shaolin, or the Sanchin kata of Karate. The scenario of a princely monk arriving at the Shaolin Monastery and using known techniques of ancient Zurkhane to strengthen the monks and teach them self-defence is difficult to prove but is not improbable.

Kalarippayattu

Bodhidharma's training of the Shaolin monks may have come from observing ancient martial schools in India. Of these, Kalarippayattu is currently the most famous, although many other styles existed. It is possible that one of these arts, or more likely an ancestor (or progenitor) style, may have contributed to Bodhidharma's understanding of martial arts.

Kalarippayattu is one of the oldest extant martial arts in the world. It originated in South India and is currently practised in India (based in Kerala), Sri Lanka and Malaysia. 'Kalari' means fighting arena and 'payat' means 'fighting system'.

This system probably originates from the Kerala and Tamil Nadu region of southern India. The early Tamil (heroic) period from the time of Alexander the Great[58] (and maybe before) to 600 BCE[59] provided a a perfect environment for the development of martial arts. During this time, three rival kingdoms started a martial-arts arms race based at Cera, Cola and Pandya.[59] Here the factions advanced their knowledge of indigenous Dravidian martial arts.

Brahmanic sages from the north began to travel and settle in the south and established a code of logic, ethics and law that allowed the systematic categorisation and development of the martial arts in these regions. The Brahmans brought with them knowledge of Dhanur Veda – a martial practice that existed as one of the eighteen basic foundations of knowledge described in both ancient Indian epics, the *Mahabharata* and *Ramayana*. By approximately 1100 CE, there were a number of descriptions of the martial expertise of Kalari warriors. The Kalari martial art then divided into two main styles, the Northern Kerala (*Vadakkan Kalarippayattu*) and the Southern Kerala (*Thekken Kalarippayattu*), which then developed subsequent substyles.

According to ancient legend, this martial art was derived from the sixth avatar reincarnation of Lord Vishnu, known as 'Parashurama' (or 'axe-wielding Rama'). He created forty-two Kalari and twenty-one masters for these arts in order to defeat his opponents. He brought Brahmans from the north to worship him, and then decided that Kalari should only be taught in that one style.

In the current era, Kalarippayattu (**Figure 8**) is recognised as three different substyles: Northern, Central and Southern, each with a characteristic emphasis on armed and unarmed combat and sprirituality. Healing is considered part of the art and is taught from the beginning alongside the fighting components. The art was traditionally practised and taught in the centre of ancient Indian villages. Today, the art entertains tourists with flamboyant jumps, kicks and sword techniques. Yet whilst these tourist entertainments do exist, deeper analysis reveals a pluralistic style with sophisticated practical techniques that offer long-range and short-range grappling, strikes and weapons training. Many of these have at some point been used in real warfare in a variety of settings, ranging from ancient Indian battlefields (where warriors would fight on foot or on horseback) to the time of the British Raj. Spiritual training and respect are important components of this style.

Kalarippayattu's combat techniques are directly comparable to Karate and Shaolin Kung-Fu. As with Zurkhane, some of Kalarippayattu's basic excercises resemble Shaolin's 18 Lo-Han Hands. The Lo-Han Hands has a particular resonance with Central

Figure 8: Kalarippayattu; the first image (left) is from Northern Style Kalari (*Vadakkan Kalari*), and the leg sweep (right) is from Southern Style Kalari (*Thekkan Kalari*). (Photographs courtesy of Nic Gill, senior instructor at the Kerala Kalarippayat Academy UK, London, featuring Nic Gill, Barney Bryant and John Watts. Photographs taken by Anna Kubik)

Kalarippayattu, which in turn has some common elements with Bhuddism, so that the forerunner of this art may have been associated with ancient Bhuddism, travelling to China via Bodhidharma. If an ancestor style (a 'proto-Kalarippayattu') or a rudimentary Kalarippayattu style existed when Bodhidharma was travelling from India to China, and if he had been exposed to this martial art system, then it is possible for him to have trained in this art and subsequently taught it to the Shaolin monks. Alternatively, Bodhidharma may have simply passed through India and immersed himself in the teachings of the Dhanur Veda, which he could have subsequently taken to Shaolin. Ancient Indian and ancient Persian martial arts may have influenced the monk Bodhidharma and sparked the training of Shaolin after his epic journey to China.

Legends of the ancient martial arts in India

India has a rich literary history that contains two colossal epics, the aforementioned Mahabharata (fourth century) and Ramayana (between the second and fourth centuries). Both recount stories of

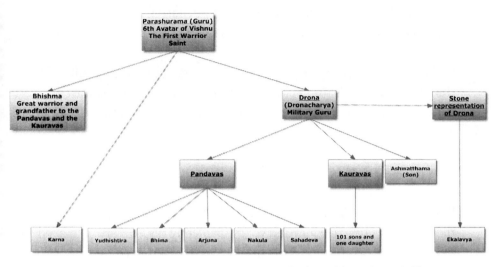

Figure 9: Legendary genealogy of martial arts in India derived from the *Mahabharata*.

hand-to-hand combat and martial arts. The Mahabharata, however, affords a deeper glimpse into the ancient legends of martial arts in India (**Figure 9**).

The book lists the first teacher of these ancient Indian martial arts as the ancient Guru Parashurama, the sixth avatar of the Indian god Vishnu and also the first warrior saint. Here again, as in China, the origins of martial arts are found in a religious warrior-patriarch.

Parashurama taught his martial arts (specifically archery) to three Kashtriya students, all of whom were (or meant to become at the time of teaching) part of the warrior ruling-elite caste system. These were namely the great warriors Bhishma and Karna and the great martial arts teacher Drona. The latter went on to teach martial arts to the ruling princes in ancient India, many of whom died in the great Kurukshetra War.

One story is of a prince of a lower caste who approaches Drona for instruction in martial arts, but is rejected on account of his low social status. He therefore teaches himself these martial skills by taking instruction and venerating a clay replica of Drona. By doing this he becomes a martial artist of equal or greater skills than Drona's own students. However, he loses his skill by purposefully cutting off his thumb at the request of the real Drona, who he continues to revere as his true master.

Clearly these are legends, but the religio-martial commonalities of the Indian, Chinese and Persian narratives may provide some extra support for a common origin of martial arts in these nations.

The medical condition of Bodhidharma

Bodhidharma is always associated with his staring gaze, sitting and meditating in his cave for nine years. Typically his eyes are displayed as extremely prominent. This may be associated with an underlying condition known as Graves' disease, an autoimmune condition of the thyroid gland resulting in its overactivity and enlargement. A hyperactive thyroid status can lead to a disturbed and increased heart rhythm (arrhythmia), muscle weakness, disordered sleep and fear of light (photophobia). Specifically, the eyes can become prominent and give the impression of 'bulging out' (also known as 'exophthalmos'). This occurs as a result of extra tissue around the orbit of the eye and its muscle displacing the eyeball.

It has been suggested that Bodhidharma suffered from Graves' disease[60] and that this is why he is portrayed on painting and sculptures with such prominent eyes. Furthermore, the muscle weakness associated with this disease, or a subsequent thyroid paralysis, may have led to the story of him sitting for long periods, and the fear of light may explain why he sat in a cave for such long hours.

Typically, people with hyperactive thyroids are usually lean, and although Bodhidharma is typically depicted as slightly obese, this has been explained by heart failure and fluid accumulation in the tissues after a prolonged hyperactive thyroid state (myxoedema of hyperthyroidism). It must also be noted that none of Bodhidharma's depictions reveal an enlarged neck mass, which is a typical finding in patients with Graves' disease. However, this has been argued away by the fact that his beard may have hidden it.

If indeed Bodhidharma did suffer from such a hyperactive thyroid state, then he may also have suffered from the associated condition of heat intolerance, and as a result may have found the cool mountain air more tolerable than other inhabitants of the mountainous Shaolin region at that time, thus explaining his tolerance of the barren cave. Of course other possibilities exist, and there are other conditions associated with exophthalmos and an obese status, including Erdheim-Chester disease.[61] This may also have explained Bodhidharma's interest in body-strengthening practices such as martial arts, and ascetic disciplines such as yoga.

6

Karate

The ancient Ryukyu archipelago harbours many hidden natural and cultural gems. This Pacific island chain (sometimes also referred to as the 'Nansei Islands' in Japanese or 'Lau Kau' in Cantonese) stretches from the Chinese mainland and Taiwan to the southern Japanese island of Kyushu. The largest island of the group is Okinawa, which carries the largest population and also acts as the capital of the broad island mass. Okinawa literally means 'rope in the ocean' (after its physical shape) and is a purely Japanese term that originally referred to the whole archipelago but primarily the main island. The name Ryukyu can be traced back approximately 1,500 years,[62] although this may have actually represented an ancient name for Taiwan as opposed to what is considered the current Ryukyu chain. Ryukyu is also the Japanese reading of the two characters 琉球 that the Chinese generally use, pronounced in their own dialect.

The evident variety of names for this small but rich island chain reflects a convoluted history of cultural interactions. In many ways the indigenous population has adopted the customs of its many neighbouring nations, whilst also consistently maintaining their own unique identity. The large number of beautiful yet hidden islands has led to an environment where people, wildlife and culture have been able to develop in the absence of external interference.

One prime example of this is the Iriomote cat (*Iriomote yamaneko*, the Iriomote mountain cat – *prionailurus iriomotensis*). This wild endangered feline is uniquely located to the Ryukyu island of Iriomote. It is approximately equivalent in size to its domestic cousin, but is considered the ancestor of a very ancient species no longer in existence. The local islanders call it *yamapikaryaa* ('mountain sparkling-eyed'), *yamamayaa* ('mountain cat') or *pingiimayaa* ('escaped cat'). Alternatively *yamapikaryaa* could mean 'mountain sparkling cat' rather than 'mountain sparkling-eyed' as *pika* and *yama* are both shared with mainland Japanese. It has dark brown spots in dense longitudinal rows that make stripes against its lighter brown fur. It has a characteristic bushy tail, and is not able to sheathe its claws.

The presence of such an island cat separated from all other cats by the Pacific is a classical example of allopatric speciation, where a species is physically separated from other species by geographical barriers, resulting in regional evolution of the species to adapt to its local environment. According to molecular phylogenetic analysis the Iriomote cat is very closely related to the leopard cat (*felis bengalensis*), which is a widespread species throughout southern and eastern Asia. Based on molecular genetic analysis, the Iriomote cat is estimated to have diverged from the leopard cat approximately 0.2 million years ago or earlier. This corresponds well to the date for geological isolation of the Ryukyu arc from the Chinese continent.[63]

Much like the Iriomote cat, Karate is likely to have arrived on the shores of the Ryukyu islands from the Chinese continent, but then developed locally and specialised over centuries to become a unique art that continues to this day. The evolution of each Karate style is analogous to each individual species evolving in its environment, much like the early findings by Darwin regarding the animals on the Galapagos archipelago. As such, Karate has undergone 'Karate speciation', such that each style has evolved as an individual 'species' due to differences in local micro-environments depending on each school's source of knowledge (instructors), the disseminators of that knowledge (students) and the local environment that would determine inter-style communication and cross-fertilisation. Before an analysis of Karate substyles can be achieved, it is necessary to consider the primary influx of Karate on Okinawa, much like the influx of a new animal on an island in the sea. This hypothetical animal (the martial art) would have come from another land, and once settled on the island, its descendants would each eventually evolve into different species (or styles). Today, Karate is among the best-known martial art in the world, and even James Bond practised Sanchin kata every day.[64] Karate is in fact considered to be the most practised martial art, with some sources quoting the number of practitioners and enthusiasts at up to 50 million people worldwide.[65]

The development of Okinawan Ti (the 'proto-Karate')

According to legend, Chinese visitors travelled to Okinawa in the seventh-century CE (maybe Taoist Buddhist monks) and possibly the same order of Taoist monks that contributed to the southern Shaolin Temple. The legend states that over many centuries the local inhabitants then developed the indigenous Okinawan martial arts of Ti (also known as Di, Dii or Tii, as the double 'ii' conveys the pronunciation better).

A varying Japanese legend reports that the veteran samurai, Minamoto no Tametomo (1139–1170), also known as Chinzei Hachiro Tametomo, of the 1156 Hogen Rebellion, had to escape after the loss of the battle and eventually arrived in exile on Okinawa. During that time, he taught fighting arts to the local inhabitants and royal family based on Okinawa, which subsequently developed into Ti. It is even claimed that he fathered the first king of Chuzan, named Shunten, by having a child with the daughter of a local Okinawan lord. According to Sho Shoken's 'Chuzan Seikan' (first history of the Ryukyu islands listed in the *Accurate Chronicles of the Kingdom of Chuzan*). There is no historical evidence of Minamoto's arrival on Okinawa, and his arrival on other islands is claimed, including Amami Oshima.

Some masters classify Ti as an indigenous grappling art that would approximate to a mixture of Aikido and Jujutsu; the ostensibly native Okinawan grappling art is also often referenced as Tuite or Tegumi. Master Choshin Chibana (former president of the Okinawan Karate Association) stated that the aboriginal practice of Ti on Okinawa was known due to the 'historical account of Oni Ogusuku' (aka Uni Ufugusuku; a famed Okinawan martial artist who was renowned for his massive height and saving King Sho Taikyu's daughter from abduction).[66, 67] The standard Romanisation of Toudi and Tuite (Okinawan) are specific terms referring to the grappling and trapping aspects of the martial art, both meaning 'taking hands' or 'taking methods'. When Tuite was mixed with Chinese Boxing or 'Chinese Chuan Fa' it became known as To-de. It is also possible that the indigenous adoption of a 'soft' grappling Chinese martial art became known as Ti and the adoption of the 'harder' Chinese Boxing added to this became To-de. Either way, most Okinawan masters claim that Ti is much older on Okinawa than To-de (the words themselves confirm this with 'to' being used to modify the base form 'di' or 'de'). 'Torite' is also sometimes employed to represent an older practice of Karate, but is a relatively common word used to refer to Jujutsu-type systems and techniques and is not unique to Karate. These terms developed in line with the evolution of Karate (**Figure 10**) in various sociopolitical contexts.

Ti developed against the backdrop of a need for naval defences and the introduction of the *New Treatise on Military Performance in 18 Volumes* by Ji Xiao Xin Shu Shi Ba Juan[5, 68, 69] – although in many ways it offered techniques of self-defence as opposed to formal group warfare. It can therefore be considered as a derivative of Chinese *quan fa* or Aboriginal Okinawan fighting arts (martial arts) from antiquity.

Okinawan Ti resembles the internal Chinese martial arts (such as Tai Chi). They both contain soft movements, dance-like techniques and some hard and fast techniques. Ti Jutsu and Tode Jutsu, or Tuite Jutsu, are amalgams of an archaic Okinawan dialect word and standard Japanese suffix that was never really used in Ryukyu martial arts until the twentieth century. It contains deflection (*tuidi gaeshi*) and reversed techniques (*ura gaeshi*) that culminate in 'The Dance of the Feudal Lords' (*Ajikata nu Meekata*).[70, 71] In its highest form, Ti provides a system where the practitioner looks totally relaxed in his combative state (*ma-ai*). Tuite (*Toudi*) was therefore a later extension of Ti as a system of locally adapted, distinct, bare-handed fighting systems (and their mixing with other arts from South-East Asia).

Modern martial-art scholarship considers that Ti refers to the old indigenous Okinawan martial practice that merged with Chinese martial arts and other influences to become Toudi. Unfortunately, its technical content has never been recorded as it was effectively superseded by Toudi before recording became commonplace – and thus can only be speculated on. There is a relationship observed between Karate and *Ryukyu buyo* (traditional folk dancing), although these movements are not formally taught in the dancing (please see the section on karate and dance at the end of this chapter).

Contrary to common belief, there is a lack of historical evidence supporting the practice of Ti as a form of self-defence practised secretly at night, but rather it suggests Ti was a martial system adopted by royal daimyo and the aristocratic shizoku class as a noble fighting system. Later on, members of the Motobu clan who were related to the Okinawan Royal House termed their secret family-martial-art *Udun-ti* (Okinawan) or *Gotente* (Japanese), which is translated as 'Palace Hand'. This was descended from Prince Sho

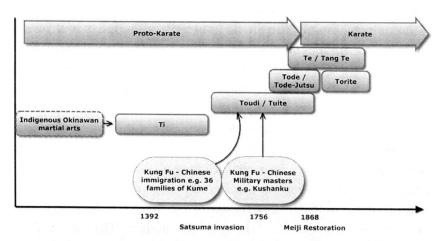

Figure 10: Karate timeline following the development of Karate from Ti and Toudi.

Koshin Motobu Oji Chohei (1648–1668), the fifth son of King Sho Shitsu. Their style consists of dancing hands (*mai-te or odori-te*), playing hands (*asobi-te or yu-te*) and fighting hands (*gassen-te*).[72] This art is considered a substyle of indigenous Okinawan Ti, specifically designed for the aristocracy. Although today the Motobu styles are generally classified as Karate, it is possible that this art may have been a hybrid of both, namely a mixture of the Chinese arts that became Karate and Okinawan Ti. In reality, the Motobu-Ryu and Gotente that preceded it are often classified as Ryukyu Kobujutsu rather than Karate per se, owing to the fact that most of the techniques are weapon-based and are quite clearly Chinese-influenced. Only a handful of modern schools teach the purported pure style of Ti; however, there is a growing belief that Okinawa's first martial art was Ti, this developed into Toudi with further influences then to Tode, Te (these can all be considered as proto-Karate) and finally into Karate (**Figure 10**): Ti → Toudi → Tode → Te → Karate.

The development of modern Karate

By the fourteenth century, Okinawa was divided into three kingdoms (tribes or *aji*), those of the Chuzan, Hokuzan and Nanzan. These kingdoms were more strongly influenced by China than their Japanese neighbours and consequently developed a satellite state-like political and diplomatic association with the Chinese Ming Empire. As a result, diplomats and envoys from Okinawa would visit China, and the Chinese would send over their diplomats to the Ryukyu Okinawan Kingdoms. It is considered that the Chinese envoys would have been knowledgeable in the Chinese martial arts, including Shaolin, and may have therefore taught these skills to the local dignitaries and subsequently the general inhabitants. As a result of this, martial knowledge among the political elite and the subsequent Okinawan martial arts acquired a prestigious status amongst the Ryukyu islanders, not unlike the prestige of Bushido and the Samurai arts on mainland Japan.

The transmission of these Chinese martial skills (Chuan Fa) from diplomats and envoys to the Okinawan populace may have happened before the advent of Ti, or could even possibly be the origin of Ti on the island. Importantly, however, this may have also been the first transmission of Karate to the Ryukyu islands.

The legends of Karate from this point onward start to gain momentum as history is finely and almost indistinguishably meshed with myth. According to popular legend, it was during these tribal leader periods that Karate's styles were developed and formalised (such as those for styles based at Shuri). The vassal-like nature between each of the Ryukyu kingdoms and China became increasingly impractical, such that by 1429, all three individual states merged into a unified kingdom. The nature of the unification of these three kingdoms was likely to have been the result of one power (Chuzan) becoming stronger than its neighbours and conquering them militarily. One prominent administrator, Sho Hashi, gained enough political and military support to overthrow King Bunei of Chuzan in 1404 and enthroned his father as king. He was able to reassure the neighbouring Chinese with his political strength and demonstrate the prospect of continued loyalty. As a result, he gained Chinese favour and was able to conquer the neighbouring areas of Hokuzan and Nanzan. Sho Hashi subsequently became the first king of the Ryukyu Kingdom in 1422 (succeeding his father as King of Chuzan and making his brother the superintendent of Hokuzan), subsequently conquering and unifying Nanzan to his kingdom in 1429. During his reign, he modernised his seat of power by structurally updating Shuri Castle. By doing this, he was able to align Okinawa's development with that of China, which in turn offered a stable line of trade and cultural exchange.

This unity would have eased the dissemination of knowledge, which could include the martial arts. In 1477 Sho Shin became king and, from his rule onward, legend indicates the birth of Karate. Sho Shi introduced a nationwide confiscation of arms known as the 'Katana gari' leading to the development of armed and unarmed fighting arts.[5, 68, 69] At this time, the full spectrum of martial arts would still have been considered to be understood by the term Ti or Te; these subsequently became distinct bare-handed fighting techniques that solidified into Toudi and, later on, Karate. The exact dating of the terms Te, Toudi and Karate are notoriously difficult to pinpoint as their use overlapped. For example the formal adoption of the term 'Karate' came in 1936, however there is evidence of the common use of the term Toudi or Tode-Justu immediately before and after this time.[178] Contrary to common belief, the weapons ban on Okinawa did not necessarily oblige the local lower-class inhabitants to adapt to an unarmed fighting system, with the poor peasant having to defend himself against a cruel Japanese Samurai sword-wielding oppressor. In reality, the upper shizoku class (much like the bushi class in Japan) aimed to preserve local fighting arts (both hand and weapon-based), and may have adopted an unarmed fighting system for self-defence (Ti/ Toudi/ Te). In fact, the term *bushi* in Okinawa traditionally equates to senior Karate practitioners,[14] whereas the use of this term in mainland Japan reflects the better-known association with the Samurai class. Evidence supporting the aristocratic origins of Karate can be noted from the opening quotation of this book, repeated below and from a poem by Nago Ueekata Chobun名護 親方 寵文(1663–1734), a Ryukyuan kindom scholar and government official who was also known according to Chinese characters as Tei Junsoku程順則 (recognition of aristocracts and politicians in the Chinese form was the preferred system of nomenclature at that time).[73] Tei Junsoku was famed as a Confucian philosopher, occasionally called the 'Sage of Nago' (名護聖人:

No matter how you may excel in the art of te ['*art of the fist*'
or Karate],
And in your scholastic endeavours,
Nothing is more important than your behaviour
And your humanity as observed in daily life.

In the Ryukyu kingdom, education was unsurprisingly the privilege of the upper classes and the aristocracy, so the mention of both 'scholastic endeavours' and 'the art of Te' implies a link between the upper classes and Te, or the early forms of Karate. Accordingly, the empty-handed fighting system in the Ryukyu kingdom was not necessarily designed for group fighting but rather for single hand-to-hand defence. This was considered a worthy goal, even if not always totally practical with weapons to hand. In such instances the lower classes (mainly farmers) would fight opponents using weapons that were readily available, such as farming implements like the *tonfa* (rice grinder handle), *bo* (wooden longstaff) or *nunchaku* (possibly a horse bridle, a communication/ travel 'indicator' or, more doubtfully, a rice flail). The story of rebellious peasants developing Karate to fight unjust weapon-carrying oppressors is a romantic flight of fancy. In either case, it is more likely for the local peasants to adopt weapons to fight and hence contribute to the development of Kobudo, whilst the shizoku class would participate and promote in the development of Toudi as a set of unarmed fighting styles to develop Karate (in a similar manner to the bushi class preserving samurai arts in Japan). Thus the aristocracy class (the royal daimyo and the shizoku class) adopted Ti and Toudi outside the common misconception of peasants practising self-defence at night or in hidden areas.[5, 68, 69] Although there would not be a complete split between individuals practising these empty-handed Karate techniques and Kobudo (as some aristocrats would have adopted weapons and some farmers would have fought with their hands), the general advances in Karate would likely have been derived from individuals who had exposure to dignitaries well versed in Chinese martial arts (*quanfa*) and local Toudi.

A number of theories as to the origin of Karate have been proposed (**Figure 11**, see p.95). No one theory can by itself explain the development of modern Karate, as the true origin of the martial art was as a composite of a multitude of overlapping elements. These are categorised below:

Chinese immigration theory – Karate developed from the Kung-Fu taught to the indigenous Okinawan populace by Chinese immigrants, the so-called thirty-six families (settling near Kume village, Kumemura) or those settling in the 'nine villages'. Some of these descendants may have been descendants of Shaolin monks. The thirty-six families are considered to have originated in Fukien (Fujian province), China and the number of thirty-six is deemed to be a figure of speech rather than an actual figure. These families, also known as the thirty-six families of Bin (Bin being an ancient term for the Fukien area), came to Okinawa in 1392.[5, 74] This was not a random migration but organised by the Chinese and Ryukyu governments to improve trade relations twenty years after the beginning of trade between the Ryukyu royal court and Ming China. Most of the thirty-six families became interpreters, trade liaisons and staff for diplomatic and tribute missions with China. The families include the Chen, Kai, Liang, Mao, Jin, Rin, Wu, Yuan and Zeng.[70, 71]

Some authorities consider that the Zheng Yiyi family was instrumental in introducing Kung-Fu to Okinawa. Although the practice of Kung-Fu by these families may have been purely for health, it is likely that the practice of such arts had a deeper meaning in the lives of the thirty-six families and the students who adopted them to develop Karate. Of note, these families are recognised as bringing the so-called bible of Karate, the *Bubishi*, to the Ryukyus from China: a text describing the innermost philosophies and techniques of a style of martial arts (based on Crane and Arhat Boxing)[75] that was fundamental to the development of modern Karate.[70, 71, 76] The Zheng family may be credited with introducing what we understand as Naha-te and started teaching their martial-arts style in Kume in 1608.[70, 71]

There is evidence that the Okinawans were informed of Ming dynasty (1368–1644) Chinese military texts such as *Ji Xiao Xin Shu* and the 241-volume *Wubeizhi*. These may have been brought by Chinese travellers such as the the thirty-six families, or others. Such treatises may have contributed to the development of Karate where the *Bubishi* gained particular prominence amongst early Karate masters. The *Bubishi* to Karate is an equivalent to the *Densho* in mainland Japanese martial arts or the 'Ninja scroll' for Ninjas. Its translation from the Chinese is *bu* – warrior, *bi* – knowledge and *shi* – mind. (武備誌 *bu* – martial, *bi* – preparation, *shi* – record or compendium). Three types of this book are listed:[70, 71, 75–78]

1. The Chinese military version with parallels to Tsun Zu's *The Art of War* from *c.*1621 written by Mao Yuan Yi of the Ming dynasty.
2. The Chinese practical version from Yong Chun village in Fukien, with White Crane (Hakutsuru, Mandarin, Paiho Chuen) and Arhat Boxing techniques,[75] acupuncture and herbal remedies.
3. Modern Japanese translations (nineteenth and twentieth century) with a mixture of historical and practical techniques.

Several prominent Karate masters, including Chojun Miyagi (founder of Goju Ryu) and Gichin Funakoshi (founder of Shotokan), regularly drew concepts from the the *Bubishi*. Modern myth claims that these texts also contain secret descriptions of nerve-point techniques such as the 'Delayed Death Touch'. In popular culture, these are known as the *Dim Ching*, *Dim Hsueh* and the famed *Dim Mak*.[79] As these terms have now surfaced in the media, it is claimed they are to be found in Kung-Fu texts, Ninja texts and recently the *Bubishi*, with little evidence. According to masters of the Goju Ryu style of Karate, the use of the term 'Go-Ju' or 'Hard-Soft' was introduced by the style's originator (Chojun Miyagi) after reading the following eight precepts from the modern *Bubishi*:

1. The mind is one with heaven and earth.
2. The circulatory rhythm of the body is similar to the cycle of the sun and the moon.
3. The way of inhaling and exhaling is *hardness and softness*.
4. Act in accordance with time and change.
5. Techniques will occur in the absence of conscious thought.
6. The feet must advance and retreat, separate and meet.
7. The eyes do not miss the slightest change.
8. The ears listen in all directions.

Whilst the *Bubishi* had a prominent role in terms of martial arts texts for the early masters, others did exist. These included the

Hyoronshi, Kokutski, Kenyushin and *Yojoho*, which were studied by Norisato Nakaima of Ryuei-Ryu when with Ru Ru Ko in the Beijing Military Academy.[80]

The Chinese immigration theory is elaborated upon in Patrick McCarthy's Matsuyama Koen theory.[81] This proposes that the thirty-six families based at Kume village would regularly practise their Karate forms at a nearby park known as Matsuyama Koen. Here the martial artists would exchange practices and techniques with the eventual amalgamation and formation of unified katas that would form the basis for today's modern Karate styles. He suggests that even though many Chinese inhabitants returned to China after the abolition of the Ryukyu Kingdom in 1879, local inhabitants would still adhere to the tradition of training at Matsuyama Koen, so that local Okinawan Karate masters would eventually determine and formalise the katas for the identifiable Karate styles of today.

In summary, the Chinese immigration theory does offer some strong possibilities as to the origins of Chinese martial arts being applied on Okinawa to become Karate.

Chinese masters (military attaché) theory – here Karate is taught to the local Okinawans by Chinese military visitors to the Ryukyu islands. Three names are mentioned: Chinto (who has a kata named after him), Waishinzan, and the Chinese visitor Kushanku (who also has a kata named after him.) Kushanku is an Okinawan rendering of what is certainly a military or aristocratic title or rank, and there is no convincing historical record of an individual called Chinto.

The late eighteenth-century document *Oshima hikki* mentions a local government scholar Tobe Yoshiteru (interviewing members of a ship) and relates how Akata no Shiohira Peichin of Shuri, aka Shiohira Peichin (possibly the ship's captain), witnessed great *quan fa* or 'grappling skills' displayed by a Chinese military officer. It states that Kushanku had come from the Chinese mainland with many disciples, and even though he was small and frail he could immediately neutralise the attack of an aggressor. These would have been differentiated from the sumo-like Chinese wrestling skills (*shuai jiao*) that had been well known in Okinawa for some time.[68, 69, 82] Shiohira Peichin was an Okinawan from Kume village in Shuri, of Chinese descent, so his surprise at Kushanku's *quan fa* skills in the late eighteenth century means that these arts may not have been practised widely until that time and probably for some time subsequently. As Shiohira Peichin was of shizoku class, some authors believe that the Okinawan aristocratic classes largely began their training in *quan fa* or Ti after the arrival of Kushanku on Okinawa.

Kushanku's visit was most likely in 1756,[68, 69, 82] and he would have been one of the special envoys of the Chinese emperor (Sappushi). These envoys would come over to Okinawa to trade and interact with the island inhabitants, and these individuals or their bodyguards may have taught Kung-Fu to the locals. The last Chinese Qing envoy went to Shuri on Okinawa in 1856. In 1857 Okinawan King Sho Tai celebrated the envoy's arrival with demonstrations of *quan fa*/Ti (performed by the shizoku class) with the attendance of the Chinese residents of Kume village (the thirty-six families originally from Bin or Fujian province). This has been described in several sources and is considered to be the first formal account of unarmed combat in Okinawa.[68, 69, 82]

The timing of this demonstration is notable in that it is just before the Meiji restoration of 1868, which ultimately led to the downfall of the shogun and warrior classes in Japan and Okinawa. Consequently some authorities believe that the Okinawan aristocratic classes developed Toudi derived from Ti between the earlier Satsuma invasion at the beginning of the seventeenth century and Kushanku's arrival in 1756. At this time the aristocracy was decimated and adopted Chinese empty-hand fighting systems. Although weapons were banned during the second Sho dynasty (1470–1879) the aristocracy could still train in unarmed combat. In fact, generally there was peace on Okinawa for almost two centuries, until 1609, owing to the state being a protectorate of China. This aristocratic adoption of martial arts would have ended with the Meiji restoration of 1868.[68, 69, 82]

One can propose that Karate developed from Toudi after the 1868 period when the Okinawan populace were in a position to adopt some of the privileges of the former aristocratic martial arts system. This contradicts the fables that Okinawan peasants developed Karate to fight off samurai warlords. More likely the Okinawan population had already developed weapons-fighting systems (Kobudo), and only embraced Toudi to develop Karate after the downfall of the warrior class. This can still be seen today in the names of the kata for Karate and Kobudo; many Karate kata are named after military men or religious and warrior concepts, and Kobudo or weapons kata are named after local inhabitants of the villages. In many ways, therefore, Karate can be considered as 'Okinawan polo' or its indigenous 'sport of kings'.

Okinawan retrieval theory – Karate developed from Okinawans visiting mainland China, learning Kung-Fu (possibly from Shaolin masters) and bringing the styles back home to the Ryukyu islands. For example, specific legends describe Okinawan fishermen falling asleep or being caught in tornadoes off the coast of the Ryukyu islands and finding themselves off the China coast. They stay on the South Chinese mainland (Fukien) and even marry and have families during their stay. During this time, they train in Chinese martial arts and become proficient in these techniques. They eventually travel back to Okinawa and disseminate their knowledge, initially within their own families and later to the general population. In the same year (1392) that the thirty-six families came from China to Kume on Okinawa, King Chuzan sent students to study martial arts in China.[68, 69, 82] More formally, individuals such as one of the fathers of Naha-te Kanryo Higaonna (1853–1916) sailed to Fuzhou in the Fukien province of China in 1873 as a translator. Whilst there, he trained with Wai Xinxian, Kojo Tatai (an Okinawan) and maybe Iwah (a hazy historical figure). Later on he trained with Xie Zhongxiang and Ru Ru Ko (controversially believed by some to be the same person, the characters for 'Ru Ru Ko' are more like a nickname or epithet) who was the chief master of Whooping Crane (often thought to be the founder of Whooping Crane). During this time he learned Sanchin kata, amongst others. According to legend, he was only taught these arts after saving Ru Ru Ko's daughter from a flood.

He returned to Okinawa in the 1880s and began his teaching to the local populace. More recently the father of Uechi-Ryu Kanbun Uechi (1877–1948) also went to China in a similar fashion to learn the style of Pangai-noon, which he brought back and taught as Uechi-Ryu (a term introduced by his students after his death, having first taught this style in Wakayama, mainland Japan).

Some scholars have actually specified particular groups of individuals (exchange envoys or martial arts students – *Ryugakusei*) as going to learn at the Chinese emperor's court.[76] There is also evidence of individuals who went over to study martial arts at the Guozijian Academy in China or attended missions to Peking where they picked up Kung-Fu.[68, 69, 82]

Other legends relate to the Pirate Lords of Nakajin (late fourteenth century), who reputedly were the first indigenous Okinawan rulers to assert democracy, meritocracy and female equality. Their rule lasted for less than fifty years and some say they brought Karate to the island after having acquired the art on their piratical travels (to China and other nations). Information on the Lords of Nakajin (who resided near or at the site of the present Nakajin Castle) is sparse as there is little written evidence on their rule and they were only in power for such a short period of time, in a relatively small area of Okinawa. Such hypotheses are therefore difficult to prove, although the origin of the kata Chinto has been reported to derive from the Nakajin Lords. Interestingly, I have already alluded to the history of Shaolin monks who successfully defended China against pirates from the east (Japan) in the mid-1500s, and it is possible these pirates were from Okinawa or had links with the island, such that their exposure to the Shaolin monks may have led to a preliminary introduction of martial arts to Okinawa. Any Shaolin prisoners taken may have also been the source of martial knowledge.

The legends of pirates introducing Karate have echoes in other legends, specifically those focusing on the Chinese master known as Chinto. He is said to have taken part in a pirate battle against the Dutch in 1625 in the bay of Wancan near Mattau (on Formosa – modern-day Taiwan), in which the Chinese pirates were victorious.

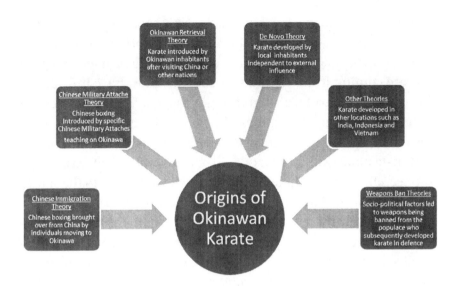

Figure 11: Theories of the origins of Karate.

This victory was short-lived, but did encourage the local Taiwanese to combat the Dutch colonial forces.

The historical and legendary components of the Okinawan retrieval theory have been intertwined to such an extent that it is practically impossible to differentiate between them. These legends describing the actions and interactions of the early Karate masters may, however, carry an element of historical accuracy.

De novo theory – it is widely accepted that Karate did not just exist *de novo* in the Ryukyu islands, but rather it evolved indigenously from an outside source (maybe the origin of Okinawan 'Ti'). Nevertheless, such a possibility does exist; but it is far more likely that much of the Karate we see today is not a discrete and entirely new martial art, but rather a unique local interpretation of a few styles of Kung-Fu.

Other theories – these are considered for completeness. Just as it is acknowledged that Kung-Fu was derived from Indian martial arts comparable to Kalaripayattu, it may have been possible for individuals to bring techniques to Okinawa from other areas. There are some purported links between Okinawan martial arts and those indigenous to Indonesia and Malaysia.[83] Finally, the origins of Tomari-te are unknown, and one individual called Annan (who may have been a pirate coming from Vietnam) is considered to have introduced this school. Tomari-te is often thought to be not much different to Shuri-te in its origins and almost the same in its lineage. Matsumora Kosaku is placed in both lineages, he is supposed to have trained in Tomari-te under KaRyu Uku (aka Giko Uku) and Kishin Teruya and also secretly under a Chinese individual who drifted on to the shores of Okinawa from 'Furuferin' on the Chinese mainland.[66, 67]

Alternatively there are legends that the originator styles of martial arts arrived on Okinawa with sailors shipwrecked on the Ryukyu islands. Over 1,400 ships are thought to have been driven onto the Ryukyu coast and survivors might have taught martial skills to the local inhabitants. The proximity of Okinawa to Taiwan, India, Korea and the Philippines makes this a possibility. One legend has it that Korean survivors of a shipwreck settled in a cave (Furu Helin) between Tomari and Naha and taught their martial arts to the local inhabitants, which may have contributed to the development of Karate.[70, 71] There was also regular trade and contact with these nations. Some specifically point to contact with Thailand and its indigenous boxing and weapon arts as having a great influence on Karate development.[76]

A number of theories have been put forward as to the reasons why Karate flourished to the extent that it did. Why was an empty-handed fighting system adopted so readily? Such theories not unreasonably focus on the lack of weapons.

Weapons ban theory 1 (under tyrannical rule) – 'farmers' and 'peasants' in the pre-Meiji period (pre-1868) developed an indigenous fighting art. This has been handed down in elaborate legends that claim these peasants were under tyrannical rule and developed empty-handed (and weapons) techniques for self-defence. It is assumed that these peasants were either banned from using weapons, or could not afford them. Karate was developed by these peasants practising their art secretly under cover of darkness, so as not to be seen practising a fighting art by their evil overlords. As already discussed, this is largely disproved by the fact that most famous Karate pioneers were aristocrats. The working-class Okinawans would not have the time or energy to develop such a system.

Weapons ban theory 2 – after a weapons ban by King Sho Sin in 1507, wealthy landowners or local police developed a system to defend their land and property. This may have been based on Kung-Fu. (The ban was only applied to the lower classes, in order to prevent revolt. The government and its allied aristocrats still had full access to weapons.)

Weapons ban theory 3 – after the Japanese Satsuma invasion and weapon ban in 1609, indigenous people or local police developed a martial art for self-defence. This may have been based on Kung-Fu, although, once again, the authorities still had access to weapons.

Shotokan's secret theory – a rather prosaic theory is that court officials in the 1850s adopted unarmed Shotokan Karate combat to defend themselves against both samurai and US marines.[84] This theory does not offer much scope for the evolution of other Karate styles in Okinawa. Gichin Funakoshi ('the father of Shotokan Karate') was not born until 1869, tending to undermine this idea.

Legends of Karate's forefathers and the first use of the term 'Karate'

A common consensus had developed by the 1950s as to Karate's origins. By then it was accepted that Karate could be traced back to Bodhidharma who travelled from India to the Shaolin Temple and subsequently developed Shaolin Kung-Fu, which in turn developed into Karate. Master Choshin Chibana who was president of the Okinawan Karate Assoication supported this view,[66, 67] and added that

Karate's uniqueness was to be found in its use of the 'grasping fist' (*nigiri kobushi*) as opposed to Kung-Fu's preference of the palm strike (*hirate*) and the chicken-beak fist (*keiko*). He noted that the Naha kata Tensho (derived form the Chinese Rokkishu section mentioned in the *Bubishi*) does not discuss the grasping fist for strikes, demonstrating that the older forms of Karate may have had more similarity to Kung-Fu than the Karate observed later in Okinawa.

As the birth of Karate likely took place in the past 200–300 years, there is some history regarding its foremost practitioners, although with the sudden explosion in popularity of the art, countless legends have been propagated regarding those luminaries. Takahara Peichin (1683–1760) was an Okinawan aristocrat who was well travelled and educated. He considered kata as a fundamental component of Karate. 'Peichin' was of a high social class in the Ryukyu kingdom. He was a Kobudo student of Chatan Yara (1668–1756), an Okinawan weapons master who studied in China for twenty years under Wong Chung-Yoh and is considered by some to have been a Shaolin Buddhist monk. His most famous student was Sakugawa Kanga (1733–1815).

Sakugawa Kanga trained with Peichin and later, on his advice, with Kushanku, so that he was subsequently nicknamed 'Tode' Sakugawa (Sakugawa – 'Chinese Hand'). His most prominent student, Matsumura Sokon, was initially considered a ruffian but following training entered the service of the royal Shoō family in 1816, and became the chief martial-arts instructor and bodyguard for the last two Okinawan kings, Shō Iku and Shō Tai. In view of his contribution to royal life and martial arts, he was titled 'Bushi' ('Warrior') Matsumura. He developed the elements of Shuri-te Karate that led to the development of the Shorin system of Karate. Matsumura Sokon (also known as Machimura Bucho), called his art 'Bu' (martial), in his book *Bucho Ikko*, and within it wrote the following letter to his last student Ryosei Kuwae (1853–1939) just before his retirement in 1882 (the scroll (makimono) on which the letter was written resides with Ryosei Kuwae's descendants):[85, 86]

To my wise and young brother/fellow pupil Kuwae Ryosei

I am writing to you as I consider that you should appreciate the true way of the martial arts (Bujutsu or military arts/Wushu) through determination and continuous training.

Bun bu ichi (文武一) – Literary arts (the art of knowledge) (bun) and (bushido) Martial/military arts, (bu), (the sword and the brush), are one (ichi) and have the same theory. In other words, the theory underpinning methods of scholarly study and the study of martial arts is fundamentally the same.

When examining methods of scholarly study and literature (bun), we find there are three distinct elements or methods in its meaning:

1.   Poetry
2.   Exegetics (extensive and critical interpretation of a text)
3.   Confucianism

The first method, poetry, is the study of powerful words and skills needed in communication and the pursuit of high-paying positions. Poetry is the knowledge of language, fluent use of the written word and knowledge of a large vocabulary. A student of poetry works at words and produces sentences, often in order to seek fame, lordship and fief.

In the second method, admonition (kind, yet earnest reproof), is the way of exegetics (extensive and critical interpretation of a text) in which one compares the wisdom of traditional literature as in the Chinese classics, and Buddhist texts in order to reach an ultimate understanding, and to teach other people, by instilling a sense of duty by way of example, yet continuing study constantly on one's own.

The person who pursues the way of admonition and exegetics may make a scholar, but can be ignorant of the world.

Despite the fact that the two methods of poetry and admonition are both unique, they fall short of comprehending the true essence of the Way and encompass only a superficial comprehension of scholarly studies. Because they cannot be considered as mastered until one has gained prestige in them, they only go towards making people chase after fame, thus they are not the true art and should be regarded as incomplete.

The third method of literary study is rooted in the philosophy of truth through a knowledge and understanding of Confucianism. This is a complete method, and allows us to understand the true nature of things.

By embracing the teachings of knowledge, honesty, and righteousness one will be able to understand matters in life and to make the mind pure and true.

It will allow one not only to manage a household and govern a family well, but also administer a country and govern a nation well.

A method that can be applied to one's family and country can also be applied to the entire world. Therefore peace could reign throughout the world.

Confucianism teaches us to:

1. Gain a more profound understanding of matters in life
2. Gain strength from our weaknesses
3. Become more sincere
4. Become more righteous and pure
5. Be more honest and true
6. Better control our emotions
7. Have more peace in our homes

If we examine martial ways (budo), we see that there are also three distinct ways of approaching them:

1. The bujutsu (martial arts) of intelligence
2. The bujutsu (martial arts) of nominals (names or insignificant ideas)
3. The bujutsu (martial arts) of Budo (the warrior's way)

The first method, the Bujutsu of intelligence, is an understanding that styles may vary. However, a style is only as good as the one who practises it. It is more like a game of psychology and tactics and the desire to be superb or excel is often scarce.

A scholar pictures many ways of training in his mind and as a consequence his movements become empty. Many of these styles have no practical application in fighting at all, and have exaggerated movements that look pretty but are superficial, much like women dancing, and of no practical use. Such movements do not work in a real defensive situation.

The second method, the Bujutsu of nominals (relating to names) is nothing more than physical exercises with a lot of ideas without execution and a lot of talk about winning.

A normal or ostensible student of martial arts is good at promising victory, but is a bad performer.

The practitioners of this method are often quarrelsome and in this, there is no virtue.

Sometimes a dispute caused by such a person can hurt other people as well as himself.

It can bring disgrace, and cause dishonour and shame to come upon members of a family, parents, brothers and sisters.

The third way, the Bujutsu of budo is the way of the true martial artist and is always performed with conviction.

This person does not idle away his time, but rather accomplishes his task with ingenuity.

He controls his mind, has pure concentration that leads to many unique ideas, and is possessed of an unconquerable calmness. There is no hesitation or disturbance in his mind even in cases of emergency. This calmness arouses a disturbance among one's enemies, who begin to fall apart mentally. It is like stealing the mind of your opponent.

Everything ripens and the mystery of nature shows its secret to the master of martial arts. He watches for a chance then grabs it, showing loyalty with the ferocity and power of a tiger and the swiftness of an eagle, defeating his enemies completely.

A master of budo can overcome the enemy without force and will keep the peace and stay away from violence ('no fight'), deal with people well, be sure in their accomplishments, and increase their wealth. Acting in a mature way gives incentive to others and causes no undue irritations.

The practitioners of this third method gain a solemn enlightenment, free of strife and depravity. It promotes loyalty among family, friends and country, and shows his loyalty and filial piety. It also promotes a natural demeanour, which develops a gallant character.

This third method, the Bujutsu of budo:

1. Prohibits intentional violence
2. Rules the actions of the warrior
3. Instructs so as to encourage intellectual, moral, and spiritual improvement
4. Promotes virtue – the establishment of distinguished services
5. Promotes peace among the people and the relief of the poor
6. Produces harmony in society and the settlement of disputes among people
7. Brings about prosperity and the enrichment of assets.

These are the seven virtues of bu. They were taught by wise men, and are contained in a book called the Godan-sho.

As I said at the outset, Bu and bun have basically the same theory. Of the three methods, a wise man does not need the first or second, they are useless. My conviction is rooted immovably in the doctrine of the third method. In this method, you will find the true way. Thus the sword and the pen are but one.

As seen in his teachings, Confucius also praised these virtues.

Therefore study the bun of Confucianism and the bujitsu of budo. Enrich the bujutsu of budo, adapt to change, and keep training with this advice in mind.

This unconquerable strength will deeply influence your judgment in recognizing opportunities and in taking appropriate action. The circumstances will always determine what the correct approach is that you should take.

I have revealed my words to you. There is nothing left secret or hidden in my mind, nothing held back.

Keep the above words in mind and practice hard. I wish you understand my unreserved words. If you accept and heed my words, you will find the true way.

Writing frankly on this occasion,

To my wise and young brother Kuwae Ryosei, my fellow pupil

Signed: Takenaga (Bucho) Matsumura
On the thirteenth day of May 1882

Itosu Yasutsune (1830–1915) nicknamed 'Anko' (Iron Horse) was considered to be the most physically advanced student of Bushi Matsumura and went on to teach many of the fathers of recognisable modern Karate styles (such that many consider him to be the 'father' of modern Karate), including the aristocratic Choki Motobu (Motobu Udun Di and Motobu-Ryu), Kenwa Mabuni (seventeenth-generation descendant of the aristocratic Keimochi dynasty and founder of Shito-Ryu), Gichin Funaksohi (Shotokan) and Chosin Chibana (Kobayashi-Ryu). In 1908 Itosu wrote to the Ministry of Education and the Ministry of War in Japan on the ten precepts (*tode jukun*) of Karate to highlight the nature of the art for the Japanese populace, specifically for the education department of Okinawa to introduce Karate into the public school curriculum (see following section).[87] He was among the first to popularise the term Karate, even though his own instructor was considered a master of Tode (or Tode Jutsu) and he also occasionally would use the terms Te ('hand') or Tang Te ('Chinese hand') for his martial arts practice. The formal adoption of the term 'Karate' took place at at 4 p.m. on 25 October 1936 in 'The Meeting of Okinawan Karate Masters' at the Showa Kaikan Hall in Naha, Okinawa.[88] It was at this meeting, hosted by the *Ryukyu Shinpo* newspaper publisher and attended by notable Karate masters, that the term was accepted for widespread use. The meeting lists the following 'Karateka' attendees: Chomo Hanashiro, Chotoku Kyan, Choki Motobu, Chojun Miyagi, Juhatsu Kyoda, Choshin Chibana, Shinpan Shiroma, Chotei Oroku, Genwa Nakasone; and also lists the following 'guests' – Koichi Sato, Zenpatsu Shimabukuro, Kitsuma Fukushima, Eizo Kita, Chosho Goeku, Gizaburo Furukawa, Sei Ando, Choshiki Ota, Kowa Matayoshi, Zensoku Yamaguchi and Tamashiro. Several core concepts were agreed:

1. Chomo Hanashiro is the first person who used the kanji 'Empty Hand' for Karate in 1905.
2. To use 'Empty Hand' for Karate as opposed to 'Chinese hand'.
3. To popularise Karate, there was a call to unify/standardise kata and to make it into a competitive sport.
4. To set a recognisable Karate uniform and to standardise the contents and forms of this art.

Another famous grandmaster, Kenwa Mabuni, also studied Tode under Arakaki Seisho (or Aragaki Tsuji Pechin Seisho, 1840–1918), who was a royal court official born near Kume village (of the thirty-six families) and noted for teaching Luohan Quan (Monk Boxing Fist). Arakaki also taught Higaonna Kanryo (one of the fathers of the Naha-te system of Karate). Both Higaonna and Mabuni had also studied Kung-Fu in the Fukien province of China, the former with Wu Xian Gui (Go Kenki), and the latter with the founder of the Whooping Crane style, Xie Zhongxiang, Ru Ru Ko and possibly Wu Xian Gui. Higaonna Kanryo's top student was Chojun Miyagi, who created the Goju-Ryu style of Karate.

Chotoku Kyan (1870–1945) was a prominent master of Shorin-Ryu working as a steward to the Ryukyuan royal house; his masters included Kosaku Matsumora (1829–1898) who contributed to both Tomari-te (studying under KaRyu Sokyu/ Uku and Kishin Teruya) and Shuri-te systems of Karate. He taught Chotoku Kyan the kata Chinto and rose to immediate folkloric fame when he disarmed a Japanese Satsuma overlord with a wet towel (unfortunately losing his thumb in the process). Stories such as this fed the legend that

Karate and its stylists (Karate-ka) were Okinawan heroes fighting against their Japanese oppressors with their empty-handed Karate fighting techniques.

In the present era, the lineages and connections of both Shuri-te and Naha-te systems with China are almost universally accepted. The origins of Tomari-te are less clear. Two Okinawans (KaRyu Sokyu/Uku and Kishin Teruya) trained under several Chinese masters (holding diplomatic rank) and included Ason (Chinese sergeant) and Wang Ji. They also trained with a master known as Annan, who ,according to legend, was a pirate who had survived a shipwreck and was living as a hermit in a cave in the mountains near the Tomari area. Although there is a Naha-te kata named Annan, the connection between these is not yet cemented, however, tradition alludes to the fact that Matsumura Sokon was taught the kata Chinto by this master. Matsumura considered Kishin Teruya as his main instructor,[89] having learned the katas Passai, Rohai and Wanshu from him, whilst he learnt Naihanchi from KaRyu Sokyu/Uku. In addition to Matsumura Sokon, there were three highly prominent students of Tomari-te under the tutelage of KaRyu Sokyu/Uku and Kishin Teruya who subsequently became masters. These were Kosaku Matsumora, Koka Oyadomari and Giei Yamada. Today the system of Tomari-te can be considered overshadowed to an extent by Shuri-te styles and Naha-te styles, but during Karate's early years there was extensive cross-fertilisation between many schools, such that the concept of a 'pure' Shuri or Naha style is unlikely. The rare style of Gusukuma-Ryu is interesting in that it derives from the Tomari-te master Gusukuma of Tomari and also Koki Gusukuma (a direct student of Ru Ru Ko and Kanryo Higaonna's Naha-te) in addition to influences from Shinpan Gusukuma (also known as Shinpan Shiroma, the originator of one of the two styles of Shito-Ryu). Each style carries a varying degree of the foundation systems of Karate (Shuri-te, Naha-te and Tomari-te) in addition to several other external martial-arts system influences (a particularly salient example would be the role of Jujutsu in modern Wado-Ryu Karate). There are even some pioneering schools that concurrently practise several different styles, including the Sekai Dentokan Bugei Renmei (Col. Roy J. Hobbs) and the Jindokai (Professor Stephen Chan) whose Karate practice includes Shuri-te from Shorin-Ryu and Motobu-Ryu through the lineage of Shian Toma and Seiki Toma (similarly named though not directly related) whilst also practising Naha-te Goju-Ryu through Yoshio Kuba and other Goju masters. (They also train in several schools of Aiki, Goshin, Jujutsu and Laido.)

Anko Itosu's ten precepts (*tode jukun*) of Karate

Anko Itosu is considered by many Karate masters as the 'father of Karate' in the modern era. His letter of October 1908 written to the Okinawan and Japanese education authorities was a water-shed moment in the popularisation and dissemination of Karate. As we have seen, the original practice of Karate was limited to the Okinawan aristocracy, however, Itosu was a luminary who made this art available to the general public.[66, 67] His ten articles are fore-runners to the art's eventual worldwide dissemination:[87]

Ten Articles of Karate

Karate is not of Confucian or Buddhist origin. Shorin and Shorei schools were originally introduced from China into Okinawa. Each of the two styles has its strength, thus both should be retained.
1. You should not practise Karate only for the purpose of developing your physical strength. What is essential is to serve your sovereign and your parents at the risk of your life in case of emergency. If you should be involved in a fight with a robber or a roughneck by any chance, you should ward off a blow. You should not harm him.
2. By practising Karate one can develop a strong body and his fists and feet can be used as weapons. Thus if boys are trained in their youth, they will become men of special ability. Such men of martial arts can make contributions to the country as soldiers if need be. When he defeated Napoleon at Waterloo, Wellington said, 'Today's

victory is the outcome of a lad's hard training on a training ground in England.' Well put. [Misquotation of dubious attribution.]

3. To master Karate in a short time is extremely difficult. The proverb goes that practice makes perfect. If you practise for one or two hours every day, you will not only become physically strong but master the art of Karate by the end of three or four years of training.

4. When you do makiwara-tsuki, keep these in mind: lower your shoulders, chest out, keep your feet and centralize your 'ki' on the abdomen. Do the tsuki practice in this manner one hundred or two hundred times.

5. When you assume a Karate posture, bear these in mind: straighten your back, lower your shoulders, keep your feet, centralize your 'ki' on the abdomen and harden the whole muscles of your body in such a way that the whole force is pulled toward the abdomen.

6. Learn various moves. But study when and how certain moves are applied and then practise the moves. There are many secrets handed down by word of mouth regarding stop moves and counter moves.

7. Study moves. Consider which move is good for building physical strength and which one is good for kumite.

8. You should practise Karate in the following manner: glare, lower your shoulders, and harden muscles as though you were actually engaged in a fight. Practise in this way, then you will be able to move naturally in case of a hand-to-hand fight.

9. Do not put too much strain on yourself while you are practising, otherwise you will get bloodshot and your face will turn red. These are signs of over-practice that will ruin your health in time.

10. Many Karate masters enjoyed longevity in the past. Through Karate one can build muscles, promote digestion, improve the circulation of blood. All of these contribute to a long life. Therefore Karate should be introduced into coursework as the basis of physical education at the schools. Thus a lot of Karate experts will be produced in the future.

By Anko Itosu
October, the forty-first year of Meiji

Development of substyles – Karate's evolution

According to Plato's philosophy, everything has a perfect form, structure and shape, although all we perceive are 'shadows' of reality. He
described this in his famous 'Allegory of the Cave' in Book VII of *The
Republic*. Many martial artists consider that there is essentially (in
the Platonic sense) only one true style of martial art or Karate and
that this naturally is the style that they themselves practise. In reality,
there are many styles, technical variations and practical nuances to
modern Karate. It is obvious that Wado-Ryu and Kyokushinkai have
clear differences despite some common origins; and Goju-Ryu and
Goju Kai, or Shotokan and Shotokai, vary despite almost identical
origins. Each style and substyle occupies its own place in a technical catalogue of practice and could be plotted on a bell-shaped curve
(normal distribution) of methods and procedures. These of course
change with time, so that the original eighteenth-century Goju
Ryu or nineteenth-century Shotokan are different to those of today.
This was defined in biology by Ernst Mayr as 'population thinking',[90, 91] and it can be seen in Karate, in which every style consists
of a varying population of practitioners who have individual differences, but who also can learn from and transmit to other styles and
practices, so each style will evolve over time. Phylogenetics can also
be applied to Karate such that each style can be linked to any other
via an evolutionary tree derived from the original founding schools
(**Figure 12**).[92–94] In this system, the most prominent schools are those
whose instructors are the best and most charismatic martial artists,
and these individuals best transmit their particular interpretations
and styles to the next generation. Each individual Karate style is
inevitably linked to all other styles.

Okinawa is a small island that makes communication fast through
large family networks. As a result, many early Karate masters would
have been in close enough proximity to generate a 'critical mass'
to forge the Karate that we see today. Recently a Matsuyama *Koen*
or Matsuyama Park theory has been proposed,[76, 81] in which many
founding fathers of Karate would exchange martial ideas around

Naha Kume's village's Matsuyama Park (including Wai Xinxian, Iwah, Aragaki Seisho, Kojo Taitei, Xie Zongxiang, Higaonna Kanryo, Maezato Ranpo, Matsuda Tokusaburo, Nakaima Norisato, Sakiyama Kitoku, and Wu Xianhui). Whether or not Matsuyama Park was the true and only hub that galvanised the modern Karate styles is difficult to know; the small size of Okinawa would have permitted cross-fertilisation of Karate ideas across many hubs (dojos, family networks, friendships, aristocratic groupings).

The evolution of Karate into a variety of schools, or 'Ryu', came about through individuals learning their art from different masters. The Karate idea of 'Ryu' is very different to the classical Japanese idea, and the term was not used at all until Chojun Miyagi was asked to give a proper name to his style so that it could be part of a royal demonstration. In Okinawa three areas developed a critical mass of Karate that then set the syllabus for almost all of today's Karate styles. These areas on the Okinawan mainland are based at Naha (Okinawa's capital city), Shuri and Tomari. Karate at that time was simply known as 'Te' – a term sometimes indistinguishable from the indigenous martial art of Ti (confusion regarding these terms exists, as Ti and Te can be romanized in the same way). Modern Karate is likely a mixture between Ti and Chinese Boxing, although according to some schools, ancient Ti still exists and can be distinguished from Karate by its grappling and intricately formed techniques opposing the fast, dynamic actions of Karate. Nevertheless, the development of Karate in the regional areas and villages led to the terms of Shuri-te, Tomari-te and Naha-te to reflect the Karate originating from each area. There is also a degree of inaccuracy in this specific division as all three areas are in in close proximity to each other.

By the eighteenth century, the vast majority of masters and scholars agree Karate was in existence as Naha-te, Shuri-te and Tomari-te (Hand of Naha, Shuri and Tomari respectively). These classifications are thought to be modern ones and nobody would refer to what they did as Naha-, Shuri- or Tomari-te at that time. Some consider that as To-de was already in existence in Okinawa, then it eventually became converted to these three primordial Karate styles. An older theory suggests that the Toudi styles actually became 'Karate' before splitting off into Ryu, although concurrent practice of different types of Karate in its early days renders this theory largely abandoned. Thus Okinawa was primed to become a hotbed of martial arts, much like the 1970s music scene in New York that gave birth to the differing styles of hip-hop, disco and punk,[95] Okinawa would develop three distinct but interlinking styles that would set the scene for Karate for centuries to come.

Although it is claimed that many of the styles of Karate were 'practised by moonlight' in order to avoid persecution by the authorities in Okinawa, there is scant evidence for this. The aristocracy created and passed on Karate, and as such any 'secrecy' was more likely based on class rather than concealment from authority. Master Choshin Chibana related that during training in his youth, he would hide from guests visiting his instructor's house and would only come out for training after the guests had left.[66, 67]

Some interaction between styles did exist. This would explain the common 'theme of Karate' (kata, basics and kumite). The addition of kihon to kata and kumite as a distinct unit of study in its current sense is thought to be a mainland Japanese addition, although such practice would undoubtedly have existed in some form or another. Each school would be heavily influenced by the style's founder or chief instructor, whose technique or performance would be followed to the letter, whether for kata, basics, or kumite. Many of Karate's early founders are said to have studied the same manuscript, considered by some as 'The Bible of Karate'.[76] This was a text focusing on Monk Fist and White Crane Kung-Fu but may have had a broader impact on the Okinawan masters.

Most modern styles are Naha-Shuri-based, with only a few Tomari elements existing in each school. In modern biology such a variation of styles in the same area could be considered as sympatric or micro-allopatric speciation, where individual styles diverge while inhabiting the same place. This would result in 'Karate Speciation', such that each style would have evolved into its current form according to its original knowledge base (instructors), its methods of dissemination and progression (students) and its local environment, which would (or would not) make style interactions possible.

The continual development of Karate has been recognised for some time. Master Choshin Chibana (former president of the Okinawan Karate Association) said: 'A pond which is not fed by a fresh stream becomes stagnant and dies ... much in the same way, so too does an ardent Karate-ka continually modify his or her art.'[66, 67]

The Naha styles have elements both of extreme strength and softness. Naha was initially called Shorei, 'the style of inspiration' (昭霊 Shorei is a Chinese word consisting of the characters 'shining' and 'spirit/ ghost') after the Shoreiji Temple in southern China. The Shoreiji Temple in turn is either a reference to the southern Shaolin Temple in Fukien or a fabrication of Itosu Anko. Later the words *Go* (hard) and *Ju* (soft) were used to characterise one of the largest Ryus in the Naha-te system, the Goju-Ryu of Chojun Miyagi, who drew the term from one of the poems in the *Bubishi*. Here there is a strong emphasis on conditioning, short-distance circular techniques, and *muchimi*, or momentum of technique (*muchimi* is an Okinawan dialect word used specifically in martial arts to refer to 'stickiness' or tension, both within the practitioner's own body and in grappling with and 'sticking to' an opponent). These are interlaced with fast, whip-like actions. Schools of Naha-te include Goju-Ryu, Ryuei-Ryu and Uechi-Ryu (derived from the Chinese Pangai-Noon southern Chinese Kung-Fu). These schools have clear links to Chinese White Crane, Whooping Crane and Tiger styles of Kung-Fu. Important masters who contributed to the development of this style include the Chinese master Ru Ru Ko and the Okinawan Kanryo Higaonna. Some Uechi-Ryu practitioners do not like to be classified as Naha-te, although the common lineage and technical base is undeniable.

The Shuri styles have strong, fast actions, applying low centres of gravity with low stances and long-reaching techniques. They also have the defining characteristic of rapid, whole-body movement as opposed to the more static, rooted Naha styles. Many of these schools are derived from masters Anko Itosu ('the father of modern Karate'), Sokon Matsumura and Sakukawa Kanga. Many of them carry the name 'Shorin' or 'Shorin-ji' literally meaning 'from Shaolin'. This name was largely taken up before the time of Shaolin popularity in 1920s mainland China, and this may represent a real connection to the original Shaolin. But it is also worth noting that the original characters used to write Shorin were different to those used in the Chinese Temple, and these were only later adopted by some modern Shorin styles. There is a significant amount of editing, unjustified connection and name-borrowing by the early Karate masters, rendering it very difficult to separate fact from fiction.

As already discussed, the origins of Tomari-te are much harder to identify and may have some connection with the pirate-infested China seas and even Vietnam (there is some similarity with the higher levels of Viet Vo Dao). Techniques are typically fast, use varied angles to engage opponents and comprise short, powerful strikes performed much higher than typically seen in Shuri schools. Matsumora Kosaku and Oyadomari Kokan are founding masters of this art. Two other masters were equally important in the spread of both Tomari-te and Shuri-te: Choki Motobu and Chotoku Kyan.

Many of these styles were transported to the Japanese mainland by masters such as the Okinawan Gichin Funakoshi (Father of Japanese Karate and the Shotokan style) in order to develop a new type of Karate there. Techniques were broken down to constituent movements, and were practised with maximum speed and power and with low stances. Many of the forms were simplified to accommodate the teaching of juniors and children (Itosu started this on Okinawa), whilst the belt system from Judo was adopted (as well as the uniform). This transformed the 'public' face of Karate into what is seen today. As a result, much of the Karate currently practised in the world is either Shotokan or has been influenced in some way by Japanese Karate.

In Okinawa before the Second World War, Karate had become accepted by the local authorities and many Karate masters (including Funakoshi) studied at a number of schools (this practice would occur more openly now, although there was a lot of cross-fertilisation even prior to Meiji). Great Okinawan masters such as Kenwa

Mabuni and Shinpan Shiroma amalgamated a number of schools to produce the vast style of Shito-Ryu (Shuri, Naha and Tomari), whilst others such as the Japanese Gogen Yamaguchi took the style of Goju-Ryu to mainland Japan and modified it to suit local philosophy and technical skill, transforming it to Goju-Kai. Yamaguchi's organisation took the name Goju-kai whilst his style was still called Goju-Ryu. The organisation name is used to differentiate from other Goju groups but it is not the same as the style name, as in the case of the original Shotokan club.

After the Second World War numerous Westerners, including American GIs, were exposed to both Okinawan and Japanese Karate and many Japanese masters travelled abroad to teach their art. This ultimately resulted in a massive cross-fertilisation that has brought about the current styles of Karate. Only a bare few can delineate pure links with their origins, although it can be argued that this is no bad thing, as styles have benefited from each other's techniques and practice.

Naha-te and Shuri-te

Defining the historical evolution of Naha-te Karate is considered to be more challenging than that of Shuri-te Karate.[5, 74] This is because early Shuri-te founders were either members or associates of the Ryukyu shizoku aristocracy, men of prominence and fame,[96] whereas the founders of Naha-te are considered to be inhabitants of Okinawa or south-east China working in local crafts and trades.

Consequently, the prevailing concept of the development of Naha-te broadly follows an initiation similar to that of the Shuri-te and Shorin schools, where Karate was developed from the thirty-six families from Fukian who settled to work in Okinawa. However, there is a subsequent perception that Karate development in Naha was pioneered by its local inhabitants, merchants and peasants of the heimin class, to draw a distinction with the development of Shuri-te by Okinawan aristocracy.

This class demarcation of Shuri-te being the Karate style of the rich aristocracy and Naha-te being the Karate style of poor peasants has recently been called into question.[5, 74] Traditional oral sources hold that Naha-te was practised by the shizoku class at Kume before the Meiji restoration.

Specifically, the ancient Naha-te style of Kojo-Ryu was founded in 1655 by Kogusuku Uekata, also known as Kojo Oyakata, who learned Chinese Boxing in China and taught this to his extended family. This clan were clearly members of the shizoku class, practising Karate at the same time as that of the developing Shuri-te schools. Additionally, Nakaima Kenri (1819–1879), the founder of Ryuei-Ryu Karate, studied Chinese Boxing under Liu Long Gong ('Sir Dragon Liu'), the head of the Quing dynasty's royal bodyguard officer training school. Training there would have been restricted to a few privileged individuals and Kenri would have paid a large sum to travel and gain certification from that school.[5, 97]

Furthermore, there was a cross-fertilisation of Shuri and Naha styles as it is recognised that the fourth inheritor of the Kojo school was also a pupil of well-known Shuri pioneers that included the Chinese master Weibo (also known in Okinawan as Iwah – either a military officer assigned to the tribute missions or an officer stationed at the royal court in Peking).[5, 74, 98, 99] He was also instructor to Shuri masters Sakugawa Kanga and Matsumura Sokon. Leading Shuri masters were performing Naha katas in the 1860s as official entertainment during state receptions. Kanryo Higaonna, who is universally accepted as one of the fathers of Naha-te, was trained by Arakaki Seisho (1840–1918), an official at the royal court of Okinawa holding the title of Chikudon Peichin, who heavily influenced both Shuri-te and Naha-te schools.

There are probably two Chinese fathers of Naha-te, both known as Ru Ru Ko. The Ru Ru Ko considered to be the father of Ryuei-Ryu (possibly Liu Long Gong or 'Sir Dragon Liu') is likely to be different to the Ru Ru Ko of modern, mainstream Naha-te (in the form of Goju-Ryu) who was probably the Chinese master Xie Zongxiang.[5, 97] Although these were two individuals, both helped to create

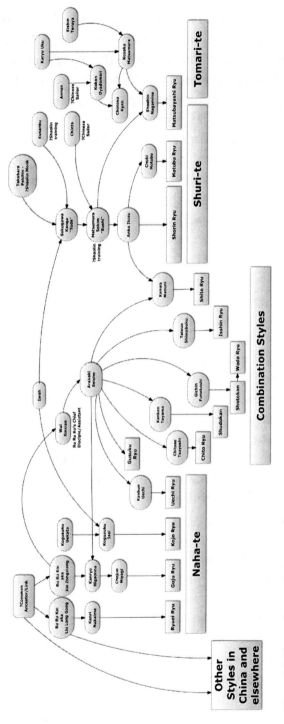

Figure 12: The evolution of Karate styles.

branches of Naha-te that are similar and have direct connections. Whether they derive from a common ancestor or an association with a middle 'link' individual needs further clarification.

There are also two masters of Okinawan Naha-te with very similar sounding names, known as Higaonna Kanryō (1853–1916, 'West Higaonna') and Higaonna KanRyu (1849–1922, 'East Higaonna'). The former trained with Ru Ru Ko (Xie Zongxiang) and Wai Shinzan, the latter trained only under Wai Shinzan.[100] Higaonna Kanryō's foremost student, Chojun Miyagi, went on to develop the well-known Goju-Ryu Karate style, Higaonna KanRyu contributed to the broad development of Naha-te in Okinawa. Higaonna KanRyu's version of the kata Seisan is continued by Juhatsu Kyoda's Tōon-ryū (Tōu'on-ryū) who trained with both masters.

Shorin-Ryu and Shorei-Ryu

Identifying Ru Ru Ko has baffled martial arts historians for many years, due to the fact that many Okinawan styles list this individual in their provenance. Commonly, three Chinese individuals are listed as being this master: Ason, Wai Shin Zan and Xai Zhong Xiang.

There is historical evidence that confirms Okinawan visits by the Chinese emperor's envoy (Saposhi) in 1838 and 1866, which included military attachés Ason and Wai Shin Zan. According to word-of-mouth, the origins of the distinction between Naha-te and Shuri-te may have begun at the time when Naha-te forefathers (including those of Ryuei-Ryu) trained with Ason, whilst Shorin-Ryu forefathers (such as Shimabukuro) trained with Wai Shin Zan. In a 1914 interview,[101] Ason said he taught 'Shorei-Ryu' – one of the early forms of Naha-te and the predecessor term for modern-day Goju-Ryu. At this tipping point in Karate, it therefore seems that two distinct but not necessarily antagonistic groups formed and marketed themselves as such, those of the Shorin-Ryu (so-named after the Chinese Kung-Fu term 'Shaolin' and mainly comprising Shuri-te and Tomari-te) and those of the Shorei-Ryu (possibly derived from the south China Shoreiji Temple and mainly compising Naha-te). This distinction remains to this day when Karate masters discuss the techniques of each style.[66, 67, 101] Shorin is more nimble and Shorei is based more on physical conditioning and strength. Many of the Okinawan Shorin stylists were aristocratic, whereas the Shorei stylists were typically less so and derived their style from southern Chinese schools and military associations.

Consequently, Ason is most likely to correspond with Ru Ru Ko in view of the broad association of this master with Naha-te-derived styles. This is supported by an interview with Seiko Higa (master of Goju-Ryu and direct student of Kanryo Higaonna and Chojun Miyagi),[102] where he states that his father knew Ru Ru Ko and Wai Shin Zan as distinct individuals – in fact they were respectively the 'left and right hands' of the Chinese Envoy in Okinawa during his visit. There is additional evidence from the Naha-te patriarch Kanryo Higaonna, who also identified the envoy's bodyguards as Ru Ru Ko and Wai Shin Zan (and subsequently trained with both, having been introduced to Wai Shin Zan by Kojo Tatei). The identification of Wai Shin Zan is clear from both sources, however, the fact that Higa's father and Higaonna both called the 2nd military attaché Ru Ru Ko, and the historical record reports the 2nd military attaché as Ason, implies that they may well be one and the same.

After 1838 the military attachés returned to China, and some of the early Naha masters reportedly went to the Chinese mainland in order to continue their martial arts training (for example, Kenri Nakaima and Kitoku Sakiyama went to train with Ru Ru Ko and the Beijing Military Academy).[80] Following the return of the attachés in 1866, the Naha masters rekindled their martial arts dialogue with their former masters (Ryuei-Ryu stylists say Kenri Nakaima did this). Interestingly, whilst we know that both Sakiyama and Nakaima trained with the same individuals in China, the former listed his mentor as Ason and the latter as Ru Ru Ko. This disparity in name may be caused by problems of transliteration (Mandarin, Fujianese, Okinawan Japanese) or they may be alternate names or nicknames for the same person. Ason may be a military rank rather than a name, and the spelling of Ru Ru Ko as Lui Long Gung by Ryuei-Ryu stylists is likely to have created futher inconsistencies. Ason and Ru Ru Ko were probably the same person, a luminary of modern Karate; particularly Naha-te.

Kanryo Higaonna is purported to recount that Ru Ru Ko had moved to the Fujian area to live by the river, where Higaonna visited him during his time in China. He furthermore recounted that Ru Ru Ko had told him to start teaching his own students in Okinawa, as he (Ru Ru Ko) had become to old too do this himself. Higaonna also wanted Chojun Miyagi (a founder of Goju-Ryu) to train under Ru Ru Ko, although this was not possible as he had passed away by this time.

Finally, when assessing Xai Zhong Xiang, there are reports that Kanryo Higaonna identified him as a basketmaker (and therefore not Ru Ru Ko, who was working as the bodyguard of the Chinese emperor's envoy, who he knew well). Furthermore, he lived between the early 1850s (likely 1852) and the First World War (likely 1915) so this does not correspond with the training of the early Karate masters of the early nineteenth century. Lastly, his name is listed in Mandarin and during the era of Ru Ru Ko, the *lingua franca* would have been Fujianese.[103]

Several Karate masters, including Iken Tokashiki, Kaicho Sensei/ founder of Gohakukai Karate-Do and Patrick McCarthy, consider Ru Ru Ko to have been Xai Zhong Xiang.[75, 104–110] They cite Ru Ru Ko/ Xai Zhong Xiang as the founder of the Whooping Crane Style (Ming He Quan). Ru Ru Ko was a student of the Crane master Pan Yuban (Kwan Pang Yuiba) who in turn was a student of Lin Shixian, the later being a direct disciple of White Crane's Fujianese female originator, Fang Qiniang. This style of White Crane is a Shaolin five-animal boxing derivative that may have its roots in Taiwanese White Crane. According to legends, Ru Ru Ko was born in eastern Fujian (Changle) into an aristocratic family but was forced into a clandestine life for political reasons.[111] As a result he became a handyman working casually as a bricklayer, builder and basketmaker. Such 'riches to rags' accounts are not uncommon in the legends of martial artists and no doubt would be welcomed to a degree by the Okinawan aristocracy, who were the intial practitioners of Karate on the island. The legends go on to specify that Ru Ru Ko befriended 'Daiji',[77, 112] an individual native to Fuzhou's village of Yong Chun (the birthplace of White Crane) and so visited the village to train under the local Crane master (nicknamed Bansho Hachi).

There is a degree of consensus that the roots of Ru Ru Ko's style are that of 'Whooping Crane' (synonymous with Shaking, Feeding, Flying and Weeping/ Crying/ Singing Crane).[76, 104–109, 113] This has been further associated with the Pan family Crane style in Yongchun (and hence Pan Yuban),[113] which also has a similarity to modern-day Uechi-Ryu (as opposed to the common belief in 'Tiger Boxing' origins).[113]

As with all progenitor styles, these have also gone through evolutionary changes, so that today when we compare styles, we do not have direct evidence of the evolutionary split, but rather we are looking back to trace inherited commonalities. Recently, Goju master Tadahiko Ohtsuka visited the grandson of Ru Ru Ko, Xie Pin Guan, in Fuzhou (Fujian, China) to reaffirm Goju Kung-Fu links. The great-grandson of Ru Ru Ko, Xie Wen Liang, visited master Iken Tokashiki (among others) on Okinawa over a period of eighteen months to teach his current Crane style to his Okinawan Karate colleagues and to compare practice.[76, 104–109, 113] Additionally, there is a recent project supported by Urasoe city in Okinawa. Here Grandmaster Tokumasa Miyagi (a Shorin-Ryu stylist and student of Yuchoku Higa), who chairs the Okinawa Dento Karatedo Shinkokai, visited Quanzhou in Fujian China with a team of ten martial artists to study Karate and Kung-Fu (Five Ancestors Fist, White Crane Fist) links in 2012. Such examples of mutual respect and transparent dialogue between like-minded individuals help us to research and understand this sophisticated martial art. Whether Ru Ru Ko was either Ason or Xai Zhong Xiang may never be known, owing to lack of evidence and legendary overlay. Whilst much of the evidence points to Ason, the broader fact is that Karate is derived from a multitude of martial sources over the past few centuries that condensed on the island of Okinawa. Some luminaries such as Ru Ru Ko coming from the Fujian and the

Chinese mainland would have offered seminal contributions to the development of this art. This highlights the pluralism of Karate and its open dialogue with Shaolin boxing arts and their derivatives to generate Karate as we know it today.

Kata

Kata is one of the true foundation elements of Karate. In numerous ways and at several levels, kata contains many of the secrets of Karate and Kobudo. It may also possibly have been an element of Ti, although there is a strong likelihood that pre-Chinese-influenced Ti would have had no kata, and any forms that exist are undeniably Chinese (in form and use). The practice of these pre-arranged forms and the understanding of their *bunkai* (breakdown and analysis) provide insights into secret techniques, deadly moves and a higher philosophy. Two levels of bunkai exist. The most basic interpretation of moves is known as *renzoku bunkai* or *chokusen*, and is based on *kuden* (or oral transmission). *Renzoku* means continuous and *chokusen* means straight line. While there are undeniably many kuden surrounding bunkai the term is not limited to it. A higher level of interpretation derived from secret movements and techniques is represented by *okuden* (deepest transmission). Kuden and okuden are completely separate terms and not two stages in the same process. Okuden bunkai can correspond to 'Hidden Waza' or 'secret techniques' in a similar way to that in Aikijutsu. As a result, kata is considered by many masters (almost universally) as the highest expression of Karate.[114-118]

In Naha-te and Goju-Ryu katas, there is an established concept of *kaisai no genri* 解裁の原理, the theory of kaisai (hidden techniques in kata) as a method to guide practitioners in understanding and correctly applying the practice of their forms. This was introduced to overcome the problem of practising the same moves over and over again without understanding them; this can lead to the introduction of significant and persistent misconceptions and mistakes in the application of Karate. Seikichi Toguchi (founder of the Goju-Ryu school of Shoreikan) championed this concept and promulgated it through his students. In addition to the importance of appreciating the meaning of each technique and its bunkai, the *kaisai no genri* are also applied practically in man-on-man simulated combat to appreciate the hands-on practical execution of each technique.

Toguchi aimed to 'clear the waters' regarding the presence of 'secret techniques' and mysticism in Karate practice. He felt that this was detracting from the pure essence of Karate as an art and practical combat sport. The concept was presented to him by his instructor Chojun Miyagi (founder of the Goju-Ryu system) through the terms *kaisai no genri, toki to musubi* and *toki to musubi no genri*. Toguchi identified three fundamentals of practising kata:[119]

1a.   Do not let the steps and movements (*embusen*) of a kata deceive you.
1b.   When moving forward (through footwork) the techniques are those of attack, when retreating (through footwork) the techniques are for blocking and defence.
2.   There is one enemy and they are in front of you.

The style of Goju-Ryu is recognised for its well-trained, tough, technically excellent and practically minded practitioners who undergo rigorous conditioning and applied training for application in real-life situations. However, there is an extensive spectrum of Karate practice, so that some other styles typically consider multiple levels of understanding of Karate kata; this is associated with technical expertise and experience (and thereby usually, but not always, with Karate rank). Kenwa Mabuni (founder of Shito-Ryu Karate) explained that even for a 'beginner's' kata, such as Pinan Nidan, there are multiple ways of examining the opening movements,[120] and as a result, multiple ways of using this kata for martial applications. For example, a move to the left could be used to engage with an assailant to the left, or conversely it could be interpreted as a side step to the left away from a combatant who came from the right.

There is massive scope for interpreting and applying movements in varying combat situations. There is, however, broad consensus that appraising kata according to its bunkai, whether through kaisai and non-kaisai methods, can be done inductively (*kinoho*), deductively (*enekiho*) or even spontaneously with free interpretation according to need (achieving the art of attack and defence – *kobo no jutsu*). So there is a Janus-like duality in kata; at one level they can be performed highly technically, almost in a machine-like manner according to a set mathematical programme, yet on the other hand their performance can have an artisitic quality, with freedom of internal expression – the 'art' element of martial art. At an even higher level, the practice of kata offers a meditative opportunity, so that for some practitioners, the moves become more than the visible combative steps, and offer a spiritual experience.

Karate kata can be defined through many variables.[103, 121] One modified classification system assesses each kata thus, according to:

1. Technical components.
2. Kata name (which often retains the name of its founder; e.g. Wansu, Kushanku and possibly Chinto).
3. The area of Okinawa where it was practised (Naha, Shuri, Tomari).
4. Spiritual or religious names or associations (e.g. Suparimpei or Sepai in Naha katas).
5. Metaphysical or transcendental elements (e.g. Sanchin or Tensho).
6. Animal forms (typical in Kojo-Ryu or Hakutsuru (White Crane form) or those hidden in many katas such as Chicken-Beak in Gojushiho).
7. Numbers (e.g. Bassai Dai and Sho, Tekki Shodan and Nidan and Sandan).

Practitioners from generation to generation have attempted to preserve these physical moves in exactly the same way that they were taught it. This is a fundamental concept in Karate – if the original kata is tampered with, it may lose some of its 'original' or secret meaning. Changing a kata for personal preference is frowned upon and can only be performed by the most senior of stylists, and then only rarely.

Nevertheless, teaching a kata from individual to individual is unintentionally subject to subtle differences in personal interpretation (whether physical or mental), and in a period before the presence of easy recording methods, katas were subject to a 'Chinese whisper syndrome' (of sorts) from one generation to the next.

It is therefore possible to study two masters who were initially taught the same kata by the same instructor and find discernible differences. Over numerous generations these changes become copied and retained with a few minor changes in each generation, such that after hundreds of years the katas can look very different.

This is an 'evolution' of kata. These changes can be compared to the biological evolution of an organism. Here the inherited genes and DNA of an organism is the kata, and the organism itself is the style. The method of translating the kata into practice is therefore akin to the way that the body translates DNA into protein. The molecules that do this, the ribonucleic acid (RNA), are the method that each instructor uses for each particular kata according to his or her individual style. Just as in kata, the DNA is replicated with massive precision, however, there are small natural flaws within every generation of cells, such that over a long period genes evolve and if these genes are consistently copied and spread, whole organisms and populations can have permanent changes, equivalent to a change in Karate style.

If katas are considered akin to genes and Karate style akin to species, as in my analogy, then we can trace the evolutionary history of each Karate species or style. For example, some authorities have traced the origins of Naha-te katas[103] to classical Shaolin Tai Chi-type schools,[78] whereas others have identified the Fujian Boxing origin of these forms.[75, 102, 110] There are countless elements of Chinese martial arts in Karate katas, and a more robust analysis can be applied to assess their 'evolutionary' origins.

As a relevant example, I have modelled the genetic or evolutionary 'phylogeny' of the kata Seisan (**Figure 13**). This is because this kata is retained by a large variety of Karate styles, and is arguably the most universally recognised Karate kata. As it is such an important 'conserved' kata, it is analogous to a 'conserved' gene that has been retained by numerous species. As a result we can compare its changes to give us an indication of the evolution of individual styles.

Seisan was first taught by Sokon 'Bushi' Matsumura in the nineteenth century to many of Karate's early masters, and was ascribed to a well known and powerful Chinese boxer named Seisan who lived in Okinawa between the proposed but unvalidated dates of 1588 and 1600. Today it is arguably practised by more styles than any other, as it is used in Naha-te, Shuri-te and Shorin-Ryu schools (where it can be called Seisan, Sesan, Sheshan and even Hangetsu). The other most universal katas are Passai/ Bassai, Kushanku/ Kanku and Naihanchi/ Naifanchi (or Tekki in Japanese styles and possibly *noy huan tsien* as its original Chinese form).

The ultimate 'look and feel' of a style is analogous to the biological 'phenotype' of an organism. In the model demonstrated, the changes in the performance of the kata Seisan quite closely reflect the changes of the style, just as changes in an important biological gene are significant in the evolution of an individual species.

Karate is particularly amenable to such phylogenetic modelling as the purported origins of each kata are relatively well known, recent and originate from only a handful of founders. Performing the same modelling for a Wushu kata (Taolu) as an alternative example is also possible but would be more complex.

The analogy between the development of Karate and the evolutionary gene pool offers further insights. So far, I have considered a *natural selection* of Karate styles. The analogy can be extended to encompass the concepts of genetic mutation and artificial selection. Genetic mutations can occur in a single generation to change an organism (and its phenotype) from its parents. In Karate, this could occur by one individual ignoring or forgetting to teach certain techniques or kata. This is not necessarily detrimental. For example, according to some

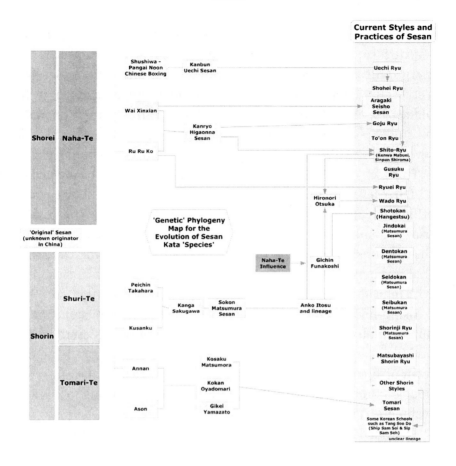

Figure 13: Phylogenetic map of the evolution of the kata *Seisan*.

sources, the famed Karate master Choki Motobu only knew three kata: Naihanchi (series), Wansu and Passai Guwa (small Passai). Some actually say he only knew Naihanchi. Either way, he taught this to his students, but the quality or depth of his teaching gave his style its distinctiveness and it did not end with him but rather flourished. Motobu's interpretation of Karate can be viewed as a mutation, but not a lethal one, rather one that had its advantages.

Then there is artificial selection. In biology, particular organisms can be purposefully mated to bring out certain selected characteristics in the next generation (such as the selection of fast racehorses or prize-winning canines). The same can occur in Karate. Masutatsu

Oyama trained in the very rigorous styles of Goju-Ryu, Shotokan and Judo to form the very hard style of Kyokushinkai; essentially Oyama merged the very tough concepts from these strong styles to develop a style characterised by strength, endurance and knockdown techniques. He also added many of his own ideas. Interestingly enough, his students carried on this evolution down a specific path and took several elements from Muay Thai, another notoriously hard style.

This idea of a kind of science of 'Paleo-Karate' can be applied at a higher level of complexity and hierarchical modelling by considering each particular move or technique within a kata. This can be used to identify style origins, but more importantly the closeness of the relationship between each kata and each style – in the same way that one can compare humans with primates (relatively close), or with marine mammals such as whales (relatively distant).

Using my previous example of the Karate kata Seisan, I have approximated the degree of homology between the different katas, and have plotted this against an arbitrary classification using the form of opening movements as one single marker of kata type: double-handed, left-handed and right-handed, according to this one technique (**Figure 14**).

The classification of each kata (which is composed of thousands of moves) would require complex mathematical analysis. The use of only one single marker of technique is basic and is provided to aid comprehension of this kind of homology mapping. Nevertheless, it is quite clear to most observers that Goju-Ryu Seisan has many similarities (high homology) to Shito-Ryu Seisan and Ryuei-Ryu Seisan, and each of these in turn has a certain degree of homology with other katas. Just as in their kata, Goju-Ryu, Ryuei-Ryu and to some extent Shito-Ryu have high degrees of 'phenotypic' similarity, which correlates well with our understanding of where this kata was derived for all these styles, probably from the master Ru Ru Ko.

Using these concepts at a broader level in Karate can also enable us to better understand its fundamental origins. The origins of Shorin-Ryu (Shaolin in Japanese), likely named by Matsumura Sokon, are in a period of Japanisation of the Ryukyu islands well before the wide-

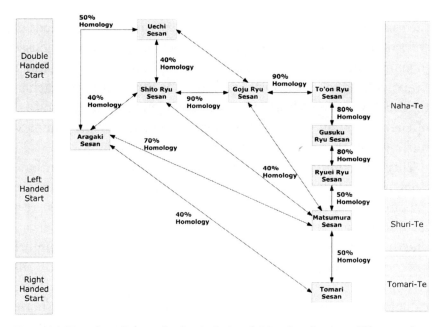

Figure 14: Homology diagram for the similarity of *Seisan* kata between different styles.

spread use of Shaolin in the Chinese popular media, representing a valid link. When applying the concepts of evolution and homology to Karate, there is a powerful link to Shaolin. For example, the numerous White Crane forms in China reflect the Hakutsuru (Japanese) of Karate, the two-man drills of the Five Ancestors fist are very similar to those in Karate (particularly Yakusoku Kumite), and the Eighteen Hand Movements or 18 Lo-Han Hands of the Shaolin closely resemble the modern Chinese Saam Chien form and the Sanchin kata of many Karate styles. The Okinawan kata Rohai has been said to represent the Okinawan pronunciation of the Chinese term Lo-Han[122] – all further adding weight to the argument for a Shaolin origin of Karate.

The Hakutsuru White Crane form is a particularly good model to study as its adoption can be located to a handful of schools in Okinawa (such as that of Kume village) so its origins can be isolated. This, however, is a relatively rare kata so only gives a partial picture of the overall development of Karate. Studying the much more universal kata of Sanchin (Chinese Sam Chien) is revealing but is highly complex owing to the high number of forms. As it is performed in the majority of Naha-based Karate styles, there are hundreds of ways of demonstrating this relatively short form. It is also practised in many Chinese schools. It can be seen in White Crane- and Black Crane-derived schools. There are also many other offshoots such as the Feeding Crane style from Taiwan. Calculating the origin and age of each form and style can therefore become incredibly complex, making 'palaeographic' analysis rather time-consuming.

This technique does, however, reveal new concepts that may have been previously forgotten. For example, it can reveal a 'lost link' or 'missing link' of Karate evolution. The Seisan kata does this. There is an observed discrepancy between the visual forms of Naha Seisans and the Shuri Matsumura Seisans (derived from Sokon Matsumura and promulgated by Chotoku Kyan). If, however, one studies the Ryuei-Ryu version of Seisan (from the Naha/Shorei school) and compares it to that of the Matsumura Seisan (seen in many Shorin schools, including those of the Shobayashi, Seidokan, Dentokan and Jindokai), although the forms may look superficially different, the techniques carry many similarities. As an example, the first technique in Ryuei-Ryu is that of a left-handed inside block (*uchi uke*) followed by a right punch and then a simultaneous right step (in a short right–front stance) and a right-handed inside block. In Matsumura Seisan (Shorin-Ryu), the first technique is again that of a left-handed inside block (*uchi uke*) followed by a punch (on the spot without moving stance) followed by a right-handed inside block and then forward step, and so on. The real difference in these forms is on the stepping motion between moves, which in modern Karate is accentuated by very long, deep and highly emphasised stances. What we know from the practice of original Karate (notable in pictures and photographs), is that the stances were typically much shorter and people performed many katas in an almost walking fashion. Based on such conspicuous similarities between these superficially different forms (Shorin versus Shorei), it is feasible that they had a common ancestor, but the performance was modified and stylised over time by different groups of practitioners who accentuated the stepping motion and emphasised the punches as a result of personal interpretation and ability. We see the Shorin-Ryu schools give heavy emphasis to the first block (left) and stance (left) then punch (right) then right block with subsequent step. The Ryuei-Ryu school, however, perform the same first block with less emphasis (almost using it as a preliminary guarding technique), before a subsequent strong punch (right) and then a simultaneous right block and step (as opposed to the right block then step of Shorin-Ryu). Such similarities can be noted in many different aspects of Seisan kata, and can also be observed in many other katas across the whole Karate compendium, and in other martial arts, most prominently Shaolin Kung-Fu, but also in other Eastern arts including Taekwondo (see Appendix 2). The commonalities of the fundamental forms of each art indicate the evolutionary process for each kata performed over generations. Even at a local club level, it it clear that individuals perform a kata according to their own physical attributes and abilities. When they demonstrate these katas for purposes of formal teaching, however, the students adopt some of the personal style of their instructor and, by doing so, perpetuate that style in a 'natural', evolutionary way.

Where does the future of Karate lie? The application of evolutionary models can be quite insightful. The rich plethora of modern Karate styles reflects the evolution of each individual style and can be considered equivalent to a Karate 'gene pool', represented in the various kata of each style. Due to various selection pressures, the kata pool has changed. The selection pressures include the introduction of modern competition Karate, the dissemination of media (books and internet) and global rapid travel and communication. As a result, it can be seen that many styles of Karate now adopt simplified techniques that cater for a mass audience and almost universally require much deeper stances that did not exist fifty or even a hundred years ago. Thanks to modern media, we can trace the history of some styles such as Shotokan Karate, and we can see the style presented by its founder Gichin Funakoshi in his book *Karate-do Kyohan*, or on one of the many film clips of him from the mid-1900s. He totally differs from modern Shotokan practitioners. Kata such as Tekki Shodan or Sochin were quite nimble in performance, but have now become rigorously powerful and robust in the Karate of modern times. There are also examples of living Karate 'fossils', exemplified by the style of Ryuei-Ryu. This Okinawan Naha style was practised amongst family members following the arrival of some of the early Naha masters, mainly via China, in the early 1800s (Ru Ru Ko and his Okinawan student Kanryo Higaonna). It was subsequently taught to the local Okinawan populace, including schoolteachers in the 1970s, and so represents a style largely untouched by outside influence until then. The gene pool or katas in this style have not interacted with other styles, so that many of the katas practised by other Naha styles, such as Goju-Ryu, are recognisable to Ryuei-Ryu practitioners, but there are obvious differences. Furthermore, this style has katas that are not present in all but the rarest of other Naha schools and were only reintroduced to the wider world by the world Karate kata champion, Tsuguo Sakumoto, who won the seventh, eighth and ninth WUKO (World Union of Karate-do Organisations) World Karate Kata Championship with his rendition of the rare kata Annan (**Figure 15**).

Shotokan Karate also demonstrates some of the kata seen in rarer Karate styles. This includes the White Crane popularised in the 1984 film *The Karate Kid*. Based on the truly ancient Hakutsuru (through the council of Fumio Demura), Hakucho or the Ryuei-Ryu Paiho, this style came from the Chinese mainland. In addition, it has other rare kata such as Ohan, Pacchu, Heiku, Paiku and Paiho, which offer some rich and flowingly beautiful yet powerful movements not seen in other Karate styles. Interaction with the rest of the Karate world has seen many luminaries, such as Teruo Hayashi of Hayashi-Ha Shito-Ryu, incorporate many of these forms into the Shito-Ryu and subsequently world Karate syllabi (such as those of the World Karate Federation – WKF) where they have taken new forms. For example, the technical precision and beauty of the kata Annan has led Karate competitors across the globe to adopt this form for competition purposes. Their demonstation of this kata has now incorporated physical elements that are heavily stylised 'to look good' and achieve contest triumphs, to some degree at the loss of

Figure 15: The kata *Annan* performed by the author.

technical martial rigour. So the Karate 'gene pool' is evolving from
the original Karate 'fossil' (Ryuei-Ryu), such that the flowing forms
of Sakumoto are now becoming an endangered species compared
to the newer, harder, more direct methods of performing these kata
seen on the competion circuit. Many other examples exist: the Unsu
kata of ancient Karate masters certainly does not hold much resemblance to the modern competition method of its performance.

Competition Karate is not the only source of selection in the kata
gene pool. Commonality is another factor. The ancient kata Sanchin
has been purported to be as old as some of our earliest understanding of what we call Karate and Shaolin Kung-Fu. So many variations
of this kata currently exist and have existed around the world. We
know of versions in Karate – Goju, Uechi, Ryuei etc. – but also in

China through White Crane, Black Crane, Whooping Crane and so on. The kata can be done in one direct line, in two lines (back and forth), in four lines (all four directions) and a broad variety therein. Today, however, this form is primarily performed in the one-lined method of Goju-Ryu and Uechi-Ryu, even by stylists whose original style does this differently. Although there are uncertainties and great variation in the kata's performance in China, it is commonly considered that Higaonna, and later Uechi, both brought to Japan a version that goes forward three steps, turns and goes back three. Miyagi Chojun was the one who replaced the turn with three backward steps and also changed the open hands to closed. The modern Uechi version keeps the turn but ends with the mawashi uke on a T-bar. This selection pressure springs from the extremely widespread success of these two schools. On the other hand, the large influence of martial arts film acrobatics has led to many martial arts schools in the United States focusing on the acrobatic elements of kata. As a result, these schools have totally reinterpreted ancient kata with high flamboyant kicks, gymnastic jumps and even music, whilst others have invented a totally new set of kata. Some of these katas go on to flourish in several schools, whilst others ultimately become extinct.

There is currently an unabating loss of thorough bunkai teaching that goes together with a focus on physical education in the Kodokan Judo mould since the end of the nineteenth century, or possibly earlier. The fact that the original intentions and meanings behind the movements became forgotten, and open to speculation, is one of the major reasons that katas change. It is unclear which generation of instructors consciously decided not to pass on detailed bunkai knowledge, but it has controversially been speculated that it was some of Karate's luminaries. Some argue that their role as luminaries should have led to the preservation of the ancient bunkai, which sadly does not seem to have occurred. Unfortunately, this has also lent self-proclaimed 'masters' the opportunity to invent false bunkai in order to promote themselves and their own interests. In the post-war period the influence of some of the modern styles and their disdain for the original kata helped to marginalise the practice. These trends were visible in the 1950s, when many individuals requested that the ancient kata be conserved in order to preserve the knowledge of Karate. Master Choshin Chibana (former president of the Okinawan Karate Association) specified: 'Studying new kata is necessary but, at the same time, preserving the old kata should be compulsory.'[66, 67]

Interestingly, the vast majority of Karate instructors still claim that their Karate is identical to that of their teachers and Karate forebears, whilst in reality there is an intrinsic and more or less unstoppable evolution of Karate kata, in the same way that language changes over time. In evolutionary biology this is generally accounted for by a small but constant mutation of the gene pool. For Karate, this is not necessarily a bad or a good outcome, it simply reflects the natural progression of the practice of any human activity over time. It is nevertheless incumbent on all martial artists to keep true to their original style and know the proper content of their martial history. Once this is clarified, adopting new techniques or concepts can be done so that the benefits of old and new can be harmoniously joined.

Karate innovation in the Rykyuan Kingdom

The Naha-te practitioners kept their styles very closely based on their Chinese schools. However, the distinct nature of Karate that differentiates it from other martial arts came from both an inherent Ryukyu interpretation of Chinese martial arts and their own indigenous forms. It is Ryukyuan openness to martial innovation that led to the development of Karate. It is notable that nearly all the first generation of Shuri-Te practitioners (who practised a Chinese-derived art) also learned Tomari-te – a practice that derived from local Ryukyuan arts, Chinese arts but also non-Chinese (possibly Vietnamese, other Asian, Pacific, Polynesian and even so-called 'pirate') arts. Hence the Shorin schools are by definition a mix of Shuri and Naha-te.

The second generation of Shuri and Tomari masters were also visionary in their adoption of Karate's technical skills. Masters such as Kenwa Mabuni adopted Naha-Te teaching so that their styles represented all three schools of Shuri, Naha and Tomari. All Karate styles today can be defined according to a spectrum of their proportional application of these three schools.

Okinawan dance (Ryukyu buyo)

Karate was not only stored in the form of kata or forms. There were other forms of physical expression such as Okinawan dance (Ryukyu buyo). The use of military dance also exists in other cultures, such as the martial Haka of the Maori (which might even have some ancestral link to the Ryukyu culture via the Pacific ocean). The history of traditional Okinawan dancing closely follows that of traditional Okinawan Karate in that it was derived from a multitude of sources, including Chinese dance and melodies and even more distant Indonesian music. Okinawa in the late fourteenth century under kings such as Satto of Chuzan and Sho Hashi (1371–1439), the first king of the united Ryukyu kingdom, maintained a cultural dialogue with her powerful neighbour, China. Commonly understood artistic styles may have contributed to the development of diplomatic allegiances and personal friendships that could translate into trade and military support. Okinawa could retain status as an international trade hub, devoid of Chinese bureaucracy and open to innovation and external goods and culture. Thus, Sho Hashi's court would wear Chinese aristocratic robes and aristocrats would wear two swords, as was the Japanese custom. Both court dancing (*kumi-odori* and *onna-odori*) and Karate was promoted, and just like Karate, the dancing was only for male aristocrats. As a result of the exposure of the same demographic segment to both dancing and Karate, there is some overlap between these physical arts. Their joint evolution has led to many commonalities:

leg movements and stances;
fist formations and hand techniques;

body posture;
body dynamics;
body shifting;
rhythms in movement patterns.

Some Okinawan dance groups developed their own school or style of dance, named *Ryu* in the same way that Okinawan Karate styles named their schools. The modern Hirae Kinjo School of Ryukyuan dance is also known as the Tamagusuku Ryu. This style is likely named after the location of an Okinawan village rather than the early fourteenth-century king of Chuzan, who lost the unity of Okinawa's three states, allowing the Lord of Nakijin to become king of Hokuzan in northern Okinawa and the Lord of Ozato to become king of Nanzan in southern Okinawa.

As early as the period of 'proto-Karate', Ti Jutsu was comprised of Tuidi Gaeshi and reversed techniques (Ura Gaeshi) that culminate in 'The Dance of the Feudal Lords' (Ajikata nu Meekata).[70, 71] By the time Karate was rooted in Okinawa, one of its early masters Choso Chibana (1847–1927) who named 'Shorin-Ryu' (and a student of Ankoh Itosu) performed traditional Okinawan dance during the 1866 investiture ceremony of King Sho Tai (*Tora No Ukanshin-Udui*). Choso subsequently recorded these dancing events in a manuscript entitled *Kanshintorai To Odori* (Crown Ship Visits and Dance). He was also the formulator of Chibana Kosokun kata and trained in Baron Nakijin's Naha Courtyard.[123] Choso Chibana identified that the young male aristocrats who took part in court dancing (*ukanshin-udui*) would be incentivised to participate by elevation in the social hierarchy of the Rykyuan kingdom.

There is evidence that the Shuri aristocracy (udun or tunchi rank), including the famed Karate family of Motobu, participated in royal dances (Ryukyu buyo). One particularly prominent Karate master, Choki Motobu, mentioned in his *Watashi no Karate-jutsu* that the well-known martial artist Tomigusuku Uukata Seiko (1829–1893) danced as a young boy in the 1839 *inu no ukanshin-udui*.[124] As a result of this, he was awarded the title of Gakudoshi (a senior musical/dance artistic title that to some extent equates with *Prima ballerina assoluta*) and went on to perform in the Japanese city of Edo (now Tokyo) either at the castle or the Satsuma estate. He became a well-known Karate master and one of the early forefathers of Gusuku-Ryu, which today is a style that has very esoteric Karate movements demonstrating a dance-like nimbleness and flow. Tomigusuku was an expert horseman and skilled Kobudo-ka as a spear specialist. In later life he was a well-known politician and was accepted as a top-ranking aristocrat, taking on the mantle of sixteenth chief of the Tomigusuku family, the head familiy of the Mo clan, which in turn was considered to be among the top five clans in the Ryukyu kingdom.

Seikichi Uehara, who was among the best Motobu-style practitioners of the twentieth century, describes how he regularly saw prominent Motobu masters such as Choyu and Choki demonstrating their interest in or performing traditional Okinawan dancing. Choyu was particularly proficient. His movements were described by Uehara (who himself became a Motobu's 'dance-ti') as 'heavenly', whilst Koyu Shimabukuro (1893–1987) described Choki as a noted dance afficionado attending stage performances, sometimes watching from backstage and eventually becoming a powerful advocate for traditional dance in Okinawa.[124] Consequently, the famous Motobu family style, *Udun-ti*, comprised core elements of dancing hands (Mai-te or Odori-te) in addition to playing hands (Asobi-te or Yu-te) and fighting hands (Gassen-te).[72]

Several individuals carrying the name Shimabukuro contributed to the cross-fertilisation between Karate and dance in Okinawa. Tatsuo Shimabukuro (1906–1975, also known as Shimabukuku) founded the Okinawan school of Isshin-Ryu (One Heart Style). He had adopted the name Tatsuo ('Dragon Man') in later life, but was also nicknamed Sun Nu Su by the mayor of Kyan (Chan) village after a dance that had originally been created by Shimabukuro's grandfather. The nickname implied that Tatsuo performed it at some point. Tatsuo's younger brother, Eizo Shimabukuro, was also a famed Karate-ka and became the chief of the Shobayashi Shorin-Ryu style that was founded by Chotoku Kyan (another Shimabukuro,

Zenryo, had also trained under Chotoku Kyan, founding Shorin-Ryu Seibukan Karate). It is interesting to note that both Shimabukuro brothers had trained in Goju-Ryu under its founder, Chojun Miyagi, and it was an aptly named Tsunetaka Shimabukuro who trained in Shorin-Ryu with the modern Goju-Ryu master, Morio Higaonna, who on the advice of Shimabukuro attended classes at Chojun Miyagi's dojo. Morio Higaonna went on to study the close associations between Karate and Okinawan dance.[14]

Two evolutionary parallels exist when considering Okinawan Karate kata and classical Okinawan dance. To some extent, they both have a distant common origin, so that whilst they have evolved divergently, they can be seen to reflect each other in distant heritable elements, analogous to alligators and crocodiles. Whilst they look very similar and one can be studied to gain insight into the other, they are distinct species. For a molecular example, through the process of molecular transcription and translation, traditional Karate kata can be considered as DNA and dance as as a complementary strand of DNA. In the correct setting both kata and dance can be interpreted into effective karate techniques. This latter analogy offers a deeper insight as there may be a molecular dialogue and even equilibrium of sorts between kata and dance, as they have likely influenced each other since their initation; they may have co-evolved for many, many years, particularly before the twentieth century.

These close links between Okinawan aristocracy, Ryukyuan dance and Karate therefore offer a largely unexplored and rich source for

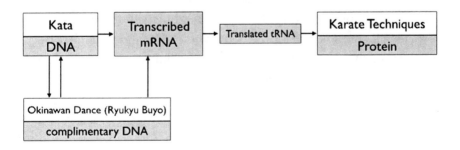

Figure 16: Okinawan dance.

understanding lost elements of Karate. Okinawan dance is a lost repository of information about ancient Karate techniques (**Figure 16**). Ultimately, the study of Ryukyu buyo may offer the chance to genetically 'reverse engineer' lost Karate knowledge, much as there are biological efforts to re-engineer lost or extinct animal species from the ancient DNA.[125] Whereas Kobudo is an ancient Okinawan martial art that remains alive in association with the training of Karate, Ti or Ryukyu buyo remain sporadic and rare, but could represent a unique opportunity to enhance modern Karate practice.

Fertile soil

In summary, the unique island culture of Okinawa and its Ryukyuan kingdom allowed a powerful cross-fertilisation of martial schools to become Karate. Its island location, the innovative nature of the people – able to adapt to new knowledge and skills – and the political backdrop of both upper and lower classes in the context of the Chinese and Japanese empires, allowed Karate and Kobudo to flourish on the Ryukyuan islands. These arts were taken to Japan by famous masters such as Mabuni, Miyagi and Funakoshi, the latter's students most notably formalising and restructuring Karate into a readily reproducible (almost conveyor-belt manufactured) and marketable phenomenon, as seen in its modern global form.

Karate's pluralism stems from its hybridisation from many wide-ranging sources, including those from northern and southern Shaolin (routed prominently but not exclusively through Fujian provice). It was adapted for the body type and fighting/ defence needs of the Okinawan artistocracy, with the backdrop of Okinawa's own indigenous art of Ti and the multilateral island influences of trade, piracy and diplomacy to finally coalesce into today's modern styles. The recent renaissance of Okinawan Karate has lent a new impetus to the appreciation of traditional Karate. The real goal of higher quality and more authentic Karate-do perhaps can be achieved from the deeper study of 'proto-Karate's' evolution into modern Karate.

7

Ninja

Ninja and the art that they practise (Ninjutsu) has captured the collective imagination of the whole world. In contrast to the other martial arts studied here, the Ninjas have been well documented since the Middle Ages. Having started out as a clandestine group of disparate mercenaries, they are now romanticised as gloriously dynamic superhumans who embody the modern concepts of power, confidence and secrecy. The underlying clandestine nature of this art has meant that there are few accepted practitioners, and there is some consensus that these arts have become extinct, or rather have been amalgamated into the other martial arts. On the other hand, some have always associated the Ninja with dark arts and black magic – representing the antithesis of the heroic, noble bushido code and its supporters the samurai, whom the Ninja would consider as their 'arch-enemies' (mainly based on legend rather than fact). Here they are seen as dangerous mercenary assassins who inhabit a world of spies and skulduggery. Despite the fact that a wealth of information exists on historical Ninja, this is outweighed by the flood of media exploitation. The apparent dual nature of the Ninja has allowed a flexibility in the interpretation of the terms Ninja and Ninjutsu, such that each individual can decide upon the meaning of these terms.

In 714, the *Kojiki* (also known as 'Record of Ancient Matters', which is the oldest manuscript of legends of Japan) describes Prince Yamato Takeru (or Yamato Dake) as a character who uses cunning, deception and clandestine techniques. This leads scholars to regard him today as the proto-Ninja. According to legend, some time between 1185 and 1189 the samurai Minamoto Yoshitsune is also reported as using furtive techniques, subsequently creating Yoshitsune Ryu Ninjutsu. Between 1294 and 1336, the samurai Kusunoki Masashige is acknowledged to have used comparable methods to create Kusunoki Ryu Ninjutsu. In reality, both characters were 'real' samurai, later heralded as Ninja masters.[126] This resulted from several accounts of ploys and manoeuvres used by them that were then transformed into Ninja-like activity in the minds of later scribes and poets. Yamato Takeru was probably a prince and Yoshitsune was, of course, a very successful general and clan lord who would have had control of espionage agents – but someone of that status is unlikely to have had the time to create and promote a school of martial arts.

According to most Ninja lore, the origins of the Ninja (**Figure 17** p. 145) can be broadly classified into three possibilities:

1. Chinese origin.
2. Indigenous Japanese origin.
3. Combined Chinese-and-Japanese origin.

Most theorists broadly agree, however, that whichever is correct, the roots of Ninja are found in warrior monks at approximately the end of the first millennium CE.

According to the 'from China' theory, the eighth-century CE was a very unstable era in China's history, with numerous wars and uprisings. This led warriors and scholars to leave their land for Japan. Amongst these were military men with knowledge of strategy in war (as mentioned in Sun Tzu's *The Art of War*), and possibly also Shaolin warrior monks or other Kung-Fu stylists. These refugees then either taught the locals their skills, or continued to practise their martial arts within their own families. Eventually they and their descendants worked as mercenaries. Examples include the Lin Kuei clan, otherwise known as the 'Forest Demons'. (Are there *any* reliable sources for the existence of the Lin Kuei?)

The indigenous Japanese origin of Ninjas involves the myths of demigods and forest spirits formulating and mastering martial arts, which they then taught to selected individuals who would then become Ninja. Classic examples include the *Tengu* ('heavenly dogs') or 'forest demons' that have magical, ghost-like powers and typically take the form of a mixture of two or three animals (classic depictions show them as bird-like humanoids; later myths gave them red skin and long noses). These semi-divine creatures would share their knowledge with mortals to teach the concepts of Ninjutsu. (Many regular schools of martial arts, especially swordsmanship, also claimed divine inspiration from Tengu.) Alternatively, just as in the case of China and its Shaolin monks, mountain mystics and priests spontaneously undertook the study of martial arts to strengthen their bodies for health and protection, whilst strengthening both their bodies and souls for arduous meditation and religious piety. Examples include mystic or esoteric Buddhists, the *Yamabushi*. These were ascetic Japanese mountain-dwelling hermits famed for their connection with nature. They have a long tradition as mighty warriors gifted with supernatural powers. One famous example considered by some to be a Ninja patriarch is En no Gyoja (born *c.*634 CE), a mountain mystic who developed the religion of Shugendo that integrated elements of Buddhism, Taoism and Shinto.

Interestingly, the mountain mystics and Yamabushi are closely associated with the magical Tengu in Japanese folklore and culture. They are renowned for being able to communicate with each other and even wear the same distinctive apparel. Whilst some Tengu can be evil spirits or ghosts, others offer protection, mentorship and even patronage to some Yamabushi and warriors. The Tengu form a hierarchy, with some considered as *Dai-Tengu* (or 'Great Tengu'). The greatest of these typically reside at Mount Kurama and Mount Atago. The Japanese Buddhist philosopher Inoue Enryo

(1858– 1919) lists the order of Dai-Tengu from the *Tengu Meigiko*. *Sojobo* of Mount Kurama is the 'King of the Tengu' (possessing the strength of 1,000 normal Tengu), and is followed in rank by *Tarobo* of Mount Atago and *Jirobo* of the Hira Mountains.

The Tengu king Sojobo (or 'highly Buddhist priest') is typically depicted with a characteristic large nose and flowing white hair. He is best known for mentoring Ushiwaka-maru, who later became the aforementioned famed warrior Minamoto no Yoshitsune (see book cover), who is subsequently credited with creating Yoshitsune Ryu Ninjutsu. The large nose and the pale features of Sojobo possibly allude to a more Western or central Asian origin for this Tengu, and his long nose and sometimes pronounced eyes are evocative of Bodhidharma (although this image is generally considered to have come later), who himself was a mountain mystic of sorts. Although there is currently no tangible evidence connecting these two characters, there may have been a subtle degree of association between the Buddhist-warrior natures of Bodhidharma and Sojobo.

The China and Japan theories are pooled to form the third theory of combined China/Japan origin. Chinese visitors and immigrants would teach local Japanese clans martial skills. These clans would subsequently master the skills and add them to their own to create Ninjutsu and would subsequently find employment as mercenaries. Interestingly, many of these warrior monks were Buddhists (non-Zen), who may have been trained by Shaolin Buddhist warrior monks from China teaching a very early form of Zen, or alternatively a varying school of Buddhism associated with the martial arts of warrior monks.

Although there is debate, the vast majority of legends associate Ninja's foundation with of a sect of warrior monks of the mid-tenth century CE. These monks were comparable to some extent to Shaolin monks in China and were known as the *Sohei* (a general word for a militarised monk and not a specific order).[127] They shared a similar philosophy to the Yamabushi and the mountain mystics, although they were not hermits and lived and acted collectively. This gave them a larger political impact and also afforded the power of a small army.

Amongst the most famous Sohei centres was the Tendai Buddhist Monastery of Enryaku-ji overlooking Kyoto on Mount Hiei; this is also the home of the ascetic *Kaihogyo* marathon monks.[128] Initially, different units of Sohei would fight each other as a result of political–religious discord between different sects of Buddhism or to contest unpopular appointments to the Buddhist religious hierarchy.

In the eleventh century the Sohei took part in the Gempei Civil War (1180–1185) between the two great warrior clans of the Taira and the Minamoto. The warrior monks fought alongside the Minamoto samurai defending the Byodo-In Temple and the bridge over the Uji River against the Taira army. Although they were ultimately unsuccessful, the monks had gained a powerful reputation and were also involved in attempting to prevent the kidnapping of Emperor Go-Shirakawa at Hojoji Palace. By the thirteenth and fourteenth centuries the rebel Emperor Go-Daigo and his son were supported by the Sohei in rebelling against the Kamakura shogunate.

The Sohei had declined by the fifteenth century; however, they were possibly precursors to the Ninja (many different sects of Sohei existed and most were not secretive organisations) who had been formally recognised by this time. Interestingly, another offshoot of the Sohei were the *Ikko-Ikki* (literally: united direction rebellions). This is a collective name for the various peasant and religious uprisings against unpopular policies by Tokugawa, and not an organised sect or group, who believed in the *Jodo Shinshu* sect. These monks were involved in a battle with Tokugawa Ieyasu, who had a strong association with the Ninja clans of Iga and Koga. Subsequently, Ieyasu defeated the Ikko-Ikki through his own warrior monks following the Jodo Shinshu sect.

The *Buke Meimokusho* mentions how Ninja were used covertly to dwell on the mountainside to gather intelligence and perform reconnaissance regarding enemy territory and politics before an orthodox armed attack.[127] The 'buke' in *Buke Meimokusho* means 'warrior families' or in context 'samurai families'. The 'bu' is the same character used in bugei, budo, bushi etc., and the 'ke' literally means 'house' but is also used to mean family, as in the medieval European use: 'the house of Lidon' etc. The *Buke Meimokusho* would translate as something along the lines of 'a written record of the warrior families'.

This may have an association with the *Buke Myomokusho* written in 1806, with very slightly differing characters but a broadly similar meaning. I am not sure if this is a misreading or simply an older reading of the name, or a different document entirely. This document is, as the name would suggest, a record of warrior families' occupations, their armaments and their writings between 887 and 1603.[82] Most probably the documents in question are the same thing. *Meimoku* and *myomoku* are simply alternative readings of the same characters.

In 1312 CE the Japanese monk Da Zhi (Chinese name) attended the Shaolin Temple to study Zen. Over a period of thirteen years, he was also versed in the Shaolin martial arts, so that in 1324 he returned home to Japan and imparted some of the wisdom and skills of the Shaolin monks. In 1335, another monk known as Shao Yuan also went to the Shaolin Temple for a period of twelve years, studying Zen, art and calligraphy and returned in 1347 to convey Shaolin concepts and techniques.

In 1487 Ninja are first identified in both Iga and Koga, described in the chronicles of the Ashikaga shogunate of the Muromachi period (*bakufu*) (written as a 'supplement to the *Nochi Kagami*'). This is the first use of the word 'Shinobi' in this context. They were reported to have the ability to enter castles covertly at will. The shogun Yoshihisa was reputed to have Ninja (Shinobi) serving him at his camp based at Magari. The Ninja were from family generations of Iga warriors, and they fought alongside regular troops. These warriors were famous, and specific mention is made of the Ninja family of Kawai Aki no kami of Iga.[126, 127, 129]

In the chronicles of the Muromachi bakufu (written as a 'supplement to the *Nochi Kagami*'), Ninja were technically recognised as *kagimono-hiki*. Importantly, the text mentions that they were also known in China ('the west') as *saisaku*.[126, 129] This is therefore the first association of Japanese Ninja to Chinese equivalents in the known literature, and such an association may represent the cross-fertilisation of cultures to derive Ninja and Ninjutsu **(Figure 17)**.

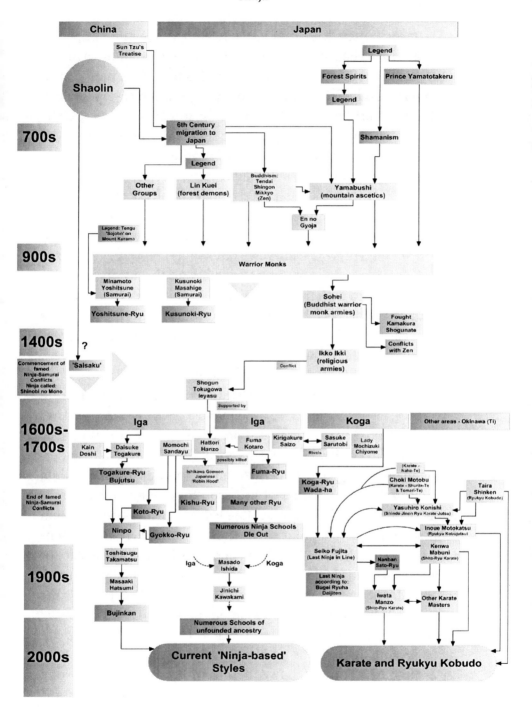

Figure 17: Ninjutsu evolution.

The term *saisaku* 細作 could be in reference to 'Ninja-like people from the past'. The characters mean 'thin or narrow' and 'to make/construct' or 'product' and are used in this order in a native word meaning 'slightly built' (as in a body type). Saisaku is very likely to be of Chinese origin due to the form of the word (two Chinese characters with no *hiragana* to clarify the reading). Consequently the word has a very generic and basic meaning such as 'slightly built' and was adopted to refer to a specific group of people.[82]

The next 200 years see a total upheaval of Japanese society and the Ninja become intimately linked with those changes in Japanese politics. Three men – Oda Nobunaga, Tokugawa Ieyasu and Toyotomi (Hashiba) Hideyoshi, known as the 'three unifiers' – are collectively credited with responsibility for the events that ultimately concluded with the unification of Japan. Ieyasu was brought up with Nobunaga as a hostage of the Oda clan and Hideyoshi was born a peasant and promoted to become one of Nobunaga's top generals. Ieyasu initially fought a number of battles with the Oda clan, although eventually became a strong ally of Oda and all three at one point ruled Japan, eventually leading to national harmony. During all of this period, Ninjas were used in most of the warfare and are mentioned in reports from that time. The first half of this time of upheaval (1467–1602) was the the era of the warring states, otherwise known as the Sengoku period. During this time the most Ninja use was in the field during warfare, scouting, laying ambushes, in direct combat and providing warfare leadership and co-ordination (contradicting the popular myth that samurai were fundamentally opposed to Ninja). The second era was known as the Edo, or Tokugawa, period (1603–1868) in which peace gradually returned, the mid-1600s representing a transition period. The 'pivot' is the victory of Tokugawa as the most famous battle in Japanese history: Sekigahara. As the wars fade away much of the work of Ninjas was based around information gathering, robbery and espionage (and assassination according to twentieth-century legends). For a long time, Tokugawa ran Japan as the world's largest ever police state, and had great need of intelligence agents.

Returning to the Sengoku period, in 1541 the Abbot Eishun of Tamon-In describes in his diary (*Tamon-In nikki*) an example of Iga Ninja (*Iga Shu*) efficiency in successfully attacking the castle on mount Kasagi. In the 1540s the *Chugoku Chiran-ki* mentions how Ninja (Shinobi) successfully fought in a battle near the shores of the Japanese inland sea (here not acting as mercenaries but in conjunction with the regular army as elite troops).

Some time between 1558 and 1562, the *Bansen Shukai* describes Igasaki Doshun (previously Tateoka no Doshun) successfully leading a team of Ninja from Iga (forty-four men) and Koga (four men) to enter an enemy's castle by subterfuge. The account names the method of entry under disguise as *bakemono-jutsu* (or the 'ghost method'). Ninja actions are described thus in the ensuing years:

1561 – the *Shima Kiroku* states that Iga Ninja were employed in setting alight to a castle during samurai warfare. The Ninja under Shima Wasaka-no-kami were successful in their task, although the samurai with which they were collaborating were not. (This was a Ninja mercenary role.)

1562 – the *Mikawa Go Fudo-ki* states that Koga Ninja (Koga Shu) were recorded as helping the shogun Tokugawa Ieyasu in performing a classic fortress Ninja raid (Ninja mercenary role). The Ninja leader was identified as Tomo Taroza-emon Sukeie or Tomo Yoshichiro Sukesada. These names indicate samurai rank and illustrate that Ninja were clearly part of the social system and their arts not as removed from the overall family of bujutsu as many would like to think.

1566 – the *Koyo Gunkan* recounts the story of a warrior called Kumawaka who had to leave a battle to go and get his clan's battle flags. For some reason he is not given access to his own clan castle, so has to resort to Ninja-like skills to collect them.

1530–1578 – toward the latter part of this period, the daimyo Uesugi Kenshin was assassinated by a Ninja concealed in his toilet, who thrust a spear through his anus. This fable is regularly mentioned in Ninja circles, and although its

origins remain untraced and unfounded, it was popularised by Don Draeger's 1969 *Asian Fighting Arts*.[130] Historical
records from the time in the *Kenshin Gunki* mention that he
experienced abdominal pains and died thirteen days later. The
Todaiki of Matsudaira Tadaaki stipulates that this may have
resulted from a stroke. The works of Arai Hakuseki (1656–
1725) in the *Sugiura* clarify that Kenshin was suffering from
a chronic disease that was likely due to oesophageal, gastric
or upper-gastrointestinal disease, and that Kenshin himself
was so aware of his imminent demise that he communicated
this in his own poem. His death was immediately blamed on
Kenshin's main rival Oda Nobunaga, or on a deadly spirit/
ghost (*Uesugi Kenshinden* in the *Sugiura*). Finally, the *Todaiki*
of Matsudaira Tadaaki postulates that Kenshin was actually
a woman and died from pregnancy complications!

1573 – according to an 1883 Toyonobu woodprint, Manabe
Rokuro was a samurai seeking revenge for his daimyo.[126, 131]
He sneaked into Azuchi Castle to assassinate Oda Nobunaga.
He was found by guards and committed suicide. He is repre-
sented as a Ninja dressed in black.

1575–1580 – the *Hojo Godai-ki* stipulates Ninja (Shinobi), also
known as 'Kusa' (grass), acted as spies and ambushed enemy
scouts. The opposing Ninja are called Rappa, and their leader
is Fuma Kotaro (or Kazama Kotaro) – one of the most famous
Ninjas of all time, who is sometimes described as an ogre-like
giant. (Here again, the Ninja are not acting as mercenaries
but in conjunction with regular army as elite troops.)

1579–1581 – during the conflict between the Iga and Ise regions,
the *Iran-ki* describes how Iga Shinobi were used for reconnaissance and the failed attempted assassination of General
Takigawa Saburohei. Both the *Iran-ki* and the *Seishu Heiran-ki*
describe a further battle against Oda Nobukatsu (also known
as Oda Nobuo – Oda Nobunaga's second son) that resulted in
the mainstream Iga Samurai forces using Ninja-like tactics to
win victory. Both the *Shinchoko-ki* and the *Iran-ki* report that

ultimately, however, Oda Nobukatsu was successful and the whole Iga region was invaded and subdued. Nevertheless, the episode revealed numerous examples of the Shinobi's success in battle. The fall of the Iga Ninjas in 1581 has been embellished by legends of the *Tensho Iga no Ran* (uprising of the Iga Ninjas). Following a second humiliation at the hands of the Iga Ninjas, who had applied guerilla-type Ninja tactics, Oda Nobukatsu decided to tackle the Iga warriors with more force. He unleashed his father's army of 40,000–60,000 men (some specify 46,000) on the Iga warriors using standard open warfare and 'scorched-earth' tactics. He was victorious against the Iga Ninjas at Kashiwabara Castle (or alternatively Heiraku-ji Temple and Tendoyama) as a result of Nobunaga having conspired with the neighbouring Koga Ninjas. The Iga warriors were led by Momochi Sandayu (teacher of another famous Ninja – Ishikawa Goemon). Variations of this legend relate that Oda's second son (Nobukatsu) had died at the hands of the Iga Ninja, so Oda Nobunaga himself managed the battle. Nobunaga's commanding general was killed in action by the Iga Ninja leader, who is sometimes listed as Momochi Tanba. There is some confusion, however, as there is another Iga Ninja of a similar name, Momochi Tanba Yasamitsu, who led the Iga warriors in the early seventeenth century. Either way, after the great battle where the Iga fell, their leader is reported as dying or escaping, and subsequently either Momochi Sandayu the 2nd, or Ishikawa Goemon, took control of the Iga Ninja clan.

1581 – the Shinobi continued to prove effective whilst aiding besieged Iga Samurai by helping to protect the Iga castles. There are accounts of Iga Ninja being assisted by Ninja from the Koga region (having previously opposed each other), notably from the family of Mochizuki Chotaro, who is recognised as one of the greatest of all Ninja. Mochizuki was not only a master Ninja, but also a top-class swordsman with the ability to defeat samurai swordsmen with ease.

The *Iran-ki* recounts an incident in north-west Iga where the Shinobi helped local inhabitants and Samurai who were under siege in the Buddhist temple known as the Kannonji on Hijiyama Mountain. These Ninja used standard combat techniques but also successful guerrilla tactics to oppose the onslaught. In this encounter we are introduced to the Hattori, considered among the most outstanding Ninja names of all. Ultimately however, these Ninja defences were unsuccessful against the Nobunaga army. One of the Hattori clan (Jonin Hattori) was killed during an attack on Kikyo Castle. The *Shinchoko-ki*, a well-known text describing Oda Nobunaga's visit to Iga after his successful invasion, does not mention the Ninja attempt to assassinate him at this time. The *Iran-ki*, however, mentions an attempted assassination of Nobunaga by three Samurai named Kido, Harada and Jindai. Of these three, Kido had Ninja training and experience and headed the assassination, which was attempted through cannon fire. This was a last-ditch attempt by the Iga Ninja to maintain independence and autonomy for the region; although it proved unsuccessful, the powerful role of Ninja was now openly acknowledged. This paved the way for a short but golden era, where many of the greatest legends of Ninjutsu were initiated. The *Iran-ki* goes so far as to say that the Ninjas of Iga were the direct successors of the group of Ninja men that tried to assassinate Oda Nobunaga.

According to legend, the famous Ninja Ishikawa Goemon tried and failed to assassinate Oda Nobunaga. His technique was to try and use poison dripping down a thread into a victim's mouth whilst being positioned in the ceiling of the room. This is mentioned in Andrew Adam's 1980 book *Ninja: The Invisible Assassins*,[131] and is copied in the 1967 James Bond film *You Only Live Twice*.

In the late 1500s and early 1600s, the *Ou Eikyo Gunki* describes a case where the Ninja help in defending a castle under siege using psychological warfare. The *Taiheiki* also describes how a young boy uses Ninja-like skills to kill his father's killer. During the Sengoku era there was a failed attempt on the life of the daimyo Takeda Shingen by an Iga-mono Ninja called Hachisuka Tenzo.

The golden age of Ninjutsu

Ninjas had now established themselves throughout Japan, and Iga and Koga Ninja warriors were dominant in terms of numbers. This concentration is almost certainly down to the central locations of Iga and Koga and their proximity to the centre of national conflicts in Kyoto and Nara, which were the major source of their employment. The fall of Iga in 1581 prompted a shift of some of these skilled warriors to other areas of Japan, serving other masters.

After Oda Nobunaga's numerous battles he finally died, caused through the treachery of one of his own generals. Akechi Mitsuhide, who had been one of his best officers, attacked him, and Oda Nobunaga subsequently committed *seppuku* (ritual suicide by disembowelment). Nobunaga's allies were now also under threat from Akechi, and amongst these, Tokugawa Ieyasu was one prime candidate. Ieyasu desperately needed to get back to his stronghold of Mikawa at speed. He had the choice of going by sea, which was a longer, more taxing route, or the faster route by land, which meant crossing Iga, with an extremely high risk of ambush by Akechi or local Iga outlaws (some of whom may have been surviving Iga Ninja).

At this point, the *Mikawa Go Fudo-ki* introduces two men called Hattori. For the brief first leg of the journey, Hattori Sadanobu helps guide the Ieyasu party, protecting them from the outlaws and Yamabushi and getting a reward for his efforts. From this point onward, however, the famous Hattori Hanzo, or Hattori Hanzo Masahige (1517–1596) ensures the party are transported safely through the region. Hanzo loosely translates as clan chief, albeit an obscure term. Rather than having to fight his way through, Hanzo uses his influence as a powerful native of Iga to ensure the safety of the group, being accompanied by 200–300 warriors from Iga and Koga. Hanzo is greatly appreciated by Ieyasu from this point onward and becomes one of his most highly respected generals. In hindsight, he is considered as amongst the most famous Ninja of them all. Other members of Ieyasu's group selected another route to that of Hanzo's and were summarily killed at the hands of the Iga outlaws. Ieyasu now realised the potential and the power of these two Ninja regions of Iga and Koga and rewarded warriors in both regions, who according to legend were all Ninjas. Hattori Hanzo Masahige was master of Omyodo (hidden arts).[132] His father was also known as Hattori Hanzo and wrote the so-called Ninja manual, *Ninpiden*.

Here we have the first account of one individual leading such a large group of Ninjas, and it can be considered the first public identification of a Ninja chief. Hattori Hanzo Masahige subsequently earned the title 'Devil Hanzo' ('Odo Hanzo' or possibly 'Oni Hanzo') and established his own Ninja team of Iga and Koga Ninjas and Sohei warrior monks who were supremely skilled in both armed and unarmed combat. Hanzo died in 1596 aged 55, and there is some evidence of his son Hattori Iwami-no-kami Masanari leading Ninja groups. According to legend, Hattori Hanzo was killed by fellow Ninja master rival Fuma Kotaro during a sea battle. Hanzo was quite clearly considered as a Ninja and is frequently depicted as such.[133, 134] However, he was one of the few individuals to bridge the gap between 'respectable and honourable' samurai adopting the 'mainstream' *Bushido* (warrior) code, whilst also having significant influence and likely leadership in the Ninja establishment that consisted of a loose hierarchy of Ninja schools. Hattori Hanzo Masahige's first son was not well liked and was killed in warfare, so that the second son became Hattori Hanzo, although by this time the family had fallen into obscurity as they could no longer offer the shogunate any useful service.

In 1590 the whole political landscape of Japan changed as Toyotomi Hideyoshi (a former officer of Oda Nobunaga) took over most of the country. He did this through the force of arms but also through strategic alliances, including one with Tokugawa Ieyasu. Hideyoshi now turned his attention to other lands and began an invasion of Korea. This was supported by a 'battalion' of Ninja who are described in the *Taiko-ki* as contributing to the successful storming of Chiguju Castle. The famed Ninjas Arakawa and Mochizuki were involved in this battle.

The invasion of Korea was a failure and Toyotomi Hideyoshi died leaving his 5-year-old son Toyotomi Hideyori in his place. At this time Tokugawa Ieyasu moved in swiftly to subdue all his rivals, so that by 1600 he could fight against Hideyori for the rule of Japan at the Battle of Sekigahara – Japan's largest internal land war.

Ninja from the Koga region proved indispensible to Tokugawa Ieyasu during the raid on and acquisition of Fushimi Castle, and approximately 100 are listed as giving up their lives during the task. Warriors in the Satsuma used Ninja-type techniques (*Ninpo*), whereby their warriors would feign death (*sutekamari no jutsu*) and as the opponents came to inspect them they would shoot their weapons. This may be an embellishment; other versions state that the troops would sit cross-legged rather than play dead. Sutekamari tactics are known to have involved a series of last stands by musket-armed detachments in order to cover a retreat and protect the general. Ninja were also physicians and surgeons, so that when one of Ieyasu's generals, Ii Naomasa, suffered from one of these Ninpo techniques, one of his own Ninja (Miura Yoeman Motosada) treated him: a Ninja treating Ninja-inflicted injuries to his master!

Tokugawa Ieyasu's war was successful so that in 1603 he became the shogun. By 1614, however, Toyotomi Hideyori was a grown man and was in a position to lead the many *ronin* samurai who had been loyal to his father, and who had been estranged and isolated under Tokugawa rule. They set up their base at Osaka Castle and Tokugawa had no choice but to address their open defiance by laying siege to the castle. Ninja were an important component of the castle siege, as this was one of their most renowned specialities. Hattori Masanari and Miura Yoeman led the Ninja from Iga, and Yamaoka Kagestsuge those from Koga.

These men were clearly rewarded for their contribution to conventional warfare but Ninja also employed techniques of propaganda, misinformation and subterfuge to achieve their goals. The siege took place through winter and summer operations, and the role of Ninja in this episode was foremost in Tokugawa's strategem and resulted in massive success.

In 1637 the Tokugawa shogunate suffered one of its last uprisings in an otherwise more or less peaceful period. The Shimabara rebellion was instigated by Christian peasants who were being perse-cuted on religious grounds and who also were incensed by the heavy taxes levied on them by the Matsukura clan for the construction of their new castle at Hara. The Tokugawa shogunate employed their trusted Koga Ninja associates to lay siege to the castle. The *Amakusa gunki* gives us another name for Ninja, *ongyo no mono*, or 'concealed ones'. One particular diary (entitled the Ukai Diary, named after famed ancestor Ukai Kanemon's descendants described the episode, mentioning the famed Ninjas Arakawa Sichirobei and Mochizuki Yoemon in the attack. Both suffered serious wounds in this siege. The Ninja forces acted as spies, then began their invasion, many wearing 'safety ropes'– possibly a forerunner of today's safety harnesses. It is clear that the Ninja themselves knew that it would be a mission from which many would not return.

In the attack, the Ninjas used air explosives to distract and confuse the enemy whilst shadowing their own actions within the cloud of debris offered by the explosives. Both Ninja masters survived, albeit with heavy losses to their squad, and the Ninja survivors were rewarded greatly for their contribution to ending the rebellion. At around this time, many samurai schools started to include espionage-type tech-niques, for example, the *Jigen Ryu* of Togo Shigekura (1561–1643) contained some teachings of Ninpo that reflected an increased aware-ness of the necessity to combat the Ninja's stealth and innovation.[135]

Rise of the modern Ninja

Until this point, Ninjas were seen both as mercenaries who were par-ticularly adept at castle warfare fighting alongside standard troops and samurai, and alternatively as masters of disguise and scouting spies. Although Iga and Koga were famous regions of Ninja strong-holds, they were by no means limited to these areas. There is no evidence that they all had a 'standard black uniform' (**Figure 18**), wielding shuriken and disappearing into thin air – the current con-cept of a Ninja!

During the relatively peaceful mid-Tokugawa or Edo period (1603–1868), stories of Ninja were embellished, romanticised and became larger-than-life. The concept of Ninja returned to its mystical origins first seen in the context of pagan magic. The Ninjas became ghost-like warriors who could fight, move and act with supernatural force and skill. Their costume of black commando dress (*shinobi shozoku*) and boots (*jika-tabi*), was derived in the popular imagination from the black theatre dress of 'special effects' *Kabuki* theatre actors hiding in the backstage or sidestage areas and moving props. This was known as *kuroko*. It became a theatrical tradition to use the same black costume as the stage-hands to show that a Ninja character was concealed.

Following the Second World War, Japan and the West would commandeer the concept of a Ninja for entertainment, for spiritual belief and only sparingly for martial arts. The media explosion in films and comics (particularly manga) meant that only the later notion of the Ninja would be popularised and would give us the 'mainstream' concept of what we call Ninja today, an image that has now pervaded every corner of the globe.

Modern authors recount stories of how Ninjas feign death such as pretending to commit *seppuku* (by using a dead animal under their clothes to give the impression of bleeding).[136] Others mention the 'test by theft',[126] where Ninjas successfully steal pillows or swords from people, testing their own skills. Others believe that

Figure 18: A 'typical' artist's impression of a ninja.

Ninjas practise these techniques as a means of psychological warfare,[137] whereby they can reveal the threat they pose when people are at their most vulnerable. The Ninjas mentioned in these 'test by theft' accounts include Nakagawa Shoshunjin, Tobi Kato, Sada no Hikoshiro, Fukami Kuzo and Yamada Hachiemon of Iga (a master of *semmen-jutsu*).[126] These sources also describe the Ninja school of Nakagwa (or *Nakagawa-Ryu*), whose founder Nakagawa Shoshunjin Yoritaka sets up his Ninja group known as the 'short-cutters', or the *Hayamichi no mono*.

A reversal of the 'test by theft' is the 'test by perception', which is used today in the fifth Dan or *Godan* test of the *Bujin-kan's Togakure Ryu* school by means of the *sakki* (literally, lethal intent) test. Members are blindfolded and asked to dodge a sword coming towards them, which represents the integration of *shinden-gokui* (heavenly transferred inner spirit),[138] where *gokui* literally means 'ultimate essence' or 'deepest meaning'.

There are many named fictional Ninja schools that have never historically existed. However, these occupy the imagination of many martial artists and non-martial artists, so that their names are uttered in the same breath as historically accurate martial arts schools. This has created a massive confusion, so that most 'information' available comes from hearsay and embellished stories rather than fact. One famous Ninja narrative is that of the Ten Heroes of Sanada (*Sanada Juyushi*) written in the Edo period about Ninjas in the late Sengoku and early Edo eras. These have featured in many Ninja stories, including those of Sarutobi Sasuke, Kirigakure Saizo and Mochizuki Jinzaemon. Whilst these characters are fictional, many contemporary so-called Ninja schools claim descent from them. There are also myriad unrecognised Ninja styles of likely fictional origin being practised around the world. Whilst there is a fair amount of information on the Ninjas of Iga and Koga, other purported styles include those of the Hikizaru, Kurohabaki-gumi Fuma clan, Mitsumono, Nokizaru, Negoroshu, Nusumi-gumi, Saikashu, Sanadashu and Shinshu-Toppa. The name Mitsumuno carries some Ninja-lore significance as the term has been used to describe a Ninja-like spy system of three warrior types (*Mami*, *Mikata* and *Metsuki*). Also named as *rappa* or *suppa*, according to legend, they were set up by the daimyo Takeda Shingen (1521–1573) to act as his spies in order to gain military intelligence.

One of the most mainstream popularisations of the Ninja occurs in the 1967 film *You Only Live Twice*. As mentioned earlier, there is an assassination attempt by a Ninja concealed in a ceiling, who attempts to drip poison into a sleeping victim's mouth down a piece of thread. Interestingly, *after* the film, this story becomes famous and is ascribed to previous Ninja masters.

In view of the flood of modern Ninja legends in popular culture, there has been a recent trend to challenge some common misconceptions. Some go so far as to claim that Ninjutsu does not even constitute a historical martial art, claiming Ninjas were masters of deception and combat, rather than belonging to a specific martial arts school. Using several weapons, they became masters of other martial arts styles including samurai and Jujutsu arts.[139] The evidence from the *Bugei Ryuha Daijiten* and Seiko Fujita opposes this. Other than *Fujita*, however, there are few ancient literary examples that provide specific evidence of unarmed Ninjutsu techniques, although the scarcity of sources renders objective proof difficult for this either way.

There are certainly some popular misinterpretations of Ninjutsu in existence. For example, there were no formal Ninja suits as we know them today – the Ninja acted as spies so they would wear ordinary clothes in order to merge into their locale for espionage purposes. Ninjas were not always obliged to die on missions. The *Shonin-ki* states that Ninja should return, although Yoshimori's '100 Ninja poems' indicates that a Ninja should die on a mission.[139–141] The romanticisation and justification of death is a common thread in the warrior ethos of ancient and medieval Japan and it would not be surprising to find its influence on Ninja groups as well.

Ninjutsu activity can be classified into light Ninjutsu (*Yo-nin*) where the actions of Ninja are done in the open (sometimes through espionage), and dark Ninjutsu (*In-nin*) where it is camouflaged and hidden in the dark.[139] There is a common misconception of the Ninja being divided into the *Jonin*, *Chunin* and *Genin* ranks, which has no historical basis. The *Bansenshukai* of 1676 was incorrectly interpreted by Okuse Heishichiro in the twentieth century, which originated this confusion.[139] The *Bansenshukai* actually states that the Jonin were Ninja with superlative skills, whereas the Chunin were ordinary people with low-level 'amateur' Ninja skills and the Genin were simply ordinary people recruited to take part in Ninja work; neither the Chinin nor Genin were formally Ninjas.

The use of the word *'shinobi'*

It is widely accepted that the first use of the word *'shinobi'* comes from the late eighth-century poem *Otomo no Yakamochi*. The poetry anthology *Man'yoshu* (a collection of myriad leaves) is the oldest surviving example of Japanese literature. As such it represents the earliest coherent record of the Japanese written language. For this reason alone it contains the first recorded usage of many Japanese words, including *shinobi* in the poem *Otomo no Yakamochi* (*Man'yoshu* volume 15, poem number 3725).[142]

However, the verbal noun 忍び 'shinobi' and its verbal form 忍ぶ 'shinobu' (the form in the *man'yoshu* is actually the classical version, 忍はむ, 'shinohamu') are actually very basic words in the Japanese language and mean 'to endure' or 'put up with'. In this poem the alternative Chinese character偲 is used with an even more specific meaning of 'to endure unrequited longing'[5] (from the *nihongo no gogen jiten* dictionary of Japanese etymology) although the root is the more general version mentioned above. Although the word *shinobi* (the noun) is used to refer to Ninja today, I am fairly certain that its verbal use in the *Man'yoshu* is purely the basic meaning and has nothing to do with our current understanding of Ninja. It is not until 1487 that the *Annals of the Muromachi Bakufu* lists the word *shinobi* in a Ninja context.

The actual Chinese characters used are probably not of great importance, especially because the word *shinobi* originates from before they were widely adopted in written Japanese (you can tell by the grammatical form it takes). This is quite a common phenomenon in Japanese (the Karate greeting '*oss*' being another good example) known as *ateji* (literally, matched characters).[82]

Today there are a flood of so-called Ninja schools listed as extinct or extant. To list all of these would be almost impossible, so the remainder of this section will focus on styles with some degree of verifiability, although this does not guarantee any objective historical validity.

The Koga master's view

Although the many sources listed so far describe Ninjas (aka Shinobi) and their art Ninjutsu (*Shinobi-jutsu*), we have very few original Ninja sources describing their style, techniques and history. This is typically explained by historians by the fact that the Ninja sect was highly secretive to the point of death, and spreading the secret ways of the Ninja masters was unreservedly forbidden. There are numerous popular legends of Ninja scrolls describing all the secrets of one style or another but few have ever been found or even reported to exist.

We have, however, an exception in the form of Seiko Fujita (1899–1966), the fourteenth and final successor (*soke*) of *Koga-Ryu Wada-Ha* Ninjutsu. He is accepted by some as the 'last true Ninja', specifically as he was the last listed master of Ninjutsu by the *Bugei Ryuha Daijiten* (Official Japanese Directory of Martial Arts).

Seiko Fujita commented extensively on the history of Ninjutsu, focusing on the development of Koga.[137] He goes on to say that Ninja history, by definition, is highly secret and in the past anyone who revealed secrets would be assassinated. He specifies that he was only able to retrieve written evidence of two Ninja schools out of what he roundly lists as a total of fifty. He says that the two main schools of Ninjutsu were Koga-Ryu and Iga-Ryu, although other schools existed, including those of Akutagawa, Negoro, Fuso, Ninbikari, Koyo and Kishu (**Figure 19**).

159

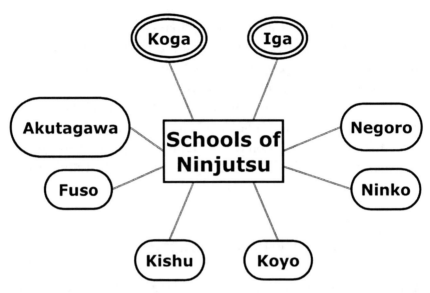

Figure 19: Schools of Ninjutsu.

Although plenty is known about the areas of Iga and Koga, the other areas are largely unknown. This is what we can glean about them:[5]

1. Akutagawa
There are places called Akutagawa in Tosa city, Kochi prefecture (formerly Tosa province) and in Takatsuki city in north Osaka. However, this may or may not be relevant as I have found references to inheritors of the *Akutagawa Ryu* lineage who bear the family name Akutagawa (Akutagawa Kuroemon Yoshitsuna and Akutagawa Sakyo Ryo). This makes it highly likely that the style is named after its founder rather than the place he came from. (Although it is vaguely possible that the family name was in use in the place itself, linking the two.) The *Akutagawa Ryu* appears to have been active in two places, Nagano (formerly Matsumoto prefecture) and Shiga prefecture, under the auspices of the two individuals mentioned above. As an aside, the most famous novelist in Japan's modern history also bears the name Akutagawa and there is a literary prize named after him.

2. Negoro

This refers to a temple rather than an area. Negoroji (*ji* just means temple) was burned to the ground in 1585 by Toyotomi Hideyoshi in his campaign to take over the country; its remains are in the south of Wakayama prefecture (formerly Kishu province in the area still known today as the Kishu penninsula). There is a story about how the monks of this temple were militarised warrior monks who fled into the hills and became guerillas fighting against Toyotomi. There is a reference to a person called Suginobo but there is no mention of his exact relationship with the monks. His name means 'priest of the cedars' and is most likely a priestly title.

3. Fuso

There is a place in Tanba city in Aichi prefecture, just to the north of Nagoya, but I have no idea if it is linked to the school that bears its name. Apparently this style was founded by an individual, Fujita Reisai, who is likely to be an ancestor of Seiko Fujita. There is also another individual mentioned, Takeuchi Shukuya, and a reference to the *Fuso Ryu Ninjutsu* being part of a larger discipline mainly focusing on theoretical martial strategy (*gungaku*).

4. Ninbikari

Almost certainly not a place name, this literally means 'hidden light', 'enduring light' or possibly even 'Ninja light'. Interestingly enough, there are suggestions that this school also claims Fujita Reisai as its founder.

5. Kouyou

There is very little evidence regarding this school. The search is complicated by the fact that this name is homophonous with the general usage word for 'nurturing' or 'enriching'.

6. Kishu

As mentioned above, this is the old name for the province at the bottom of what is now Wakayama prefecture. There is apparently a separate *Kishu Ryu* derived from the Iga school but there are few references to it other than in the *Shoninki*.

Koga-Ryu

Seiko Fujita traces the origins of the Koga-Ryu Ninja to the prehistoric period of the age of the gods and Emperor Jimmu, the legendary founder of Japan. The emperor sends Michi no Omi no Mikoto to govern some of his territory. He subsequently changes his name to Otomo and arrives in Koga. His descendants are the people and warriors of Koga. Later on, Prince Shotoku (573–621) requests Hosoiri Otomo to describe his techniques for reconnaissance, and uses the characters from *Man'yoshu* to designate Otomo as 'Shinobi' – hence its first use.

He lists famous Ninja of the time: 'Tateoka no Mimotsugu, Nomura no Ootakimagotayuu, Shindō no Kotarō, Shimotsuge no Kisaru, Ueno no Hidari, Yamada no Hachiemon, Kōbe no Kominami, Otoba no Kido, Kamiyama no Taroushirō.'

Regarding the development of Koga-Ryu (**Figure 20**), Seiko Fujita describes its source as the 'House of Isomi in the Kōga District of Shiga

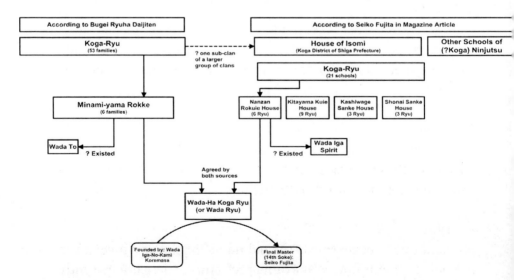

Figure 20: The Eevolution of Wada-Ha Koga-Ryu.

Prefecture'.[137] He credits the house of Isomi as the birthplace for the majority of Koga Ninja schools, which are categorised into four sub-houses, which then developed into twenty-one different schools:

Shonai sanke house – three Koga-Ryu Ninja schools;
Kashiwagi sanke house – three Koga-Ryu Ninja schools;
Kitayama Kuie house – nine Koga-Ryu Ninja schools;
Nanzan Rokuie house – six Koga-Ryu Ninja schools.

San, ku and *roku* are all multiples that should probably be 'houses'. Nanzan is a place just outside Nagoya but could equally be a family name. Fujita himself was of the Nanzan Rokuie House under Wada Iganokami Koremasa, which came into existence in 1591 (although in the mid-1900s he claimed his style to be 500 years old),[143] the same year as Tokugawa Ieyasu went to Edo Castle, also coinciding with the birth of Iga-Ryu. Although he recounts the story of Hattori Hanzo protecting and guiding Tokugawa Ieyasu through Iga territory under the protection of 200 Ninjas, he also mentions two other Ninja leaders alongside Hanzo, these were Sanosuke Tsugi and, interestingly, Anayama Beisetsu. The latter is reported in most accounts as having taken a different route to Ieyasu, and as a result being killed.

Following this episode, Fujita says that the Ninjas of Iga settled in Iga-Cho in Yotsuya (Edo) under Ushizō Hattori, and were separated from their Koga compatriots. He goes on to say that the Iga region was a subsection of the larger Koga region, and that the Iga warriors co-operated with neighbouring groups in the Ayama and Naka districts of Mie prefecture, which also housed Fujita's own Ninja house. As a result, this made Seiko Fujita, according to his own testimony, not only the successor of Koga-Ryu, but also 'the 14th successor of the Wada Iga Spirit'.[137] He went on to identify the Kanda area in Tokyo as the location where Tokugawa Koga spies would reside, and where the Koga-shi would base their activities and training.

According to the *Bugei Ryuha Daijiten*, Watatani's understanding of Fujita's line is that Wada-Ha was part of the *Minami-yama Rokke* (six strong families). *Minami-yama* is just an alternative reading of *nanzan* (above) and literally means southern mountain, although this is likely to be just a family name or place name. The translation of *Minami-yama Rokke* would be the six families of Minamiyama. These were also known as *Wada Iga-shu*. These 'six strong families' were a subgroup of a total of fifty-three families that made up the Koga-Ryu Ninjutsu system. Watatani lists the founder as Wada Iga no Kami Koremasa and that Seiko Fujita was the last *Soke* (head) of this style. As far as Watatani understood, Seiko Fujita did not teach this style to any others.[144]

The Wada clan from Koga were well-known as accomplished Ninjas. Their area of domination corresponded to a river valley that contained a number of mountain castles. As a result of their influence, it has been reported that the founder of the Wada-Ha school, Wada Iganokami Koremasa (1536–1583) provided sanctuary and protection to Ashikaga Yoshiaki in Koga during the political instability after the murder of his elder brother Ashikaga Yoshiteru. At the time of the murder, Ashikaga Yoshiaki was known as Kakukei, the abbot of the Ichijoin in Nara; he eventually became a shogun himself, being formally acknowledged by Emperor Ogimachi in mid-November 1568.[126, 145] Interestingly, there is a disparity between the time line of Wada Iganokami Koremasa (1536–1583) and the year that Seiko Fujita claims that Wada-Ryu came into existence (1591). This mismatch may indicate either a simple misinterpretation of dates or that the Wada School of Koga Ninjutsu might have been formally commenced by a successor of Wada Iganokami Koremasa.

Watatani's manuscript also quotes Fujita as mentioning a Koga school of Ninjutsu known as *Wada-To*. Watatani believed this to be a guess by Fujita, as there was no evidence of any masters or lineage for this style.[144]

Fujita classifies Ninjutsu into two categories:[137]

Yojutsu – where Ninja are termed *Ichimei Younin*, or infiltration Ninja. Here individuals are masters of strategy and military advancement and penetration.

Injutsu – where Ninja are termed *Younin*, or covert Ninja. Here individuals are expert spies and masters of disguise and concealment.

'*In*' and '*Yo*' are the Japanese readings of yin and yang and carry with them all the weight of Chinese cosmology. In this case it appears that the light and dark – overt versus covert dichotomy – is being stressed. *Injutsu* consists of:

Shukei-jutsu;
Katsura-jutsu;
Jyukei-jutsu;
Hisanoichi-jutsu;
Satori-no-jutsu (*satori* is the Buddhist concept of nirvana or enlightenment);
Minomushi-no-jutsu (*minomushi* is a bag worm);
Hotarubi-no-jutsu (*hotarubi* is the glow of a firefly);
Fukurotobi-jutsu (*fukuro* can mean a bag, or the longer sounding *fukuroo* is an owl; *tobi* can mean to jump or to fly, or a kite);
Tentsuban-no-jutsu;
Ikeyumi-jutsu;
Yamabiko-no-jutsu (*yamabiko* can mean a mountain echo);
Shiroyarinin-no-jutsu;
Kanin-no-jutsu.

Yojutsu ('magic' or 'witchcraft') consists of:

Ryokuhon-jutsu;
Geinyuu-jutsu;
Youja-jutsu;
Sansa (there is a Japanese folk dance called *sansa odori* and it also has some kind of unspecified Buddhist meaning);
Mizuki (this could be moon reflected on the water);
Taniiri (this could represent entering a valley);
Ryohan.

Fujita denies the existence of *Ton-no-jutsu* (methods of escape) in his style. In Fujita's family style, there is a system of *Suiton-Katon-Mokuton* (escape using water, fire or trees):

> *suiton*: concealment in (escape using) water;
> *hiton*: concealment in (escape using) fire ('*katon*' and '*hiton*' would be two ways to read the same characters);
> *mokuton*: escape using forest or woodland.

According to the definition given, the various types of *ton-no-jutsu* do not necessarily limit them to hiding but apply to any means used to escape. For example, *katon/hiton* does not mean hiding in fire but would involve setting fires to cover escape and distract pursuers. *Ton-no-jutsu* initially meant the use of fire to spar with an opponent, stealing or manipulating the opponent's spirit or the water's spirit to get away. Fujita claims that there are 10,000 such techniques within Ninjutsu.

He states that Hakuunsai Tozawa founded Koga-Ryu, although he may not have initially resided in Koga (likely a mistake by Yamajoumori Yamanaka) and that there is no strong evidence of his existence. On the other hand, he lists Momochi Santayuu as the founder of Iga-Ryu, as there may be substantial evidence of his existence. He may have lived at a mansion based in Tomoumura Jikuiyo Shirogatani. Fujita goes on to say that Ippusai Hashimoto, a short, thin man with dangerously powerful and flexible fingers, was the second successor of Koga-Ryu.

He lists the three most famous Ninja as Bisasuke Saruto, Resaizou Kirigaku and Hakuunsai Tozawa. He also lists other well-known Ninja:

Mukeisai Takahashi, from Nagaoka;
Echigo-han (current-day Niigata prefecture);
Kurouemon Akutagawa;
Kannosuke Akutagawa;
Matsumoto, Shinshuu;
Zennemon Uehara was living in Okachimachi;

Hannmabou from Iga was based at Izuha;

Kutayuu Ikeda was in Yoshida;

Sansu was also in Yoshida.

According to Fujita, Ishikawa Goemon was not a thief, but also not a great Ninja. Furthermore, he complains that Goemon taught the *Shitate* (inferior) arts, whereas he felt that Ninja should always raise their level higher.[137]

The true origins for a formal style of Koga-Ryu remain unknown, although today many unsupported accounts and legends exist. One account includes the first formal appearance of the Koga-Ryu clan members as a result of Rokkaku/ Ashikaga discord. The Rokkaku clan governed their own homeland and also the adjoining area of Koga. Two members of this clan (Masayori and his son Takayori) were targeted by the ruling Ashikaga shogunate as a result of general insubordination. They fled to Koga Castle, which was successfully attacked by General Yoshihisa Ashikaga. Father and son escaped a second time and took refuge in the Koga mountains. Over the subsequent three years the local Koga warriors helped the Rokkaku family to attack Ashikaga's army using advanced guerrilla warfare methods. Yoshihisa Ashikaga was eventually killed during these attacks, so a truce was achieved. From that time on the Koga families who had provided the warriors were named as the 'fifty-three families of Koga' and the formal identification of Koga-Ryu came into existence. Whilst it is claimed that this was the first demonstration that Ninja were recognised according to a traditional samurai military hierarchy, there is no current historical evidence to back this narrative.

The Iga point of view

The identification of Iga Ninjas and Ninjutsu is multifaceted but fortunately has some traceable roots. The Bujinkan is an international organisation of martial artists who practice *Bujinkan Budo Taijutsu*, an art that itself consists of interrelated systems:

Gikan-Ryu Koppojutsu;
Gyokko-Ryu Kosshijutsu;
Gyokushin-Ryu Ninpo;
Kuki Shinden Happo Bikenjutsu;
Koto-Ryu Koppojutsu;
Kumogakure-Ryu Ninpo;
Shinden Fudo-Ryu Dakentaijutsu;
Takagi Yoshin-Ryu Jutaijutsu;
Togakure-Ryu Ninpo Taijutsu.

The style is headed by the world-renowned *Soke* (official inheritor) Dr Masaaki Hatsumi who largely purports to teach *Ninpo* (a word popularised by Yamada Futaro in the twentieth century and used to mean codes and laws of the Ninja, as opposed to Ninjutsu or Ninja art/skill). He is the 'lineage holder' of this style following the transference of this position by his direct predecessor Toshitsugu Takamatsu (1889–1972), who had been given the privilege of copying the *Kukishin Ryu* scrolls and the *Amatsu Tatara* scrolls of the Kuki family.[138, 146–148] According to the *Bugei Ryuha Daijiten*, from 1968 onward Toshitsugu Takamatsu and Dr Masaaki Hatsumi are associated with the following arts: *Gikan-Ryu Koppojutsu, Gyokko-Ryu Kosshijutsu, Gyokushin-Ryu Ninpo, Kuki Shinden Happo Bikenjutsu, Koto-Ryu Koppojutsu, Kumogakure-Ryu Ninpo, Shinden Fudo-Ryu Dakentaijutsu* and *Takagi Yoshin-Ryu Jutaijutsu*.

The Bujinkan associate several of these styles with the Iga Ninja tradition, most notably *Gikan-Ryu Koppojutsu, Gyokko-Ryu Kosshijutsu, Koto-Ryu Koppojutsu* and *Shinden Fudo-Ryu*. Others, however, are linked to samurai schools, namely *Kuki Shinden Happo Bikenjutsu* and *Takagi Yoshin-Ryu Jutaijutsu*. In addition, Dr Hatsumi also lists himself as *Soke* of *Amatsu Tatara Hichi Buku Goshinjutsu* (Amatsu Medicine). The term *goshinjutsu* simply means self-protection so its use as a medical discipline would be relatively unique in the martial arts.

The Bukinkan further associate their style with Iga Ninjutsu through the school of *Togakure-Ryu*. According to Toshitsugu

Takamatsu and Dr Masaaki Hatsumi, the mythical style originated with a Chinese general known as Ikai and the historical style originated with a Daisuke Nishina of Togakure village. After a defeat by Heike soldiers, he escaped from Nagano and settled in Iga, where he assumed the name Daisuke Togakure and formulated Togakure-Ryu. As a result, they state that this style is now over 800 years old and that Dr Masaaki Hatsumi is its thirty-fourth grandmaster. The evidence for this has not been independently verified and it is widely regarded that the oldest extant *koRyu* is the Takeuchi-Ryu, which is only around 450 years old.

According to this Iga-related tradition, the following are listed as the eighteen levels of Ninjutsu training:[146]

1. *Seishin teki kyoko* (spiritual refinement);
2. *Taijutsu* (unarmed combat);
3. *Ninja ken* (Ninja sword) or Kenjutsu (sword fighting);
4. *Bo-jutsu* (stick and staff fighting);
5. *Shuriken-jutsu* (throwing shuriken);
6. *Yari-jutsu* or *Sojutsu* (spear fighting);
7. *Naginata-jutsu* (naginata or halberd fighting);
8. *Kusarigama-jutsu* (kusarigama or chain-and-sickle weapon fighting);
9. *Kayaku-jutsu* (pyrotechnics and explosives);
10. *Henso-jutsu* (disguise and impersonation);
11. *Shinobi-iri* (stealth and entering methods);
12. *Ba-jutsu* (horsemanship);
13. *Sui-ren* (water training);
14. *Bo-ryaku* (strategy and tactics);
15. *Cho ho* (espionage);
16. *Inton-jutsu* (escaping and concealment);
17. *Ten-mon* (meteorology);
18. *Chi-mon* (geography).

These skills all require application of the overriding philosophy of *kyo-jitsu ten-kan ho*, which requires the interchanging of falsehood and truths in order always to gain the upper hand by deceiving an opponent whilst keeping one's own reality and purity of heart (*seishin*) and not getting lost.[146]

Some extra evidence on the Iga style of Ninjutsu can be derived from the *Shoninki* – a short Ninja manual written by Natori Masazumi in 1681–82. The manual is formulated for the style of Kishu-Ryu (likely separate to that of the Koga-Ryu school) and its Natori-Ryu subschool. The text focuses heavily on techniques of strategy, covert activity and penetration, and the lack of specific Ninja hand-to-hand fighting techniques have led some to conclude that Ninjas were expert military tacticians as opposed to specifically martial artists.[139]

Some authors have outlined evidence for a lost Ninja scroll entitled the *Fukashima Ryu* document of the Nojiri clan. The mention of this document was identified in transcriptions at the Iga Ueno Ninja Museum. They assert that they have searched the Japanese national archive and found out that such a document did exist but that it has disappeared. These authors also mention that Seiko Fujita donated the transcription of the *Fukashima Ryu* document to the Iga Ueno Ninja Museum in the 1950s and that, coincidentally, the *Fukashima Ryu* document went missing from the Japanese national archive at this time. Consequently, it is controversially suggested that there may be an association between Seiko Fujita and these lost scrolls, which may still remain with the Iga Ueno Museum.[140]

Another text is the *Bansenshukai* (Sea of Myriad Rivers Merging), which is claimed to have both an Iga version and a Koga version. From the Koga point of view, Seiko Fujita never mentioned it, and the Iga version once again focuses on broad strategy, weapons, astrology and Ninja philosophy. The authorship in 1676 is ascribed to Fujibayashi Yasutake or Fujibayashi Yasuyoshi, and even the Fujibayashi Sabuji of Iga province.

Despite the relatively lengthy lists of masters and martial associations, the very secret nature of the Ninja has made identifying legitimate masters and schools practically impossible. In fact, although the *Bugei Ryuha Daijiten* mentioned Seiko Fujita as the last-known

Ninja, some doubt even this. As a result, the world of so-called Ninjutsu is a spawning ground for fake claims and bogus martial heritages associated with Ninjutsu that would make the unlikely survival of a true Ninja school even harder to recognise amidst the masses of unfounded schools. The word Ninja can bring a practitioner new students, wealth and media attention. Jinichi Kawakami is reported as having met a certain Masado Ishida in the park when he was a boy. He went on to become an electronics worker, but later claimed that Masado Ishida was the last Koga Ninja, and that he was Ishida's last student, making him a bona fide Ninja master. As a result, Kawakami became an honorary curator at the Iga Ueno Ninja Museum.[149] Whether or not the many claims such as these are true or false is beyond the scope of this book, nevertheless the development of Ninjutsu as one of the biggest martial arts phenomena of the twentieth century cannot be denied, and this wealth of martial influence is likely to have a significant impact on the melting pot of modern martial arts in general.

8

Karate–Ninja Connections

There are numerous similarities between open-handed martial arts styles. In addition to the basic punches and kicking techniques, these similarities can run to the core of several arts. Although many stylists have traditionally considered powerful links to exist between both Okinawan Karate and Shaolin, there have been a few associations between Karate and other Japanese empty-handed martial arts. There are well-established links between Karate and Jujutsu; several luminaries have become prominent masters of both martial arts. Examples include Shogo Kuniba (1935–1992) who was the *Sandai Soke* of *Ryukyu Karate Motobu-ha* and a noted expert in Jujutsu who developed his own style of *Goshin Budo Jujutsu* (or *Kuniba-Ryu Goshindo*). Sadatomo Harada (associated with the Kuniba line) became president and later *soke* of the Shito-Ryu Seishinkai Karate Japan and president of the All Japan JuJutsu Federation in 1999. Minoru Mochizuki (1907–2003) trained in Karate with Shotokan Karate's founder Gichin Funakoshi; Judo at the famed Kodokan (in 1925) with its founder Jigoro Kano; Aikido with its founder Morihei Ueshiba; and, amongst the oldest extant Japanese *koRyu bujutsu* (traditional Japanese martial arts) in the style of Tenshin Shoden Katori Shinto-Ryu. In the United States Albert C. Church, Butch Velez and Dentokan's founder Col. (Ret) Roy J. Hobbs (whose backrounds all include lineage from Kuniba) are recognised hanshi masters in several styles of Okinawa Karate and Japanese Jujutsu (amongst others). In addition to these recognised Karate-Jujutsu associations, there are some Karate-Ninjutsu connections that are less well known but represent an important relationship in the evolution of modern martial arts. Beyond the apparent parallels between open-handed Karate, Ti and the associated Kobudo weapons systems with the Ninjutsu's Taijutsu and Ninja weapons styles, there may be some further underlying links amongst these arts.

The life and death of Seiko Fujita

According to Kiyoshi Watatani's *Bugei Ryuha Daijiten*, an 'official' encyclopaedia of historical martial arts schools and their genealogy, Seiko Fujita (**Figure 21**) is the final listed Ninja master who was recorded as the fourteenth *soke* of *Waha-Ha Koga-Ryu* Ninjutsu. Although the book has some critics, who consider the text incomplete, Fujita is nevertheless considered by some classical martial artists of the *KoRyu* to be the final and last true master of 'official' Ninjutsu.

Fujita was born on 13 August 1899 in Asakusa, east of Tokyo on mainland Japan, with the name Isamu, as the second of two sons (Rokugo being the elder by five years) and with an older sister (by four years).[143] His father, Morinosuke, was a police officer who was a master of *Ichiden-Ryu Hojo-jutsu* (capturing and binding) and his grandfather, Shintazaemon (with the nickname Shinosuke), was thirteenth *soke* of his familial style Wada-Ha Koga-Ryu Ninjutsu, which was over 500 years old, commencing with the use of spies during the Tokugawa shogunate.[150]

Shintazaemon Fujita was born in Okinawa and was a lifelong martial artist, although it is unclear why his son Morinosuke was not bestowed with the soke-ship of the family Ninjutsu style. It is reported that although a committed individual, Morinosuke went through three jobs: as Shibetoro hospital director (having been pro-

Figure 21: Seiko Fujita. (Pictures courtesy Sylvain Guintard)

moted form doctor's assistant), Ishikawa Island prison guard and, finally, a Tokyo Metropolitan Police officer.[137]

At the age of 5, Seiko Fujita suffered from a likely episode of cardiorespiratory arrest, possibly as a result of what Fujita himself says was diphtheria. The doctors at the time were unable to revive him, as he could not breathe due to a blocked upper airway as a result of throat swelling – and he was pronounced dead. His mother Tori was able to intervene and resuscitated him by placing a tube down his throat (we know that Seiko Fujita's sister died at an early age from an undescribed condition).[143]

The term 'Quick's oedema' has been used to describe this disease,[151] but this is a misspelling of the disease, which is hereditary angioedema (also known as Quincke's oedema).[152] This is an autosomal dominant inherited disease caused by low levels of the plasma protein C1 inhibitor (C1-INH):

It can cause sudden swelling of the throat and visceral (including abdominal) organs.

It presents in family history.

Children are particularly at risk as the majority of sufferers have attacks during childhood (40 per cent before the age of 5).

Triggers include trauma, infection and stress.

This would not only explain Fujita's near-death experience but possibly also his sister's early death. If this was the case, Fujita's mother Tori may have been forewarned of Seiko Fujita's condition and may have been taught previously how to place the tube in his throat (known as intubation) to revive her son. She died unexpectedly from gastrointestinal bleeding (intestinal and colonic haemorrhage) on Fujita's seventh birthday on 13 August 1906.

At that time, the nature of Fujita's condition of hereditary angioedema was not well known, and as result Fujita entered the world of martial arts. Today, however, sufferers are asked not to enter confrontational situations or to take part in combat sports, as these activities can prove fatal. Nevertheless, there are some individual cases of very advanced martial artists who have this condition.[152]

As a result of Fujita's family situation, his father's job changes and his inherent character, he was a boisterous and aggressive child. According to his memoirs, when he was 10 years old he successfully attacked his brother's 15-year-old assailant in an act of revenge.[143]

Fujita, who was purported to have an excess of energy and an ability to withstand injury (such as when falling downstairs), was taught traditional Japanese budo by his grandfather from the age of 3 (including the techniques of seppuku!). Following the attack on his brother's assailant, Fujita was taken to the Buddhist temple at Daiji-dera at Itsuka-cho with the rank of *shinpochi* (lowly student) in order to calm his aggression (without success). However, after the death of his mother he undertook a period as a Yamabushi monk, while his father searched for his lost son, fearing his death.

After approximately three or four months (Fujita says 100 days), Fujita's father and brother found him on Mount Mitsumine and took him home. During this time Fujita claims to have witnessed the Yamabushi arts of extrasensory perception and remote viewing.[143] Furthermore, he claims to have learned Yamabushi long-distance walking skills (not dissimilar to the chi Shaolin walking skills) and *Daien-Ryu Jojutsu* from a Yamabushi Shugenja called Daien (Large Circle).[144]

On his return in the autumn of 1906, his grandfather Shintazaemon felt him worthy to be taught the family style of Wada-Ha Koga-Ryu Ninjutsu. Shintazaemon commenced tutelage with the samurai sword-crossing oath ceremony of Kincho.[143]

Fujita lists a gruelling training schedule of extreme physical stamina, fighting arts, sense-enhancement training and exposure to alcohol and smoking. His grandfather passed away on 10 September 1910, passing on the soke-ship of their so-called orthodox Koga-Ryu family style to Fujita (aged 11) after approximately four years of formal training.[143] On his deathbed, Shintazaemon is recounted as having given Fujita two ancient secret Ninja scrolls describing the essence of their family Wada-Ha Koga-Ryu style. One of these may correlate with a scroll dated to 1544 entitled *Ninjutsu Hisho Ogiden no Kan* (the secret essence of Ninjutsu) that was photographed and revealed in Fujita's obituary in 1966.[150]

One year later, aged 12, Fujita spends two more months with the Yamabushi and learns the ascetic religious skills of Kuji Kiri and Kuji Goshin Ho. He also claims that around this time and a little earlier, before his grandfather's death, he developed a keen interest in paranormal phenomena, spent time with soothsayers and also claimed to have honed his skills of extrasensory perception. He completed secondary school in 1914 and graduated with a degree in religious studies in 1919 from Nippon University. Although he was a young graduate, it seems that he had to work part-time as a journalist for local newspapers to earn extra money, and he is also reported to have been expelled from Meiji, Tokyo and Waseda universities (this may be an embellishment, as the top three universities in the land taking on the same difficult student is unlikely, let alone the prohibitive costs of such an undertaking) on account of his unfortunate proclivity for fighting. His time as a journalist with the *Chugai*, *Yamato*, *Hibi*, *Kokumin* and *Houchi*, may have given him the tools with which to communicate his Ninjutsu skills, but may also have helped him to add his own journalistic spin.[143, 153]

As a 15-year-old, he encountered Hashimoto Ippusai, the second *soke* of *Nanban Satto Ryu Kempo* (**Figure 22**), a Jujutsu-type style based on grappling. This style is unrelated to Okinawan *Nanban Satto Ryu Kempo*, but according to the *Bugei Ryuha Daijiten* was founded in the Edo or Tokugawa period (1603–1868) by Hashimoto Ippusai (who had the same name as his descendant) and whose style is related to *Nanban Ippo Ryu Jujutsu*, which in turn is derived from *Torite-jutsu* of the Nobeoka- Han in Hyuga province in the time of the Sengoku period (mid-fifteenth century to early seventeenth century). Fujita himself became the third *soke* of this style, which he taught to many of his subsequent Karate students, including Inoue Motokatsu (grandson to the former prime minister of Japan, Katsura Taro) and Konishi Yasuhiro who would go on to form *Yui Shin Kai Karate Jutsu* and *Shindo Jinen Ryu Karate Jutsu* respectively. Furthermore, through his close association with Kenwa Mabuni (also a friend and colleague of Konishi Yasuhiro) who was the founder of Shito Ryu Karate, he taught this style to a student of both of them, Iwata Manzo, who would be given the fourth soke-ship of this style (becoming Fujita's *uchi deshi* (live-in) student). Iwata Manzo first inherited Fujita's Daien-Ryu Jojutsu in 1943 and Nanban Satto Ryu Kempo in 1948; his son

Iwato Genzo would be given the fifth soke-ship in turn, who is then reported as having passed on Nanban Satto Ryu only to his highest Karate student (in Shito-Ryu), Sakagami Ryusho. The grandfather of Iwata Manzo was a good friend of Morihei Ueshiba (1883–1969), the founder of Aikido. As a result of this Manzo also received training in Aikido, but it is also reputed that through this connection Fujita and Ueshiba had met and demonstrated mutual respect and admiration.

Although Hashimoto Ippusai also taught this style to other individuals (**Figure 22**), for example to Miura Hayato (giving him the *Menkyo Kaiden* of this style), Fujita was clear in stating that he did not pass his Ninjutsu to any inheritor; but many have subsequently claimed to have been taught Nanban Satto Ryu by him or an intermediary as a basis for their so-called knowledge of Koga Ryu Ninjutsu.

Fujita's association with certain innovative Karate-ka allowed him to bridge the worlds of traditional mainland Japanese 'KoRyu' samurai-based martial arts with those of the island of Okinawa. One such association was with Yasuhiro Konishi (1893–1983) the founder of Shindo Jinen Ryu and *Japan Karate-Do Ryobu-Kai*. His martial background included Muso-Ryu Jujutsu and Kendo, and later acquaintance with the founder of Aikido, Morihei Ueshiba. Through exposure to Okinawan Karate via a University of Keio classmate (Tsuneshige Arakaki of Okinawa), he trained with many luminaries of twentieth-century Karate, including Choki Motobu (*Motobu-Ryu* and *Motobu-Ryu Udundi*), Kenwa Mabuni (Shito-Ryu) and Chojun Miyagi (Goju-Ryu). As a result, he founded the first university Karate club in Japan with Gichin Funakoshi (the founder of Shotokan) at his alma mater Keio University and helped to develop modern competition sparring (*kumite*). Konishi and Fujita were friends and Konishi was reported to appreciate Fujita's Nanban Satto Ryu, as he felt this aligned with his background in Jujutsu, whilst considering Aikido to be overy circular and traditional Karate as overly straight. As a result of their friendship Seiko Fujita would be exposed to Konishi's network of famous Karate-ka, including Choki Motobu and the great weapons Kobudo master Taira Shinken (1897–1970). Furthermore, both Fujita and Konishi would co-supervise the progression of Motokatsu Inoue and the development of his Yui Shin Kai School. Whilst Motokatsu primarily credits Konishi as the inspiration for the developmemt of his school, he clearly identifies the role of Fujita in guiding him towards tutelage under both Yasuhiro Konishi and Taira Shinken to advance his martial studies, which subsequently enabled him to develop Yui Shin Kai Karate Jutsu.

Fujita went on to list his style as containing the following:

Iaijutsu (art of drawing the sword);
Kusarijutsu (chains);
Kusarigama (sickle and chain);
Daien Ryu Bojutsu (school of the long staff of the Great Circle);
Shingetsu Ryu Shurikenjutsu (throwing weapons of the school of the New Moon);
Heiho (military strategy);
Shinto Muso Ryu Jojutsu (short staff);
Ichiden Ryu Torite (restraining techniques);
Tenmon (psychological sciences related to espionage);
Muso Ryu Kenjutsu (long and short sword);
Yawara (Jujutsu);
Towatejutsu (hand weapons and diversions);
Yarijutsu (spear);
Suiheijutsu (different forms of swimming with armour);
Kayakujutsu (handling of explosives);
Naginatajutsu (halberd);
Yumi (bow);
Hinawajutsu (firearms);
Mushu no Jutsu (the art of not exposing one's odour – also associated with enhancing one's own sense of smell;
Nanban Satto Ryu Kempo (empty-hand fighting).

Seiko Fujita was clearly a talented martial artist, but was also highly sensitive to the role of the media in popularising Ninjutsu. He himself describes a vast library of martial arts scrolls listing various schools, or Ryu. These included: '1140 for Kenjutsu (fencing), 442

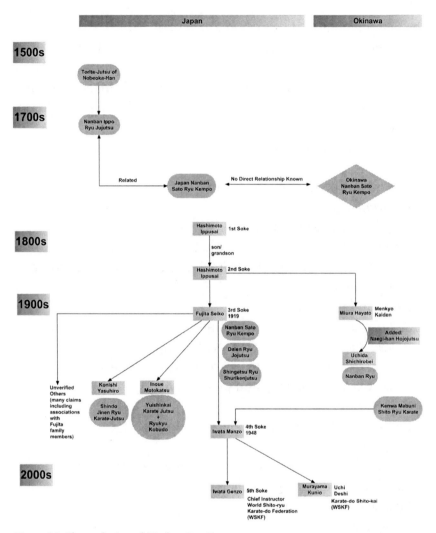

Figure 22: The evolution of *Nanban Sato Ryu.*

for Jujutsu, 273 for Iai (drawing one's sword to kill and sheathing it), 262 for Soujutsu (spearmanship)'. He even mentions that he had a manuscript written by famous samurai including Miyamoto Musashi (1584–1645) and Kamiizumi Ise-no-kami Fujiwara-no-Nobutsuna (*c.*1508, originator of the *Shinkage Ryu* 'New Shadow School'). In total, he mentions 3,830 manuscripts, which he planned to combine to produce a manual that listed 1,452 methods.[137]

After enrolling and departing from several universities (including Waseda and Meiji), and working briefly as a journalist, Fujita became a professional martial artist. He started to gain a reputation as the last-known Ninja, and was able to publicise his knowledge through interacting with a number of well-known martial artists and teaching some prominent students such as Inoue Motokatsu and Konishi Yasuhiro. He even worked as a part-time bodyguard for Inoue Motokatsu's father, General Inoue Saburo. He also became a member of the *Nihon Kobudo Shinkokai* in 1935 for the preservation of Japanese Bujutsu, where he regularly demonstrated at their annual meeting. Here he was closely associated with Shimizu Ryuji/Takaji of Shinto Muso Ryu Jojutsu, a subject that he would subsequently write a book on in 1953,[154] and Ryushou Sakagami Karate (Shito-Ryu) and also Kendo, Muso Jikiden Ryu Iaido and Taira Shinken Kobujutsu.

Fujita's circle of friends was purported to include:

Nakashima Atsumi[155] – *Katayama Hoki Ryu Jujutsu* and *Tenjin Myoshin Ryu.*

Ueno Takashi (sixteenth-generation head of ancient koRyu Japanese art of *Asayama Ichiden-Ryu*), instructor to Masaaki Hatsumi (head of today's style of Bujinkan and Ninpo) and who were both students of Takamatsu Toshitsugu.[138] Asayama Ichiden-Ryu consists of striking (*atemi*), reversal techniques (*gyakute*), Jujutsu, *gyakute-jutsu* (a rare weapon-based reversal art) and empty-handed combat skills (*taijutsu*). The term taijutsu is used in many modern Ninjutsu-based schools as their foundation of empty-hand techniques. This school originated in the Aizu region, which coincidentally is the same area in which *Daito-Ryu Aiki-jujutsu* (or *Daito-Ryu Jujutsu*) was developed. Interestingly, the *Bugei Ryuha Daijiten* identifies Ueno Takashi as the nineteenth head of Shinden Fudo-Ryu after Kenei Mabuni, with the founder of Shito-Ryu, Kenwa Mabuni, as its seventeenth head. This school comprises one of the nine martial traditions of Bujinkan. In return, Kenwa Mabuni benefited from studying Asayama Ichiden-Ryu and Shindo Tenshin-Ryu from Ueno Takashi, thus reflecting the reciprocal nature of the Karate–Ninjutsu dialogue.

Specifically he taught at the Japanese Army University (Rikudai), Military Officers Academy (Rikugun Shikan Gakko), the Naval University (Kaidai) and Toyama Academy of the Japanese Army. He was famed for conflict with the Japanese mafia (*yakuza*), and from 1937 and during the Second World War he held a teaching position at the famed Nakano Spy School (Nakano Gakko).[156] He was also instructor to various Tokyo police bodies as a Bujutsu instructor at the headquarters of the regiment of military policemen. He occupied instructor posts at Kobo Kinmu-in Joseisho and the Kokumin Seishin Bunka Kenkyusho (Cultural Institute of National Spirit). By definition, his time here would have been purposefully shrouded in mystery, and Fujita in all likelihood probably used this to his advantage. The lack of solid evidence from this period has led many to claim that they were instructed in the secrets of Ninjutsu by Fujita during this time. Fujita was of course a showman on one level; one example of his self-promotion is the story that he cut away and ate a piece of his own thigh in front of a reporter in order to demonstrate his skill and cool demeanour when exposed to pain and revulsion.

Fujita went on to describe Ninjutsu in the context of modern spying during the war in his 1942 book *Ninjutsu Kara Supai Sene* (From Ninjutsu to Modern Espionage). The father of French Shotokan Karate, Henri Plée, later wrote a book in 1998 entitled *L'Art Sublime et Ultime des Points de Vie* (The Sublime and Ultimate Art of Vital Points). He proposed that during the war Fujita had worked in the Nihon Bujutsu Kenkyu Jo to preserve Japanese martial arts and philosophy, where many masters of Japanese martial arts would document and teach many of their deadliest and vital point techniques for use in the war against the Allies. Fujita went on to write *Kempo Gokui Atemi No Sakkatsu Ho Mikai*, and Plée asserts that Fujita may have come to describe these techniques after experimenting with them on Allied prisoners of war. There are no official sources to support this and the Nihon Bujutsu Kenkyu Jo came into existence after the war, in 1951, as did Fujita's book *Kempo Gokui Atemi No Sakkatsu Ho Mikai*.

After the war, Fujita continued his teaching and exposure to the martial arts, though there is no evidence that he taught his Ninja skills to any students. He continued to write books on his Ninja heritage such as *Doron Doro, Saigo no Ninja*:[157] '*Doron doron*' is the 'sound effect' for when Ninja disappear; *Saigo no Ninja* means the last Ninja, so the title could be translated as something like 'the last Ninja disappears into darkness'. He lists himself as a grandmaster and fourteenth patriarch of Koga-Ryu Ninjutsu. He asserts at length that he did not teach his Ninjutsu to any students and that he is the last Koga Ninja.

The largest group of martial artists associated with Fujita from the 1930s onward were Karate masters. Starting with the politically well-connected Inoue Motokatsu, whose father (General Inoue Soburo) was guarded by Fujita, a number of Okinawan Karate masters befriended Fujita. In fact Fujita passed on only one soke-ship in his career (*Nanban Satto Ryu*) to a student (Iwata Manzo) of one of his closest martial arts colleagues, Mabuni Kenwa (he also awarded Iwata the Shihan licence for *Taien Ryu/ Daien Ryu Jujutsu* and conceivably *Shingetsu Ryu Shurikenjutsu*). The Okinawan masters with whom Fujita interacted at a high level included the following (see also **Figure 20,** page 162):

Mabuni Kenwa – Karate (Shito-Ryu), Founder.
Motokatsu Inoue – Karate-Jutsu (Yui Shin Kai), Founder.
Konishi Yasuhiro –Karate-Jutsu (Shindo Jinen-Ryu) and Japan
    Karate-Do Ryobu-Kai (JKR), Founder.
Motobu Choki – Karate (Motobu Udun Di, Motobu-Ryu),
    Founder.
Miyagi Chojun – Karate (Goju-Ryu), Founder.
Manzo Iwata – Karate (Shito-Ryu), subsequent *soke*.

Shinken Taira – Kobudo, Karate (Ryūkyū Kobudo Hozon Shinko Kai), Founder.

Ryushou Sakagami – Karate (Shito-Ryu, Founder of Itosu Kai) and also Kendo, Hanshi in Muso Jikiden Eishin Ryu Iaido and Taira Shinken Kobujutsu.

Fujitani Masatoshi – Karate (Tani-Ha Shito Ryu/ Shukokai, Founder of Myobukai/Meibukai and second master of the Bujutsu Kenkyusho).

Fujita met regularly with these masters and discussed many aspects of martial arts. They often shared students such as Motokatsu Inoue. Many of these masters attended Ueno Takashi's research meetings (*kenkyukai*), which were also attended by Seiko Fujita. These masters would teach each other. Ueno Takashi would teach the Okinawan masters elements of Japanese martial arts (*koRyu*) so that, for example, Ryushou Sakagami trained and received from him a mastership certificate (*menkyo kaiden*) in Asayama Ichiden-Ryu and Shinto Tenshin-Ryu, whilst Takashi would himself learn *Shinden Fudo-Ryu* and possibly *Hontai Kijin Chosui-Ryu Dakentaijutsu* from Mabuni. According to Okinawan Karate sources, there was a deep respect between Fujita and these Karate luminaries. Many of these masters were considered true innovators of their time, whereas Mabuni, Konishi and Miyagi are considered among the first to introduce Karate to mainland Japan. Other kenkyukai-type meetings were also in existence, an example of which is that of Mr Kishumoto's house in Wakasa, attended by masters such as Chojun Miyagi and Choyu Motobu.

Fujita died on 4 January 1966 at the age of 67, and was subsequently hailed as the 'last Ninja', or as the 'last Koga Ninja' (implying other non-Koga Ninja schools still existed or exist). He died with no objective evidence that he ever passed on his Ninja arts to any individual. Some claimed he died in a car crash with three of his most senior Ninja students, but the records show he died from the complications of hepatic (liver) cirrhosis at his home at Nezu 1-24-3, Bunkyo-ku, Tokyo. In modern Japan, this condition most commonly results from hepatitis (infection of the liver) or excess alcohol consumption.[158] In Fujita's case, the effects of angioedema (C1 esterase inhibitor deficiency) seem to have decreased with age, but his exposure to large volumes of alcohol from a young age, when his grandfather tried to build his tolerance to the effects, may have initiated a lifelong alcohol consumption that finally led to his death.

Seiko Fujita's funeral was attended by a large number of martial arts luminaries, including the following as listed in an obituary (I have added the descriptions):[150]

Motokatsu Inoue – Karate-Jutsu (founder of Yui Shin Kai, first kaicho of Ryûkyû Kobujutsu Hozon Shinkôkai).

Manzo Iwata – Karate (Shito-Ryu and founder of Shito Kai, fourth-generation heir of Nanban Satto Ryu and Taien-Ryu Jojutsu).

Ryushou Sakagami – Karate (Shito-Ryu, founder of Itosu Kai) and also Kendo, Hanshi in Muso Jikiden Eishin Ryu Iaido and Taira Shinken Kobujutsu.

Katsutani/?Fujitani Masatoshi – Karate (Tani-Ha Shito-Ryu/ Shukokai, founder of Myobukai/ Meibukai and second head master of the Bujutsu Kenkyusho).

Masaru Watanabe – Karate (founder of Seiki Kai and possibly Kenyu-Ryu).

Zeniya Kunii – Kenjutsu (eighteenth-generation *soke* Kashima Shin-Ryu, possibly Kagoshima Shinto-Ryu).

Ono Jiusai (likely: Sasamori Junzo) – Kenjutsu (sixteenth *soke* of Ona-Ha Itto Ryu, former Japanese parliamentary politician with close ties to the practitioners of Muso Jikiden Eishin Ryu Iaijutsu).

Ryuji Shimimizu or Kiyomizu (likely Shimizu Takaji) – Jojutsu (twenty-fifth head master of Shindo Muso Ryu Jodo).

Hon Reik (likely: Kono Minoru Hyakuren) Iaido (twentieth *soke* Muso Jikiden Eishin Ryu – MJER) and founder of the All Japan Iaido Federation (Zen Nihon Iaido Renmei – ZNIR) also a Jujutsu master.

Ogasawara Kiyonobu – Kyujutsu (*soke* of Ogasawara Ryu who had close ties with the practitioners of Muso Jikiden Eishin Ryu Iaido – MJER).

Kobayashi Sei(o) – Naginata (Menkyo Kaiden of Toda-Ha Buko Ryu, founded the the Nihon Joshi Naginata Gakuin – Japan Women's Naginata Institute. She also befriended Golda Meir who became prime minister of Israel).

Ikeda Toki (?) (Ikeda Takashi Seiko) – Naginata (Tendo Ryu) and if Ikeda Takashi Seiko: twenty-second consecutive *soke* Muso Jikiden Eishin Ryu – MJER Iaido [Hokiyama-ha] – Seitokai. President of the of the All Japan Iaido Federation, Zen Nihon Iaido Renmei – ZNIR.

Saito (Sa)toshi/Akira – Shurikenjutsu (*soke* of Negishi Ryu), Shirai Ryu, Shuriken-jutsu (GanRyu/ Ganritsu Ryu), Iaijutsu (Yamamoto Ryu – Kuwana Handen). Disciple of Naruse Kanji (renowned Shuriken jutsu master).

One third of these individuals are Okinawan Karate masters, which represents by far the largest group. Three of these Karate-ka (Manzo Iwata, founder of Shito Kai, Ryushou Sakagami, founder of Itosu Kai and Masaru Watanabe, founder of Seiki Kai) had received the 'Shihan no Menjo' (or master/ expert teacher certificate/ diploma) from Fujita's friend Kenwa Mabuni (founder of Shito-Ryu). Almost half of Mabuni's senior students received this certification (the others included Ken Saiko of Shito Kai, Hakuru Seiki, founder of HakuRyu Kai, Ryusei Tomoyori, founder of Kenyu-Ryu and Chojiro Tani, founder of Tani Ha Shito-Ryu and subsequently Shukokai) as well as the right of heritage of Mabuni's sons (Kenei and Kenzo, whose roles as *soke* of this style are disputed). Motokatsu Inoue had trained under one of Mabuni's colleagues, Yasuhiro Konishi, on the advice of Fujita, who also named Motokatsu Inoue's style of *Yui Shin Kai*. The reason why Fujita's funeral was attended by such a large number of Okinawan Karate-ka, when Fujita himself was a Japanese Ninja master, requires further consideration.

Why Karate?

Although Fujita shared warm friendships with his Okinawan Karate colleagues, it is unlikely that he spent such a high proportion of his time with them, purely on account of amity. He would have had significant exposure to the various Japanese martial artists in Tokyo, who would have practised arts closely allied to his own and, according to many purists, Karate did not warrant serious consideration since it was not an official Japanese *Ryuha* derived from Samurai Bushido tradition, but rather had originated in China and Okinawa.

Karate is not mentioned in any of the 'great texts' of Japanese martial arts such as *Go Rin No Sho* (Book of Five Rings) or the *Hagakure*, and it only arrived in mainland Japan in the 1920s with Funakoshi's official demonstration, whereas Ninjutsu had a much longer provenance in Japan. Although Ninjutsu has several 'unarmed combat' elements that are superficially akin to the 'empty hand' of Karate, such a comparison requires a deeper analysis.

According to the popular interpretation of Ninjutsu, the unarmed fighting elements are known as Taijutsu and only comprise a small proportion of the techniques. These are mainly based on grappling (or Jujutsu) and rather unlike the straight punching and kicking seen in most Karate styles. Furthermore, the weapons used in Okinawan Kobudo vary greatly from those of traditional Ninjutsu.

Fujita's affinity with Okinawan Karate could have stemmed from there being such a significant difference to his own art that he studied it to complement his skills; or alternatively he found such significant similarities in history, philosophy and technique that he felt a fundamental link between Okinawan Karate and the Ninjutsu he practised. I consider the latter more probable for several reasons.

If we study Fujita's association with Karate-ka through his network (**Figure 20**), it becomes clear that most of his encounters are with exponents of the Shorin-Ryu schools. These include the father of Shito-Ryu Karate, Mabuni Kenwa, Motobu Choki and Inoue Motokatsu. Mabuni and Motobu are among the most prominent Karate-ka of all time, and it is through Mabuni connections that

Fujita attended the Toudi Kenkyukai conference sessions of many of Karate's forefathers. These meetings were attended by individuals such as Miyagi Chojun (founder of the Naha-te style Goju-Ryu) but they mainly consisted of Shorin stylists.

So what similarity did Fujita identify between his style of Ninjutsu and Shorin-Ryu Karate? It is fair to surmise that he did not feel closeness to the Shorin stylists, based on their elementary forms, steps, punches or kicks.

The term Shorin-Ryu was first utilised by Ankoh Itosu (1831–1915) to indicate the Chinese origin of his Okinawan Karate deriving from Shaolin Kung-Fu. There is authenticity in the use of the word in this context as it literally means Shaolin in Japanese Okinawan, and importantly, the word was introduced in Okinawa in the 1800s, well before the popularisation of Shaolin Kung-Fu in China in the early 1900s (although Itosu did use different characters).

A Ninjutsu connection with China and Shaolin is reconcilable. Fujita's Ninjutsu and Okinawan Shaolin (Shorin) may have been separate concepts in Fujita's texts, but a fundamental similarity in martial arts techniques may have been a real possibility. Fujita may have therefore found an affinity with Okinawa Shorin-Ryu through a common ancestry with his Ninjutsu, back to ancient Shaolin Kung-Fu.

Technical evidence to support this theory is lacking. We have little direct evidence of Fujita's style or techniques. We do have indirect evidence of Fujita's Nanban Satto Ryu, which he clearly differentiated as a non-Ninjutsu school. Most of our current evidence therefore rests in the network trail left by Fujita through his associations with Okinawan Karate and Kobudo experts.

The specific relevance of Okinawa Shorin-Ryu to Fujita rests on the evolution of Shorin-Ryu within the context of a Japanese/Bushido cultural Ryu system. He could assess the Shorin style within a common frame of reference to his indigenous Ninjutsu; this may not have been so clear to him if he had encountered modern Shaolin Kung-Fu directly; Ryu in Karate are a very modern thing and bear little resemblance to traditional mainland Ryu in their organisation or practice. The Shorin/ Shaolin systems nevertheless have a number of physical and spiritual elements that share corresponding motifs and demonstrate high concordance.

In terms of physicality, many of the basic punches and kicks can be found almost universally in Eastern martial arts. The areas that distinguish Karate are its coded message hidden in kata (forms) and its interpretation in Bunkai. This is particularly developed in the Shorin schools that have the largest selection of, and longest, katas. These are associated with an even larger number of Bunkai interpretations.

The teaching of bunkai across most styles follows a clear methodology. The most basic interpretation for a given form is taught first to junior practitioners (known as kuden, which refers to all oral transmission at any level and, if anything, more commonly refers to higher-level knowledge and 'secrets'). As the seniority of a martial artist increases, so does the variety and complexity of kata interpretations. Finally, the deadliest, most secret techniques are taught to the most senior students who are considered to have achieved a level of responsibility and worthiness commensurate with the level of bunkai taught to them (okuden, or deepest transmission). In the modern era three terms for bunkai are utilised, (i) *Omote* or obvious 'as you see it' application, (ii) *Ura* or hidden application and (iii) *Honto* or 'real-life' true application.

This of course adds to the mysticism encountered in each style. The whole system can be dynamic: many practitioners do not achieve the seniority to be taught all bunkai interpretations, some instructors forget some of their most complex syllabus, others may add new interpretations. There is also a very common attitude on Okinawa that the true value of kata is not so much in individual techniques or their interpretations but in how they condition the body and ingrain martial principles unconsciously through endless refining and repetition. This is especially true of *tanrengata* like *sanchin* or *naihanchi*. Among the most senior Okinawan Karate masters, kata and bunkai are considered the heart and essence of their art.

The highest level of bunkai contains much more than just punches and kicks. It includes more complex manoeuvres, including grappling. It imparts combinations of body movements, sometimes communicating several moves ahead of time; it bestows strength of foresight similar to that of a chess master predicting the future moves of an opponent. Bunkai can offer even more, for it can help a practitioner achieve a higher mental level, which can increase focus and confidence and decrease stress and fear.

The strengths of bunkai, however, can become its weakness. With inappropriate instruction, knowledge can be watered down and students can be taught a type of voodoo mysticism devoid of any true content. Furthermore, such a lack of teaching quality would be difficult to prove because of the associated secrecy.

It is likely that Fujita's encounter with some of the foremost stylists of Shorin would have ensured a high level of authenticity in their styles and teaching. At this much higher level, the secret techniques of Koga Ryu Ninjutsu may have been comparable to the teachings of the Shorin stylists and could have evoked warm feelings of recognition in the Ninja master. (It should be noted, however, that although there may have been some technical similarity, the scope and purpose of the two arts is vastly different. Karate has always been concerned with the civilian individual; Ninjutsu was a military skill involving far more than unarmed fighting.)

There is some evidence that Fujita came into contact with the Naha styles at the Toudi Kenkyukai conferences through the father of the Goju-Ryu school, Chojun Miyagi. Furthermore, his close colleague Kenwa Mabuni was well versed in Naha-based Karate (in addition to his knowledge of Shorin), so that Fujita may have noted some affinity with Naha-te Karate and his Koga Ninjutsu. Interestingly, a tangible Naha Ninja link might be discernible in the 'unknown' Karate style of Ryuei-Ryu. Quite recently, this became public knowledge in the 1970s and 1980s after centuries of family secrecy, seen as an authentic Naha style untouched by modern influences. I have previously alluded to this style as a living fossil of the early days of Karate, and the style offers an explosive mix of Karate power with softer, artistic elements that many believe are directly derived from Chinese Kung-Fu (likely Fukien). This style was popu-

larised by Tsuguo Sakumoto, who was the Karate world kata champion three times in a row. In an interview, he described his style: 'The
techniques of Ryuei Ryu consist of basic Chinese Kempo techniques
called "Mutensho", augmented by "Heiho" tactics, "Yojoho" (techniques of healing) and "Ninja" skills.'[159]

Such a revelation regarding ancient Okinawa Karate and the Naha
school is also cited in some of the other rarer extant styles of ancient
Karate today. Although formal Ninjutsu is no longer clearly discernible in these Karate *Ryuha*, Fujita may have noted them during his time
with the elite Karate-ka. This may have derived from a local Ninjutsu
presence on the island of Okinawa or may relate to a common ancestor style of Karate and Kung-Fu. Many Karate masters consider these
ancient Okinawan Ti and many of the katas of such ancient Karate
styles contain certain techniques and bunkai that have a degree of
commonality with confidence-boosting psychological manoeuvres
described as 'mind-control techniques'. In these ancient Naha and
Shorin styles, these manoeuvres typically exist at the beginning of
katas, although they are also sometimes found within the main body
of katas as well. These techniques share an affinity with the Ninja
tradition of Kuji Kiri practices and point towards a deeper connection
between Okinawan Karate and Ninjutsu.

Kuji Kiri

According to Ninjutsu lore, there are a series of 'magic' hand-
knotting movements associated with meditation that correspond
to different levels and compositions of the 'four basic elements' –
Chi (earth or solids), *Sui* (water or liquids), *Ka* (fire or burning) and
Fu (wind or gases). By using these movements, the practitioner is
thought to be placed in spiritual alignment with these elemental
forces and can derive energy from them.

These hand movements are known as the Kuji Kiri – the nine cuts
or nine seals are not only known to Ninja practitioners but are also
practised by a number of religious sects of the East, including those

of Buddhism and Hinduism. Kuji Kiri (nine magical cuts) should be differentiated from Kuji-in (nine meditative seals). These are believed to originate in the ascetic and shamanistic practice of Mikkyo Buddhists and by the Yamabushi and *En no Gyoja*. They are derived from the ancient Indian Sanskrit *Mudras* but were later accompanied by Buddhist *Mantras*. These movements are considered to have been first transcribed onto paper in China by Boa Pu Zhi and later taken to Japan.

It is considered that there are a total of eighty-one ways of knotting or intertwining fingers, although nine levels are considered as the foundation forms, or so-called magical cuts:

Rin – strength of body and mind.
Kyo – direction of energy.
Toh – harmony with the universe.
Sha – healing (oneself or others).
Kai – premonition.
Jin – knowledge of other's thoughts.
Retsu – mastery of time and space.
Zai – control of natural elements.
Zen – enlightenment.

The Kuji Kiri are used in displays of Japanese martial arts and in traditional religions, and may be demonstrable in some of the forms of Okinawan Karate kata and subsequently derived forms (such as those of Taekwondo). For example, the opening technique of the Okinawan kata *Kushanku* (known in mainland Japanese styles as *Kanku* and in Korean Taekwondo as *Kong Sang Koon Hyung*), ascribed to the Chinese envoy of the same name, is interpreted as being a wrist-lock technique. It does, however, have some resemblance to the Kuji Kiri sign of Zai (**Figure 23**). Fujita may have noted this in some of the katas demonstrated to him by Mabuni and Iwata. Interestingly, several other katas demonstrate these Kuji Kiri-type techniques. Some of these have been demonstrated since the death of Fujita. For example, the Naha-te style of Ryuei-Ryu was kept as a

Figure 23: The author performing the opening sequence of the Okinawan Karate kata *Kusanku* (known in mainland Japanese styles as *Kanku* and in Korean Taekwondo as *Kong Sang Koon Hyung*). The hand formation resembles the Zai element of *Kuji Kiri* signs.

father-to-son secret family style until the 1970s, when it was taught to several schoolteachers and Karate enthusiasts. Many of the commencing sequences of Ryuei-Ryu katas have Chinese start motifs similar to Kuji Kiris. These may, of course, simply represent ancient Chinese wrist locks and techniques, but examples similar to these may have led Fujita to consider Okinawan Karate as offering a mystical depth that enabled a close comparison with his style of Ninjutsu.

Here the circle may be closed. The Shaolin origin of Shorin Karate and the possible Shaolin origin of Ninjutsu may have finally re-encountered each other in the ostensibly unlikely association between Shorin Karate masters such as Mabuni Kenwa and Seiko Fujita. In addition, Fujita may have seen a close similarity between his Ninjutsu grappling and the indigenous Okinawan art of Ti, or To-de. The origins of this style are complex and it might be derived from earlier Chinese-Okinawan interactions, or other external sources beyond Okinawa, though our evidence on this art is sparse at best. Other possibilities may exist, of course, but gradually become more improbable. Speculation as to the possibility of an Okinawa Ninja style influencing Karate styles remains speculation. However, the close connection between Fujita and Shorin stylists provides one tangible link upon which to base the conjecture that Karate and Ninjutsu had fundamental similarities that could imply a common origin.

9

Conclusion: Shaolin, Shorin, Shinobi

There are tangible connections among the vast majority of authentic martial arts schools today. They may be the result of the public conception of what a good martial arts school should offer, based on accessible worldwide media. Alternatively, however, they could represent a relationship that has roots spanning well over two millennia. These two views are not necessarily opposed and the truth probably lies somewhere in between.

The idea of interconnection can be applied between each martial art in a broader sense, but also can be applied to each individual school and even individual class. Each school must by definition start somewhere and have an ancestry traceable to the present day (**Figure 24**) that passes along an evolutionary tree from instructor to pupil. However, this is rarely the whole story. In today's martial arts world it is unusual for a single artist to have only ever trained in one art with one instructor. Many people start with one martial art, then change to another that they find suits them mentally and physically, and that also suits their lifestyle and fits in with their commitments. In this process each individual comes into contact with many fellow artists and instructors. This is not only limited to the modern era: such fluidity in training (albeit with less variation) also occured in the ancient world.

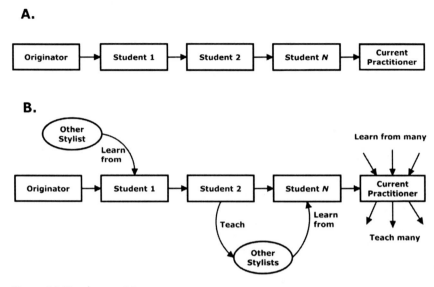

Figure 24: Development 1.

Although there are periods where the interaction amongst styles and stylists was limited (such as during the attempted ban on martial arts in Okinawa), eventually inter-style relations invariably recommenced (analogous to the spread of DNA among subspecies of animals). Just as in evolutionary biology where today's surviving species are a product of heredity and evolutionary environmental pressures, then most surviving martial arts styles are the sum of their core knowledge in the form of combative techniques, katas/forms and mental elements (heredity) being passed on by individual martial artists to a body of trainees in a particular socioeconomic and sociopolitical culture who adopt them (environment). Just as every species had to undergo sequential evolutionary changes to suit its environment (climbing 'mount improbable'),[160] every martial art has progressed and survived only if it was adopted by the appropriate trainees ('at the right place and the right time') who were prepared to study and promulgate the style. The existence of current styles therefore reflects a complex dialogue between styles and their practising audiences, so that although many currently exist (despite the improbability), many have become extinct.

In examples of styles where there have been only a few founding influences, dissecting out their origins is feasible. When considering more complex martial arts trees, this task increases exponentially in complexity. The development of martial arts styles and schools is comparable to analysing and modelling the development of biological organisms and species through their genetic and phenotypic phylogeny trees (**Figure 25**). Each specific martial art can be considered as a 'species' and each school or substyle can be considered a 'subspecies'. In addition to its epistemological attraction, this may prove useful in analysing each style to clarify its origins, with the ultimate goal of increasing the comprehension and validity of each art. Using further analytical tools, it is also possible to calculate the degree of similarity, or homology, between each school. No one style is whole unto itself and each would have developed from varying amounts of dynamic interaction between individuals or groups of different styles. Such networks can be complex and may be displayed in two-dimensional and three-dimensional network maps to represent the fluidity of the spread of knowledge within martial arts. The deeper

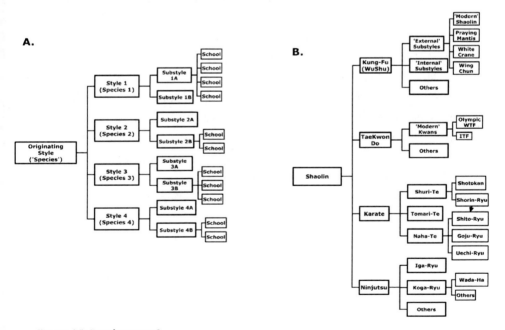

Figure 25: Development 2.

study of current martial arts styles can offer a largely unexplored way of understanding lost elements of ancient arts. As such, the evolutionary analysis of current martial arts may offer the ability to 'genetically reverse engineer' lost martial arts knowledge, much as there are biological efforts to re-engineer lost or extinct animal species from the study of ancient DNA.[125] This is gradually taking place as instructors identify knowledge in their own schools and practise with similar and dissimilar styles in order to identify commonalities and origins.

The development of martial arts through Shaolin origins (that may have been derived from more ancient roots in Persia or India) can be proposed. The teachings of Bodhidharma or other Kung-Fu patriarchs probably spread their original style across borders (**Figure 26**). Subsequently, a number of martial arts would evolve from the original style, modified by local need, geography and sociopolitics (analogous to 'selection pressure' in evolutionary biology). The role of individual masters and teachers is also fundamental. They would act as 'nodes' or 'forks' along the developmental pathway of an art, adopting certain techniques and forms, modifying these on occasion and then teaching them to their students. Generation by generation, each martial art would carry its own ethos and techniques, such that their dictionary of forms would transform them into unique independent styles and schools.

Of course, there is no conclusive evidence as yet whether Bodhidharma's teaching or Shaolin are the originators of modern martial arts. Nevertheless, there is a strong case for the prominent role of Shaolin in many of these Eastern martial arts. The extremely close ties between ostensibly opposing styles of Karate and Ninjutsu are but one example where the arts are comparable at a deeper level than just how to perform individual techniques. Shaolin may have led to Shorin (and Shorei) Karate as well as Shinobi schools, and the meeting of these styles may have re-enlightened some of the original concepts of the Shaolin, so the circle may have been closed.

The evolutionary analogy for the development of the martial arts offers insights into style development. In evolutionary biology, when different species try to occupy similar environmental niches, they acquire a similar phenotype or characteristics to address evolutionary pressures for survival; this a process known as convergent evolution. A typical example is vision and the similarities between eyes in many varied species around the world (all eyes have a lens, photosensitive retina, optic nerve, and a circular capsule). Similarly, the recently extinct thylacine (*Thylacinus cynocephalus*) was a marsupial carnivore with body structure and ecological status similar to the biological family of canids that includes wolves, foxes and dogs, despite having no immediately related genetic origins. 'Form follows function'.

In martial arts there are equivalent evolutionary pressures and niches in the form of fighting needs. Quite simply, 'a fight is a fight' and without weapons the tools with which to win are consistent in the form of the human body (armaments are clearly different as they have evolved dramatically over time). As a result, the same tools of arms, legs, feet, fists, head, thorax and abdomen are consistent and largely unchanged in the current era (excluding body enhancements and bionics), so that common patterns of winning a fight can be seen in different styles. In this way, convergent evolution can be seen in different martial arts schools; the application of body throw dynamics is very similar, whether in Brazil or Mongolia.

Modern media platforms exhibiting martial performances and combative competitions enhance the dissemination and then congruence of modern technical practice. This is not necessarily damaging, it results from individuals adopting the 'best' or 'perceived best' elements of what is out there. This may slow some evolutionary processes by homogenising how techniques should be performed, but nevertheless beneficially offers martial information to countless enthusiasts worldwide.

Just as in biology, the theory of convergent evolution does not undermine the idea of a single origin of Eastern martial arts. One typical example is the giant tortoise (*Aldabrachelys gigantea*) from the atoll island of Aldabra in the Indian Ocean, now part of the Seychelles. Aldabra and many of its adjoining islands have long been part of an ancient trade network where the indigenous giant tortoises carry various distinct characteristics,[161] however, despite these variations there is clear genetic evidence of a common ancestor.[162, 163] Similarly, whilst there are myriad martial arts schools and styles derived from the Far East and South-East Asia, a *common phylogenetic* origin possibly from Bodhidharma and Shaolin offers an explanation for the plurality of technical, practical and spiritual similarities noted. There is now genetic evidence that the Aldabran giant tortoise likely originated in Madagascar and travelled to inhabit Aldabra,[161, 163, 164] subsequently undergoing periods of local extinction and subsequent reoccupation in its evolutionarily competitive niche. In a similar way, modern martial arts styles and techniques may have an original ancestor that subsequently occupied a combative or martial niche, only to become extinct (as in many styles of Karate and Ninjutsu), only to come back into existence as a result of technical needs. Unfortunately, there is little evidence of these martial evolutionary patterns as we only have a quantity of martial arts videos from the twentieth century, a handful of technical descriptions from before and very little else during the millennia of mankind's martial arts. We find nothing trapped in amber. Consequently, it is difficult to ascertain whether the forms or combative techniques of a modern school of martial arts such as modern Karate, Jujutsu or hybrid martial arts (such as MMA – mixed martial arts) were in existence in a similar form some time ago, though it is possible.

The concept of a 'martial arts fossil' indicates, however, that modern-day Karate, Ninjutsu, Taekwondo and other martial arts may not be descendants of Shaolin (or Indian or Persian arts such as Kalaripayattu or Zurkhane). Rather these arts may have been derived from an ancestral progenitor form, so that 'proto-Shaolin' may be the common link between them, which may in turn have been derived from progenitor Indian or Persian martial arts ('proto-Kalaripayattu' and 'proto-Zurkhane' respectively). There may even have been one or several 'proto-Bodhidharma(s)'. In the same way, a domestic cat is not a descendant of a modern lion, but is a descendant of a common feline ancestor, so Karate and Ninjutsu are not

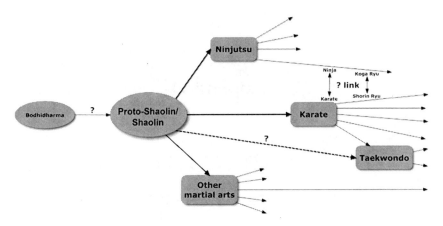

Figure 26: Development 3.

direct descendants of modern Kung-Fu, but are likely descendants of a common martial (likely Shaolin-type) ancestor.

The task for the next generation of martial artists is to continue developing their own styles, whilst addressing the core principles each school has provided over the centuries. Knowledge of martial history can only enhance current theory and practice, and an increased appreciation of current knowledge within the context of developmental pathways encourages communication and cross-fertilisation. These arts are not fully formed leviathans but dynamic philosophies and vibrant ways of life. Many talented individuals have dedicated their whole existence to enlightening others through the communication of these values. Martial artists of all styles need the resonance of ancient interpretations to cultivate the skills of the future.

Appendix 1

The Death of Bruce Lee: A Medical Perspective

A 32-year-old American-born Chinese movie star and celebrated martial artist was presented to his local hospital in the Kowloon region of Hong Kong as an emergency brought in by ambulance on the night of 20 July 1973. He had been found to be unresponsive for approximately two hours, having initially complained of a headache three hours earlier, for which he had taken an over-the-counter single tablet of Equagesic® (200mg meprobamate and 325mg aspirin)[165] – typically a medication used to treat musculoskeletal pain and associated anxiety.[166]

Past medical history revealed that until the age of 30, he had only suffered from cryptorchidism (undescended testicle) that was treated in childhood, and did not have any other significant medical complaints. Over the preceding two years, he had intermittently taken anabolic-androgenic steroids and diuretics for modifying his athletic abilities, body mass and form. An electric muscle stimulator was also used on occasion to improve muscle bulk and function. He would take Darvon® Compound-65 (each tablet containing 65mg propoxyphene hydrochloride, 389mg aspirin and 32.4mg caffeine) for simple analgesia. He consumed various Chinese herbal remedies and would drink variable amounts of alcohol, whilst on occasion he took cannabis. X-rays of his hip, lumbosacral and thoracic spine taken in 1970 had been normal, however, in view of persisting joint pains, he received regular cortisol injections to his back, knees and hands.[165]

Although his physical prowess had remained high in terms of cardiovascular fitness, strength and technical ability, he had lost 9kg over the past two years, resulting in a body mass of 57kg with a height of 17cm. In keeping with his reputation for almost super-human fitness, colleagues talked of a resting heart rate well below 40bpm (although this was never formally documented). The subject was universally acknowledged as being among the greatest martial artists of all time. He was renowned for feats of extreme speed during his offensive strikes, being famed for a 'One Inch Punch', where he would appreciably throw off-balance a 90kg opponent face-on from a 1-inch striking distance and would regularly perform feats such as performing one-hand push-ups using only two fingers and completing biceps curls of 36kg for eight repetitions.

Eight months previously, whilst working in Hong Kong, in addition to symptoms of weight loss he had complained of severe acne (likely secondary to anabolic-androgenic steroid use) and axillary hyperhidrosis (excessive underarm sweating) for which he underwent open surgical adenectomy (Skoog procedure, the excision of glands). At two months prior to this admission, having reputedly stopped taking anabolic-androgenic steroids, whilst in a dubbing studio, he suffered from an acute episode of lethargy and malaise that progressed to intermittent loss of consciousness, vomiting and seizures that required prompt hospitalisation and emergency medical review.

At that time, he was pyrexial (feverish) and comatose on arrival, being intermittently apnoeic (not breathing) with rigidity in all limbs. Pupils were pinpoint and non-reactive, with fundoscopy (eye examination) revealing gross vascular spasm. Reflexes were depressed and plantar responses were negative. Administration of the osmotic diuretic mannitol resulted in a return of consciousness, spontaneous respiration, and a temporary right and left rotary nystagmus (eye oscillation), which subsequently resolved. Lumbar puncture (including a VDRL test), blood cultures and blood haematology were unremarkable, as was blood biochemistry other than a mildly raised Sodium (154mmol/L), and mildly low blood urea nitrogen (BUN) (9.2mg/dL or 3.3mmol/L).[167] This had caused significant misunderstanding at the time, as there had been a likely typing error omitting the decimal point in the 9.2 value, giving an erroneously high value for blood urea nitrogen.

He was diagnosed with cerebral oedema and cannabis poisoning and was prescribed Valium® (diazepam). During subsequent follow-up in the United States, the patient admitted to insomnia, work stress, anger episodes, continued anxiety over weight loss and chronic diuretic abuse. General clinical examination, computed tomography of the brain, electroencephalogram, and bilateral carotid angiography were all normal, as were a repeat blood haematology and biochemistry screen. A subsequent diagnosis of idiopathic grand mal epilepsy was made, and Dilantin® (phenytoin) was commenced, although this was discontinued by the patient shortly after.

It had been reported that an hour previous to the existing admission following the consumption of Equagesic®, he was unresponsive, was not respiring, had a weak pulse, and had pupils that were not fully dilated. On arrival at hospital he was deeply comatose, apnoeic, with no pulse and fixed unreactive pupils. There was evidence of loss of all brainstem reflexes. He had no stigmata of chronic liver disease, with no hepatosplenomegaly (enlargement of liver and spleen). Diagnosis of brain death was declared, and he was pronounced as deceased soon after arrival.

An autopsy examination of the nasal cavity, mouth, pharynx and larynx was normal. The lung surfaces displayed minor haemorrhaging and moderate congestion. There were minimal bilateral pleural effusions, with microscopy revealing congestion of some of the smaller airways and blood vessels, with resultant micro-haemorrhages. There was no evidence of pneumonia, although the findings were consistent with a coryzal-type (cold viral infection) illness or mild respiratory tract infection. The brain showed evidence of considerable diffuse cerebral oedema, and had enlarged to a mass of 1.575kg compared with the normal 1.4kg. The brain vasculature was unremarkable with no evidence of tissue ischaemia (lack

of oxygen supply), excluding the diagnoses of infarction or haemorrhage. The remaining organs were normal, including the liver, with
no evidence of poisoning, and although the presence of cannabis
was found in gastric and ileal contents, forensic scrutiny deemed this
of negligible medical significance. Biochemical and general toxico-
logical screening did not reveal any irregularity.

The coroner's final verdict was 'death by misadventure', resulting
from acute cerebral oedema as a result of a hypersensitivity to the
constituent drugs of Equagesic®, namely meprobamate, aspirin,
or a combination of the two.[165] The patient was the famed Kung-Fu
legend Bruce Lee (**Figure 27**).

What was the cause of death?

It seems unlikely that the patient died secondary to drug-induced
hypersensitivity, as this would have been reflected in the post-mortem pathology.[168] Furthermore, alternative theories of death to date
also fail to correlate with the forensic findings, these include death
by poisoning, drug overdose, numerous conspiracy theories and
even the supernatural (the so-called 'delayed death touch').

Some sources do allude to the possibility of adrenal insufficiency
as the cause of death.[165] This theory correlates well with a number
of details in the history. The patient had been intermittently taking
anabolic-androgenic steroids, an acute withdrawal of which can
lead to acute adrenal insufficiency.[169] This condition can rarely be
present with cerebral oedema,[170] and might explain both the collapsing episode two months previous to death (that responded well to
mannitol administration) and the events leading to the case herein.
Furthermore, the first episode was associated with a pyrexia, whilst
the second revealed the possibility of a mild respiratory tract infection, both intimating an underlying infection that may have poten-
tiated the exacerbation of acute adrenal insufficiency. Conversely,
although adrenal insufficiency is considered a great clinical masquer-
ader, presenting with an array of non-specific symptoms, neither

episode revealed any typical biochemical or pathological findings of such a condition. Importantly, the common finding of hyponatraemia (lowered salt levels in the blood) was not present,[171] and indeed serum sodium was slightly raised in the first episode, even though a history of chronic diuretic abuse usually leads to hyponatraemia.[172]

The history and pathology reveal that cerebral oedema was the cause of death, with a background of a likely mild respiratory infection. If we thus reconsider the obvious culprit Equagesic®, and its two constituents, meprobamate and aspirin, it becomes clear from the medical and pharmacological literature that meprobamate is not known to instigate cerebral oedema,[173, 174] whereas for aspirin, there is a demonstrable association, namely through Reye's, or Reye's-like, syndromes.[175]

The term 'Reye's syndrome' has now been largely replaced by 'Reye's-like syndrome' due to the fact that the condition is now considered to represent a cluster of heterogeneous disorders whereby febrile illnesses and infections can lead to acute encephalopathy and hepatic (liver) dysfunction when initiated by underlying mitochondrial, metabolic or toxic dysfunction.

Classically this is a rare condition affecting children who suffer from a two-stage illness, first a viral prodrome from an upper respiratory tract infection (typically influenza), or other viruses such as varicella. This is followed several days later by a non-inflammatory encephalopathy with precipitous vomiting, convulsions and cerebral oedema in association with selective hepatic dysfunction and fatty infiltration of the viscera, which can lead to rapid severe neurological damage and death. Its occurrence has been associated with administration of aspirin during the viral prodrome (pre-onset symptom period), being primarily given for use as an analgesic and antipyretic.

Although an unequivocally direct causation is controversial and still contested in the literature, with a variety of other factors implicated (such as anti-emetics), a well-known association between the role of aspirin and its metabolite salicylate in Reye's syndrome is widely established, with several large public health reports demonstrating vigorous evidence alluding to this. One such study revealed that approximately one-third of their Reye's syndrome cases were correlated to aspirin administration, further supported by the evidence that its incidence has fallen in conjunction with the decrease in the use of aspirin in the paediatric population.

Reye's or Reye's-like syndromes can occur in adults, and have been reported in over thirty cases in the literature. Differential diagnosis includes multiple drug overdose, valproic acid hepatoxicity, chronic alcohol abuse with paracetamol use, connective-tissue diseases with chronic salicylate ingestion, systemic carnitine deficiency (lack of an amino acid), chronic pancreatitis, obesity with dehydration, septic encephalopathy and others. The majority of these differentials allude to a cause of encephalopathy associated with some degree of liver failure, as is usually the case with Reye's syndrome. However, in our case there seemed to be no biochemical or pathological evidence of hepatic dysfunction, and indeed liver involvement is not *condicio sine qua non* for Reye's-like syndromes, a fact that discernibly reflects more than one of a number of likely multifactorial mechanisms that can lead to encephalopathy in these patients. Cases of encephalopathy devoid of hepatic dysfunction therefore may represent instances where the speed and onset of disease seemingly prevents significant biochemical and structural changes from occurring in the liver.

Just as in the paediatric population, long-term neurological damage and death can ensue in adults, and therefore prompt action is necessary. Treatment includes control of intracranial pressure within the context of intensive supportive care. This includes hyperventilation in the short term and the use of the osmotic diuretic mannitol. Mortality can be as high as 50 per cent of hospitalised patients, though if recovery from encephalopathy is achieved, liver and visceral dysfunction usually resolves.

In the case described, the post-mortem pathology was consistent with a mild respiratory tract infection, which, combined with the use of the aspirin-containing Equagesic® could have led to a Reye's-like syndrome. Additionally, the collapsing episode occurring two months before death may have also been a Reye's-like syndrome as the patient had suffered from a pyrexia that may have represented a

Figure 27: Statue of Bruce Lee. Avenue of Stars, Tsim Sha Tsui Promenade, Hong Kong.

viral illness, coupled to a long-standing consistent use of analgesia-containing aspirin (Darvon® Compound-65). This earlier episode may have been a 'warning' episode whereby ensuing long-term neurological injury and death were successfully prevented by the prompt diagnosis and management of intracranial hypertension with mannitol.

Many athletes worldwide continue to take aspirin or aspirin-containing medications for their analgesic and anti-inflammatory properties. Although proven to be of long-term cardiovascular benefit, some individuals may be at risk of a Reye's-like syndrome if aspirin is administered during a viral illness. This condition may have been the cause of the untimely death of Kung-Fu star Bruce Lee. Aspirin use therefore warrants judicious dispensation and dissuasion from use during viral infections. Furthermore, strong vigilance for symptoms of central nervous and hepatic dysfunction is essential, as the recovery from Reye's-like syndrome is best achieved upon rapid medical referral and prompt management.

Appendix 2

Taekwondo

The development of Taekwondo follows a similar pattern to that of Karate in that they both likely originate in Shaolin Kung-Fu (**Figure 28**). Many established authorities consider Bodhidharma as a fore-father of Taekwondo.[176] The essence of Shaolin could have been passed via a series of monks or intermediaries to the ancient Korean martial arts, which can be divided into the ancient *Subak Taekkyon* arts based at the ancient kingdoms of Goguryeo, Silla and Baekje, much like the Naha, Shuri and Tomari of Karate.

The ancient Hwarang Warriors of these three martial centres practised *Hwarang Do*. This martial arts system was essentially comprised of the nine kwans. The historical record does not reveal a pattern of development according to a timeline.[177] Some consider that Hwarang Do was more of a martial ideology than a system of martial arts, analogous to Japanese Bushido, as opposed to technical practices such as Jujutsu or Kenjutsu.

More recently, the influence of Okinawan Karate, and largely the dominance of Shotokan Karate via General Choi Hong Hi (the second Dan in Shotokan) led to today's development of modern Tang Soo Do and Taekwondo (**Figure 28**). This can be readily observed when studying the kata/ forms of Shotokan Karate (derived from Okinawan Karate kata) and Taekwondo, which have recognisable equivalents (**Figure 29**).

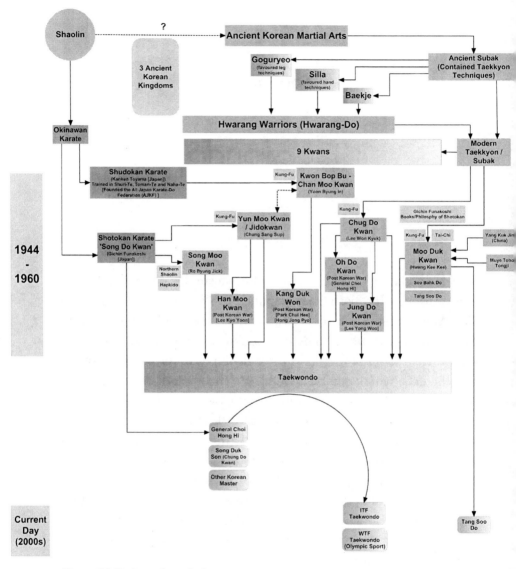

Figure 28: Taekwondo evolution.

Okinawan Kata	Shotokan Style Kata (mainland Japan)	Taekwondo Form Equivalent
Kushanku	Kanku	Kong sang koon hyung
Passai	Bassai	Palsaek hyung
Naihanchi / Naifanchi	Tekki	Chulgi hyung
Pinan	Heian	Pyonghan
	Taikyoku / Kihon	Kicho Hyung

Figure 29: Taekwondo forms derived from Shotokan Karate and their Okinawan origins.

These early events in the development of Taekwondo coincided with the twentieth-century Japanese occupation of Korea and the systematic programme to replace native Korean arts and culture with Japanese equivalents. More recently, since it stopped being a colony, there has been a compensatory and steady campaign to try to reabsorb authentic Korean martial arts. Today there is an undeniable association between mainstream Taekwondo and the Karate of the mid-twentieth century, a foremost contributor to modern Taekwondo.

Notes

1. Shahar, M. Epigraphy, 'Buddhist Historiography, and Fighting Monks: The Case of the Shaolin Monastery'. *Asia Major*; 2000; 13: 15–36.
2. Seidel, A. 'A Taoist Immortal of the Ming Dynasty: Chang San-Feng', in William Theodore de Bary, *Self and Society in Ming Thought*. New York: Columbia University Press; 1970.
3. Henning, S.E. 'Ignorance, legend and Taijiquan. *Journal of the Chen Style Taijiquan Research Association of Hawaii*; 1994; 2: 1–7.
4. Shahar, M. *The Shaolin Monastery: History, Religion, and the Chinese Martial Arts*. Honolulu: University of Hawaii Press; 2008.
5. I am grateful to Gavin J. Poffley whose expertise in Japanese translation was most helpful.
6. Order of Shaolin Ch'an. *Shaolin Grandmasters' Text: History, Philosophy, and Gung-Fu of Shaolin Ch'an (revised)*. Beaverton, Oregon: Order of Shaolin Ch'an; 2007.
7. Spencer, R. 'Putin, minus his black belt, on Kung-Fu pilgrimage' – 23 March 2006 in the *Telegraph* (UK).
8. Alley, R. 'Sung Shan, The Central Peak'. *Eastern Horizon*; 1965; 4.
9. Smith, R.W. *Secrets of Shaolin Temple Boxing*. Rutland, VT: Tuttle Publishing; 1964.
10. Dumoulin, H. Early Chinese Zen Re-examined: A supplement to Zen Buddhism: a history'. *Japanese Journal of Religious Studies*. 1993; 20: 31–53.
11. Jenner, W.J.F. *Memories of Loyang: Yang Hsuan-Chih and the Lost Capital (493–534)*. New York: Oxford University Press, USA; 1981.
12. Broughton, J.L. *The Bodhidharma Anthology: The Earliest Records of Zen*. Berkeley: University of California Press; 1999.
13. Yang, H-c. *A Record of Buddhist Monasteries in Lo-Yang*, trans. Yi-t'ung Wang. Princeton Library of Asian Translations, Princeton University Press; 1984.
14. Reid, H. and Croucher, M. *The Way of the Warrior: The Paradox of the Martial Arts*. London: Leopard Books; 1995.

15. Mackenzie, D.N. *A Concise Pahlavi Dictionary*. London: Routledge Curzon; 2000.
16. Monier-Williams, M. *A Sanskrit–English Dictionary: Etymologically and Philologically Arranged With Special Reference to Cognate Indo-European Languages*. Delhi: Motilal Barnasidass; 2002.
17. McRae, J.R. *The Northern School and the Formation of Early Ch'an Buddhism*. Studies in East Asian Buddhism, No. 3. Honolulu: University of Hawaii Press; 1987.
18. Dumoulin, H. *Zen Buddhism: A History, India and China*. Bloomington: World Wisdom; 2005.
19. Satomichi, T. 'Bodaidaruma to sono shuhen (i): Doiku to sofuku ni tsuite'. *Toyo Daigaku Toyogaku Kenkyujo Kiyo* [Journal of the Toyo University Oriental Studies Research Department]. 1978; 12: 117–121.
20. Dumoulin, H. *A History of Zen Buddhism*. London: Faber and Faber; 1963.
21. Chang. C-Y. 'Ch'an Buddhism: logical and illogical'. *Philosophy East and West*. 1967; 17: 37–49
22. Suzuki, D.T. *Manual of Zen Buddhism*. London: Rider & Co.; 1974.
23. Tonami, M. *The Shaolin Monastery Stele on Mount Song* (trans. P.A. Herbert, (ed.) Antonino Forte). Kyoto: Italian School of East Asian Studies (Istituto Italiano di Cultura / Scuola di Studi sull' Asia Orientale); 1990.
24. Sasaki, R.F., Iriya, Y., Fraser, D.R. *The Recorded Sayings of Layman P'ang: A Ninth-Century Zen Classic*. New York: John Weatherhill; 1971.
25. McRae, J.R. 'The Antecedents of Encounter Dialogue in Chinese Ch'an Buddhism', in (eds) Steven Heine and Dale S. Wright, *The Koan: Texts and Contexts in Zen Buddhism*. New York: Oxford University Press Inc., USA; 2000.
26. Sekiguchi, S. *Daruma No Kenkyū*. Tokyo: Iwanami shoten; 1967.
27. Nearman, H. The Denkoroku: *Or The Record of the Transmission of the Light, by Keizan [Jokin] Zenji ('Zenji' Meaning 'Zen Master')* – [translated from Japanese]. California: Shasta Abbey Press 2001.
28. T'ieh-yun, L. *The Travels of Lao Ts'an* (trans. Harold Shadick). Westport, CT: Greenwood Press reprint; 1986.
29. *Illustrated Explanation of Shaolin School Methods*, 1922 old text, (ed.) Li Yingang, annotated Tang Hao and Xu Zhedong. Hong Kong: Unicorn Press; 1968.
30. Zun, W.C. *Shaolin Quanshu Mijue* [Secrets of Shaolin Boxing]. Taipei: Zhonghua Wushu Chubanshe; 1971.
31. Secrets of Shaolin Boxing [Chinese] by the 'Master of the Study of Self Respect', annotated Tang Hao and Xu Zhedong. Taipei: Zhonghuawushu Press; 1971.
32. Guo, S. *History of Chinese Physical Culture* [Chinese]. Shanghai: Commercial Press; 1919.
33. Henning, S.E. 'The Chinese martial arts in historical perspective'. *Military Affairs*. 1981; 45: 173–179.
34. Kolatch, J. *Sports, Politics, and Ideology in China*. New York (Middle Village): Jonathan David Publishers; 1972.
35. Matsuda, R. *Zhongguo Wushu* Shilue [Chinese]. Taipei: Danqing Tushu; 1986.
36. Tang, H. *Shaolin Wudang Kao* [Chinese]. Hong Kong: Qilin Tushu; 1930.
37. Tang, H. *Shaolin Wudang Kao* [Chinese]. Hong Kong: Qilin Tushu; 1968.
38. Tang, H. *Wang Zongyue Taijiquanjing Yanjiu* [A Study of Wang Zongue's Tai Chi Chuan's Classic]. Hong Kong: Unicorn Press; 1969.
39. Tang, H. *Taijiquan Zongshi Wang Zongue Kao* [A Study of Tai Chi Chuan's Honoured Master Wang Zongue]. Hong Kong: Unicorn Press; 1969.

40. Xu, J. *Taijiquan Kaoxinlu* [investigation of the Facts of Tai Chi Chuan]. Taipei: Zenshanmei Chubanshe; 1965.
41. Xu, J. *Taijiquanpu Lidong-Bianwei Hebian* [Correct Approach and Recognition Towards False Aspects of Tai Chi Chuan Manuals – combined edition]. Taipei: Zenshanmei Chubanshe; 1965.
42. Tang, H. and Gu, L. *Taijiquan Yanjiu* [Tai Chi Chuan Research]. Hong Kong: Yixin Shudian; 1965.
43. Personal communication with Richard F. Gombrich, Academic Director, Oxford Centre for Buddhist Studies and formerly the Boden Professor of Sanskrit at the University of Oxford.
44. Faure, B. *Chan Insights and Oversights: An Epistemological Critique of the Chan Tradition*. Princeton: Princeton University Press; 1993.
45. Taylor, J. *The Dragon and the Wild Goose: China and India*, with new epilogue (Contributions to Study of World History, No. 8). New York: Praeger Paperback; 1991.
46. Rahman, A. *India's Interaction with China, Central and West Asia*, (project of *History of Indian Science, Philosophy & Culture*, volume 3 part 2). New Delhi: Oxford University Press; 2002.
47. Dutt, R.C. *A History of Civilization in Ancient India, Based on Sanscrit Literature: Volume 3. Buddhist and Pauranik Ages*. London: Adamant Media Corporation 2001.
48. Wiesehöfer, J. *Ancient Persia*. London: I.B. Tauris & Co. Ltd; 2001.
49. Bielenstein, H. 'The six dynasties (volume i)'. *Bulletin of the Museum of Far Eastern Antiquities (BMFEA)*; 1996; 68: 5–324.
50. Raymond, A. *Flash Gordon: The Time Trap of Ming XIII* (adapted Con Steffanson, pen name used by Bruce Cassidy). New York: Avon; 1974.
51. Daryaee, T. *Sasanian Persia: The Rise and Fall of an Empire*. London: I.B. Tauris & Co. Ltd; 2009.
52. Rawlinson, G. *The Seven Great Monarchies of The Ancient Eastern World – Volume 3: Parthia and Sassania*. Piscataway, NJ: Gorgias Press LLC; 2002.
53. Mair, V.H. 'Old sinitic myag, Old Persian maguš and English magician'. *Early China*. 1990; 15: 27–47.
54. Zurcher, E. *The Buddhist Conquest of China : The Spread and Adaptation of Buddhism in Early Medieval China*. Leiden: Brill; 1959.
55. Catling, C. 'Cyrus Cylinder'. *Current World Archaeology*. 2010; 8.
56. Luijendijk, D.H. *Zoor Khane: History and Techniques of the Ancient Martial Art of Iran*. Boulder, Colorado: Paladin Press; 2006.
57. Boyce, M. *A History of Zoroastrianism – Volume II, The Early Period*. Leiden: E.J. Brill; 1975.
58. Chugg, A.M. *Alexander the Great in India: A Reconstruction of Cleitarchus*. AMC Publications; 2009.
59. Zarrilli, P.B. *When the Body Becomes All Eyes: Paradigms, Discourses and Practices of Power in Kalarippayattu, A South Indian Martial Art*. New Delhi: Oxford University Press; 1998.
60. Greer, M.A. 'Daruma eyes: the sixth-century founder of Zen Buddhism and Kung-Fu had the earliest recorded graves' ophthalmopathy'. *Thyroid*. 2002; 12: 389–391.
61. Ashrafian, H. 'Familial proptosis and obesity in the ptolemies. *J R Soc Med*. 2005; 98: 85–86.

62. WeiZheng. *Suīshū* [The Official History of the Chinese Sui Dynasty]. 636.
63. Masuda, R., Yoshida, M.C., Shinyashiki, F., and Bando, G. 'Molecular phylogenetic status of the iriomote cat felis iriomotensis, inferred from mitochondrial DNA sequence analysis'. *Zoolog Sci.* 1994; 11: 597–604.
64. Gardner, J. *Licence Renewed*: London; Orion Publishing; 2011.
65. WebJapan. Japan fact sheet: Martial arts – from ancient tradition to modern sport. http://web-japan.Org/factsheet/en/pdf/e16_martial_art.Pdf.3.
66. Nagamine, S. Interview with Choshin Chibana – 1, 24 September 1957 (trans. Patrick McCarthy and Yukio McCarthy), (McCarthy ref: http://irkrs.Blogspot.Com.Au/. *Okinawa Times*. 1957.
67. Nagamine, S. Interview with Choshin Chibana – 2, 25 September 1957 (trans. Patrick McCarthy and Yukio McCarthy), (McCarthy ref: http://irkrs.Blogspot.Com.Au/. *Okinawa Times*. 1957.
68. Iwai, K. *Motobu Choki and Ryukyu Karate*. Tokyo: AiRyudo; 2003.
69. Poffley, G.J. Master of arts (MA) thesis: 'The development of the Ryukyu empty-handed fighting Arts translated from iwai kohaku (iwai tsukuo), motobu choki and Ryukyu Karate (aiRyudo, 2003). The department of the languages and cultures of Japan and Korea, School of Oriental and African Studies. London: School of Oriental and African Studies (SOAS), University of London; 2008.
70. Hokama, T. *History and Traditions of Okinawan Karate*. Los Angeles: Rising Sun Productions; 2009.
71. Kogel, H. *The Secret Karate Techniques: Kata Bunkai*. Maidenhead: Meyer & Meyer Sport (UK) Ltd; 2010.
72. Sells, J. *Unante: The Secrets of Karate*. Hollywood, CA: W.M. Hawley; 2000.
73. Kerr, G.H. *Okinawa: The History of an Island People*. Boston, Massachusetts: Tuttle Publishing; 2000.
74. Higaonna, M. Interview – Koukai! Okinawa Karate no shinjitsu: kimi ha honmono no Karate wo mita koto ga aru ka? [Japanese] (Exposed! the truth about Okinawan Karate: have you ever seen the real Karate?) edited by full com. Okinawan Karate column 2: The history of nahate and rū rū kō 1. Osaka: Toho Shuppan Publishing Co. Ltd; 2009.
75. Tokashiki, I. *Okinawa Karate Hiden Bubishi Shinshaku* [Okinawa Karate Secrets: A New Interpretation of the Bubishi] (gendai goshaku to giho no kenkyu). Naha; 1995.
76. McCarthy, P. *The Bible of Karate: The Bubishi*. Boston, MA: Tuttle Publishing; 1995.
77. Alexander, G.W. and Penland, K. *Bubishi: Martial Art Spirit*. Florida: Yamazato Publications; 1993.
78. Otsuka, T. 'Okinawa den Bubishi' [The transmission of the Okinawa Bubishi]. Tokyo: *Bêsubôru Magajinsha* [Baseball Magazine]); 1986.
79. Kim, A. *Ninja Death Touch*. Boulder, CO: Paladin Press; 1983.
80. RyueiRyu_Karate_Kobudo_Association. The official site of the RyueiRyu Association (http://RyueiRyu.org/history.html). 2011
81. McCarthy, P. Matsuyama koen [park] theory, 30 September 2011, http://web.Me.Com/patrick_mccarthy/personal_web_site/blog/entries/2011/9/30_matsuyama_koen_%5bpark%5d_theory.Html. 2011
82. Poffley, G.J. Personal communication. 2010.
83. Haines, B.A. *Karate's History and Traditions (Revised Edition)*. Rutland, Vermont:

Charles E. Tuttle Company; 1995.

84. Clayton, B.D. *Shotokan's Secret: The Hidden Truth Behind Karate's Fighting Origins*. Black Belt Communications; 2004.

85. http://www.Rogersheldon.Com/shinseido/resource_pages/pages on website/ bucho_ikko.html.

86. http://www.Shoshinkanuk.Blogspot.co.uk/2008/05/sokon-matsumuras-letter-about-martial.html.

87. Anko Itosu's ten precepts (*tode jukun*) of Karate – http://web.archive.org/ web/20030509024139/www.Ihadojo.Com/origins/anko.html. North American Beikoku Shido-kan Association's 25th Anniversary Celebration Commemorative Journal. 2001.

88. Toyama, K. Master Chojun Miyagi at the meeting in 1936 – part of the meeting records in the appendix of the book, 'Karatedo dai hokan', by kanken toyama (trans. Sanzinsoo), 377–392. Tsuru shobo; 1960. (http://uk.Geocities.Com/ sanzinsoo/index.html).

89. Nagamine, S. and McCarthy, P. *Tales of Okinawa's Great Masters* [translated]. North Clarendon, VT: Tuttle Publishing; 1998.

90. Mayr, E. 'The role of systematics in biology'. *Science*. 1968; 159: 595–599.

91. Mayr, E. 'Processes of speciation in animals'. *Prog Clin Biol Res*. 1982; 96: 1–19.

92. de Queiroz, A. and Gatesy, J. 'The supermatrix approach to systematics'. *Trends Ecol Evol*. 2007; 22: 34–41.

93. de Queiroz, K. 'Ernst Mayr and the modern concept of species'. *Proc Natl Acad Sci USA*. 2005; 102 Suppl 1: 6600–6607.

94. de Queiroz, K. 'Species concepts and species delimitation'. *Syst Biol*. 2007; 56: 879–886.

95. Whalley, B. (director) *Once Upon a Time in New York: The Birth of Hip Hop, Disco and Punk*. BBC; 2007.

96. Heinze, T. *Die Meister des Karate und Kobudo*. Norderstedt: Herstellung und Verlag: Books on Demand GmbH; 2009.

97. Higaonna, M. Interview – Koukai! Okinawa Karate no shinjitsu: kimi ha honmono no Karate wo mita koto ga aru ka? [Japanese] (Exposed! The truth about Okinawan Karate: have you ever seen the real Karate?) edited by full com. Okinawan Karate column 3: The History of Nahate and Rū Rū Kō 2. Osaka: Toho Shuppan Publishing Co. Ltd; 2009.

98. Funakoshi, G. *Rentan Goshin Karate Jutsu* [Japanese] – (Techniques of Karate for Self Protection and Physical Training). Tokyo: Okura Kobundo; 1923.

99. Funakoshi, G. *Karate-Do Kyohan*. Tokyo: Kobunsha; 1936.

100. Hokama, T. *100 masters of Okinawan Karate*. Okinawa: Ozata Print; 2005.

101. Azato interview (trans. George W. Alexander and Scot Mertz) (http://www. Ryuhokan.Com/azatointerview.Php). Ryukyu Shimbun. 1914.

102. Kinjo, A. *Karate Denshinroku* [True History of Karate]. Okinawa: Okinawa Tosho Center; 1999.

103. Swift, J. and McKenna, M. A brief overview of the etymology of modern goju-Ryu Karate-do kata (http://www.Fightingarts.Com/reading/article. Php?Id=623). FightingArts.com. 2000–12.

104. Swift, J. Karatedo kurofune – interview (http://www.KoRyu-uchinadi.org/ Karatedo_kurofune_interview.pdf). International Ryukyu Karate Research Society. 2012.

105. Whitehead, C. Karatedo kurofune – part 1 (http://www.KoRyu-uchinadi.com/contents/

en-us/docs/kurofune1.pdf). International Ryukyu Karate Research Society. 2012.

106. Whitehead, C. Karatedo kurofune – part 2 (http://www.KoRyu-uchinadi.com/contents/en-us/docs/kurofune2.pdf). International Ryukyu Karate Research Society. 2012.

107. Whitehead, C. Karatedo kurofune – part 3 (http://www.KoRyu-uchinadi.com/contents/en-us/docs/kurofune3.pdf). International Ryukyu Karate Research Society. 2012.

108. Whitehead, C. Karatedo kurofune – part 4 (http://www.KoRyu-uchinadi.com/contents/en-us/docs/kurofune4.pdf). International Ryukyu Karate Research Society. 2012.

109. Whitehead, C. Karatedo kurofune – part 5 (http://www.KoRyu-uchinadi.com/contents/en-us/docs/kurofune5.pdf). International Ryukyu Karate Research Society. 2012.

110. Tokashiki, I. Gohaku-Kai Nenkanshi (yearbook). Naha; 1991.

111. Jones, M. Ryu Ryu Ko – Essays of Okinawan Karate and Kobudo, 27 September 2010 (http://yushikan.blogspot.co.uk/2010/09/Ryu-Ryu-ko.Html). Yushikan. 2010.

112. Alexander, G.W. Okinawa: The trip of a lifetime (http://www.Worldblackbelt.com/pages/dec08.01_georgealexander.Asp). WorldBlackBelt.com.

113. McCarthy, P. International Ryukyu Karate Research Society (http://irkrs.Blogspot.com.au). 2013.

114. Funakoshi, G. *Karate-Do Nyumon – The Master Introductory Text*, (trans. John Teramoto). New York: Kodansha International Ltd; 1988.

115. Urban, P. *The Karate Dojo*. Rutland, Vermont: Charles E. Tuttle Company, Inc.; 1967.

116. Nagamine, S. *The Essence Of Okinawan Karate-Do (Shorin-Ryu)*. Rutland, Vermont: Charles E. Tuttle Company, Inc.; 1976.

117. Higaonna, M. *Traditional Karatedo – Okinawa Goju Ryu*. Tokyo: Sugawara Martial Arts Institute, Inc.; 1986.

118. Bishop, M. *Okinawan Karate – Teachers, Styles and Secret Techniques*. A & C Black (Publishers) Ltd; 1989.

119. Toguchi, S. *Okinawan Goju-Ryu II: Advanced Techniques of Shorei-Kan Karate*. Black Belt Communications; 2001.

120. Mabuni, K. and Nakasone, G. *Kobo Kenpo Karate-do Nyumon* (2nd edition); 1938.

121. Hokama, T. *Okinawa Karate-do Kobudo No Shinzui* [The Essence of Okinawan Karate and Kobudo]. Haebaru-cho, Naha, Okinawa, Japan: Shuppansha; 1999.

122. Iken, T. 'Karate-do and Kobudo – A Basic Investigative Report', Okinawa Prefectural Board of Educaton; Vol. 2; Ginowan: Nansei; 1997

123. The_Chibana_Project. http://chibanaproject.Blogspot.co.uk/2008/01/gekkan-translation-ii.html.

124. Motobu, N. (trans. Aaron Meldahl – http://www.Motobu-Ryu.org/library/Karate-ka/%5D. 2007

125. Nicholls, H. 'Darwin 200: Let's make a mammoth'. *Nature*. 2008; 456: 310–314.

126. Turnbull, S. *Ninja: The True Story of Japan's Secret Warrior Cult*. Poole, Dorset: Firebird Books Ltd; 1991.

127. Turnbull, S. *Warriors of Medieval Japan*. Oxford: Osprey Publishing; 2005.

128. Stevens, J. *The Marathon Monks of Mount Hiei*. Boston: Shambhala Publications; 1988.

129. Sugiyama, H. *Sengoku daimyō* (nihon no rekishi, 11). Tokyo: Chûô Kôron-sha; 1970.
130. Draeger, D.F. and Smith R.W. *Asian Fighting Arts.* San Francisco: Kodansha International Ltd; 1969.
131. Adams, A. *Ninja: The Invisible Assassins.* Burbank, CA: Ohara Publications; 1980.
132. Cummins, A. *Hattori Hanzo: The Devil Ninja, A Life and Times.* Vesta Publishing; 2010.
133. Hayes, S.K. *The Ninja and Their Secret Fighting Art.* Rutland, Vermont: Tuttle Publishing; 1981.
134. Hayes, S.K. *Ninjutsu: The Art of the Invisible Warrior.* Chicago, Illinois: Contemporary Book, Inc.; 1984.
135. Durbin, W. *Koga Ryu Ninjutsu.* Boulder, Colorado: Paladin Press; 2004.
136. Draeger, D.F. *Ninjutsu: The Art of Invisibility.* Rutland, Vermont: Charles E. Tuttle Company Inc.; 1989.
137. Fujita, S. I am the Ninja master, I am the herald of Ninjutsu [translated from the Japanese] (online version available at: http://www.Robertg.com/Ninjutsu_articles.Htm). *Liberal* [Japanese]. 1952: 72–77.
138. Ettig, W. *Takamatsu Toshitsugu: The Last Shinobi.* Schmitten, Germany: Verlag Wolfgang Ettig; 2006.
139. Cummins, A. *Shinobi Soldiers: An Investigation Into the Ninja.* Vesta Publishing; 2009.
140. Cummins, A. and Minami, Y. *True Path of the Ninja: Translation of the Shoninki, a 17th Century Ninja Training Manual.* Tuttle Shokai Inc; 2010.
141. Masazumi, N. *Shoninki, The Secret Teachings of the Ninja: The 17th Century Manual on the Art of Concealment.* Inner Traditions International; 2010.
142. Vovin, A. *Man'yoshu, vol. 15* (a new English translation containing the original text, kana transliteration, romanisation, glossing and commentary). Honolulu: University of Hawaii; 2009.
143. Fujita, S. *Biography of The Koga Ryu Ninja* [Japanese – Koga Ryu Ninja Ichidaiki]. 1968.
144. Watatani, K. and Yamada, T. *Large Encyclopedia of Martial Arts* [Japanese – Bugei Ryuha Daijiten]. Tokyo: Shin Jinbutsu Ourai Sha; 1969.
145. Yuki. *Scenery of the Koga Castle District* [Japanese – Koga Jokakyu Gun].
146. Hatsumi, M. *Ninjutsu: History and Tradition.* Orange, CA: Unique Publications; 1981.
147. Hatsumi, M. *Essence of Ninjutsu – The Nine Traditions.* Lincolnwood (Chicago), Illinois: Contemporary Books; 1988.
148. http://www.Bujinkanbritain.org/amatsu.html.
149. Dillon, T. 'When East meets West: the last Ninja', Saturday, 27 October, (http://search.Japantimes.co.Jp/cgi-bin/fl20071027td.Html). *Japan Times* Online. 2007.
150. 'Obituary' (14 January 1966; showa 41): Fujita Seiko. Daily Tourism [Japanese – Nikkan kankou]. 1966
151. Guintard, S., Watanabe-Guintard, M. and Lombardo, P. 'Saiko fujita…au-delà du réel'. *Karate Bushido.* 1999; 267: 52–56.
152. Ashrafian, H. 'Hereditary angioedema in a martial arts family'. *Clin J Sport Med.* 2005; 15: 277–278.
153. Hevener, P.T. *Fujita Seiko: The Last Koga Ninja.* Xlibris; 2008.
154. Fujita, S. *Illustrated Shinto Muso Ryu Jojutsu* [Japanese – Shinto Muso Ryu Jojutsu Zukai]. Bujutsu Kenkyu Jo; 1953.

155. Mol, S. *Classical Fighting Arts of Japan: A Complete Guide to KoRyu Jujutsu* (foreword by Fumon Tanaka and Atsumi Nakashima). New York: Kodansha International Ltd; 2001.

156. Mercado, S.C. *The Shadow Warriors of Nakano: A History of the Imperial Japanese Army's Elite Intelligence School.* Washington, D.C.: Brassey's Inc.; 2002.

157. Fujita, S. *The Last Ninja* [Japanese: Doron Doro Saigo no Ninja]. Tokyo: Shuhousha; 1958.

158. Michitaka, K., Nishiguchi, S., Aoyagi, Y., Hiasa, Y., Tokumoto, Y. and Onji, M. 'Etiology of liver cirrhosis in Japan: a nationwide survey. *J Gastroenterol.* 45: 86–94.

159. MacLaren, I.S. 'Sakumoto and Ryuei Ryu: the 'unknown' karate style of a world champion'. *Fighting Arts International.* 1992: 41–43.

160. Dawkins, R. *Climbing Mount Improbable.* New York: W.W. Norton & Company Ltd; 1997.

161. Palkovacs, E.P., Gerlach, J. and Caccone, A. 'The evolutionary origin of Indian Ocean tortoises (Dipsochelys)'. *Molecular Phylogenetics and Evolution.* 2002; 24: 216–227.

162. Balmer, O., Ciofi, C., Galbraith, D.A., Swingland, I.R., Zug, G.R. and Caccone, A. 'Population genetic structure of Aldabra giant tortoises'. *The Journal of Heredity.* 2011; 102: 29–37.

163. Palkovacs, E.P., Marschner, M., Ciofi, C., Gerlach, J. and Caccone, A. 'Are the native giant tortoises from the Seychelles really extinct? A genetic perspective Based on MTDNA and microsatellite data. *Molecular Ecology.* 2003; 12: 1403–1413.

164. Austin, J.J., Arnold, E.N. and Bour, R. 'Was there a second adaptive radiation of giant tortoises in the Indian Ocean? Using mitochondrial DNA to investigate speciation and biogeography of aldabrachelys (reptilia, testudinidae)'. *Molecular Ecology.* 2003; 12: 1415–1424.

165. Bleecker, T. *Unsettled Matters: The Life & Death of Bruce Lee.* Lompoc, California: Gilderoy Publications; 1996.

166. Scheiner, J.J. and Richards, D.J. 'Treatment of musculoskeletal pain and associated anxiety with an ethoheptazine-aspirin-meprobamate combination (equagesic): a controlled study. *Curr Ther Res Clin Exp.* 1974; 16: 928–936.

167. Royal Hong Kong Police Force. Statement/report of Dr Peter Wu Hin-Ting; http://www.Dekoele.Nl/dood van een legende.html, 1973.

168. Ratajczak, H.V. 'Drug-induced hypersensitivity: role in drug development. *Toxicol Rev.* 2004; 23: 265–280.

169. Higgins, G.L. 'Adonis meets Addison: another potential cause of occult adrenal insufficiency'. *J Emerg Med.* 1993; 11: 761–762.

170. Geenen, C., Tein, I. and Ehrlich, R.M. 'Addison's disease presenting with cerebral oedema'. *Can J Neurol Sci.* 1996; 23: 141–144.

171. Oelkers, W. 'Adrenal insufficiency'. *N Engl J Med.* 1996; 335: 1206–1212.

172. Copeland, P.M. 'Diuretic abuse and central pontine myelinolysis'. *Psychother Psychosom.* 1989 ;52: 101–105.

173. Charron, C., Mekontso-Dessap, A., Chergui, K., Rabiller, A., Jardin, F. and Vieillard-Baron, A. 'Incidence, causes and prognosis of hypotension related to meprobamate poisoning'. *Intensive Care Med.* 2005; 31: 1582–1586.

174. Ramchandani, D., Lopez-Munoz, F., Alamo, C. 'Meprobamate-tranquilizer or anxiolytic? A historical perspective'. *Psychiatr Q.* 2006; 77: 43–53.

175. McGovern, M.C., Glasgow, J.F. and Stewart, M.C. 'Lesson of the week: Reye's syndrome and aspirin: lest we forget. *BMJ.* 2001; 322: 1591–1592.

176. Rhee, J. *Chon-Ji of Tae Kwon Do.* Santa Clarita, CA: Ohara Publications; 1970.

177. Kim, S.H. *Muye Dobo Tongji,* (by Yi Deokmu and Pak Jega −1790 BCE) – the comprehensive illustrated manual of martial arts of ancient Korea [translation from Korean]. Wethersfield, CT: Turtle Press; 2000.

178. Itoman, Morinobu (Seijin). *The Study of China Hand Techniques 'Toudi-jutsu no Kenkyu',*1934 [translated by Mario Mckenna in 2013]

Index

If you enjoyed this book, you may also be interested in…

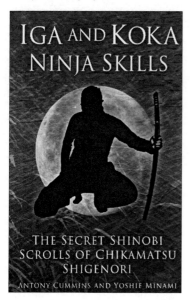

Iga and Koka Ninja Skills

Antony Cummins & Yoshie Minami
978 0 7509 5664 2

£12.99

'A retainer of our domain, Renpeido Chikamatsu Hikonoshin Shigenori, each morning washed his face and hands, dressed himself in Hakama and prayed in front of the kamidana alter …His prayer was thus: "Please afford me success in war." He kept to this routine all through his life.' Through patient and scholarly detective work, Antony Cummins and the Historical Ninjutsu Research Team have unearthed a Shinobi treasure. The 18th-century military historian Chikamatsu recorded the oral traditions of the Ninja and passed on those skills in lectures he gave at his Renpeido school of war in Owari domain during the early 1700s. Chikamatsu wrote specifically about the Shinobi of Iga and Koka, regions from which warriors were hired all over the land in the days of war. The lost scrolls are filled with unknown Shinobi teachings, skills that include infiltration, assassination, explosives, magic and commando tactics, including an in depth commentary on Sun Tzu's famous 13th chapter, 'The Use of Spies'.

In Search of the Ninja

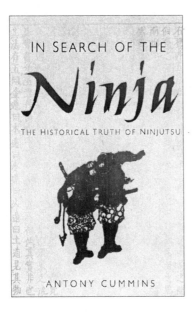

Anthony Cummins

978 0 7524 9210 0

£12.99

Who were the real Ninja, what skills did they possess and how were they employed in warfare? Lost in modern myth, false history and general misinterpretation, the ninja have been misrepresented for many years. Recently, a desire for a more historical view has emerged and here Antony Cummins fulfils that need. *In Search of the Ninja* is based upon the Historical Ninjutsu Research Team's translations of the major ninja manuals and consists of genuinely new material. Here for the first time the connection of the famous Hattori family warriors with the ninja is explained. The Samurai versus ninja myth is dispelled and the realities of ninja skills are analysed. The book explores newly discovered connections to ancient Chinese manuals, lost skills and the 'hidden' philosophy that the Ninja followed. In some ways the truth is more remarkable than the fantasy. The ninja were no myth, they were an important part of the military assets of warlords for centuries and their skills were prized and paid for across the country. *In Search of the Ninja* is the first historical look at the shinobi of ancient Japan.

The Samurai: Swords, Shoguns and Seppuku

Ben Hubbard
978 0 7509 5589 8

£12.99

The true nature of the Japanese samurai warrior is an elusive and endlessly fascinating enigma for those in the West. From their inauspicious beginnings as barbarian-subduing soldiers, the samurai lived according to a code known as bushido, or 'way of the warrior'. Bushido advocated loyalty, honour, pride and fearlessness in combat. Those who broke the code were expected to perform seppuku, or suicide through stomach-cutting. By its very design, seppuku aimed to restore honour to disgraced warriors by ensuring the most painful of deaths. However, the bushido virtues of loyalty and honour fell into question as the samurai grew powerful enough to wrest control from the emperor himself. Accompanied by vivid colour illustrations, *The Samurai* offers a complete, concise account of samurai history and culture. It tells the story of the rise of the samurai as a martial elite, the warriors' centuries-long struggle for power and their long slide into obsolescence.

Visit our website and discover thousands of other History Press books.

www.thehistorypress.co.uk

Lightning Source UK Ltd.
Milton Keynes UK
UKOW04f0442270614

234141UK00004B/34/P